THE HEARTBREAK OF STATIC CLING

The Heartbreak of Static Cling
Copyright 2022
by Robert Starr

First eBook Edition February 2024
First Hardback Edition February 2024
First Paperback Edition March 2025

Hardback ISBN 978-1-59092-995-7
Paperback ISBN 978-1-59092-994-0

Cover design by Robert Starr
Interior design by Robert Starr

All rights reserved, including the right to reproduce this book or portions thereof in any form whatsoever, except in the case of short excerpts for use in reviews of the book.

For information about film, reprint, or other subsidiary rights, contact blueforgegroup@gmail.com

This book is a memoir. It reflects the authors' present recollections of experiences over time. While all the stories in this book are true as the author remembers them, some names and/or identifying details may have been changed to protect the privacy of the people involved.

Blue Forge Press is the print division of the volunteer-run, federal 501(c)3 nonprofit company, Blue Forge Group, founded in 1989 and dedicated to bringing light to the shadows and voice to the silence. We strive to empower storytellers across all walks of life with our four divisions: Blue Forge Press, Blue Forge Films, Blue Forge Gaming, and Blue Forge Records.
Find out more at www.BlueForgeGroup.org

Blue Forge Press
7419 Ebbert Drive Southeast
Port Orchard, Washington 98367
blueforgepress@gmail.com

For Don Hall

CONTENTS

INTRODUCTION	1
SOMETHING MORLEY	3
CAPTURED BY THE CULT	40
SAINT BROADWAY	55
UNIVERSITY PLACE	66
ALWAYS CAROL	71
DRELLA	74
HALLSTARR	79
THE BIG TIME	81
FINDING AN IRVING PLACE	83
FATE	89
BEING BOB	97
THE COMEBACK	101
MAD AVE MESHUGASS	106
THE INVITE	112
WHAT'S BELLPORT?	115
STORM GATHERING	133
DEEP IN THE HEART OF HARLEM	137
THE BELLPORT BLITZ BEGINS	140
DOWN TO BUSINESS	144
FATHERS AND SONS	149
GET ONBOARD	156
PUT TO THE TEST	158
A NEW NORMAL	163
BALL BUSTER	169
LAYING DOWN TRACKS	177
WORKING IT	180
THE MAIN EVENT	186
GIVE US A BREAK	190
AND NOW FOR A COMMERCIAL BREAK	200
ANOTHER DAY ON THE JOB	204
LEVERAGE	211
ZIGGY AND BOOTS	215
LIKE A ROLLING STONE	218
BACK TO BACKER	221
TAKE THREE	225
MERGER MANIA	227

SUSPENDED DISBELIEF	230
PHOTO GALLERY	234—249
THEY CALL IT AN AD AGENCY	250
GRIEF TAKES THE F TRAIN	253
WHERE AM I?	265
LIVING WITH JEN	270
BOOM TOWN	274
WORK IT OUT	279
EXIT IRVING PLACE	286
TO LIVE AND DUI IN LA	291
WHAT'S AN EX-CON TO DO?	301
THE ONE MAN SHOW	306
ART SUPPLIES MAKE A BUCK	308
JUST LOOKING	313
SEX DRUGS AND VIDEOS	318
THE BEST HE COULD	323
SIX FOOT BUNNY CROSSES THE BORDER	326
YOU WON'T SEE MONDAY	334
LET'S HAVE LUNCH	345
STEALING ZELDA	349
SLEEP OVER	353
JUST ONE DRUNKEN NIGHT	358
FAST LANE DETOUR	365
SEEING RED	375
HOLLY'S FIREWORKS	380
SLOW MOTION	389
SMASH HIT AT THE GETTY	394
THE BEACH HOUSE	397
MONSTER UNLEASHED	401
A "TEMPORARY" MOVE	406
MARIE'S CRISIS	412
STILETTO GLADIATORS	422
YOU GOT TO MOVE	426
MOMENTS OF TRUTH	433
THE PROXY	436
A SEND OFF AND THEN SOME	453
AMONG THE STARS	458
SAIL ON	460
EPILOGUE	463
INDEX	465

ACKNOWLEDGEMENTS

A big thank you to my most supportive friends: Mary Kay Stolz, who for years has been my champion and I'm forever grateful. Ruth Strasberg, who expressed such enjoyment while also meticulously hunting down and identifying stealth typos—thank you! A great friend and author, Jeff Copeland, who connected me with Blue Forge Press. Thank you, it was meant to be. Also, to wonderful Delphine Mann, who savored each chapter with enthusiasm and perception. What a gift, a thank you is not nearly enough. And to my dear cousins, Ronna and Elyse Goldberg, a big thanks for your excitement and enthusiasm.

Paul Caranicas, I'm so grateful for our many years of friendship, and to the Antonio Archives for including Antonio's work in the photo gallery. And thank you, Anton Perich, for the video clips of my past. Also, thank you, Denise George, for your excellent design collaboration.

Everyone at Blue Forge Press, thank you for the gift of recognizing my vision and publishing this memoir. It's truly a joy working with you.

Jennifer Connelly, I treasure our times together. You lifted me up when I was most vulnerable. And Frank Steifel and BJ Dockweiler, I'm so grateful for our years of friendship and your gift of shelter when I needed it most.

Helen Glasser, our outrageous escapades are cherished and thank you for your passionate support. And much love and thanks to, Deanna Drew, (formerly, Deanna Cohen), my co-conspirator in the ad world and great friend who rescued me several times, and never regretted it.

Thank you, Constance Cooper/Robert Sherman, Todd Geyer, Brent Watson, Hank Rosenzweig, Sherry Steinberg, V.F.Cole, and my sister, Carolyn Starr, for encouragement that reinforced my determination to complete this memoir.

And especially to the most spectacular ones who are no longer here but live in my heart and on these pages, my deepest gratitude.

THE **HEARTBREAK** OF *STATIC CLING*

ROBERT STARR

BLUE FORGE PRESS
Port Orchard ✹ Washington

INTRODUCTION

HOW DO YOU BEGIN? That mystery plagued me. I had to find a key, a key to the door of my story. Frustrating years passed with no clue and then finally, lightning! This is not about me, it's about them, and how they shaped me. You don't know who you are, where you fit and where you don't, but this kid from Coney Island knew there would be nothing normal about his life.

      A strong attraction to the different, the creative, and the unconventional motivated me to find them, be inspired by them, and guided by the outrageous creatures I needed. And then it began to happen. Artists, inventors, rebellious crackpots, magical magicians, actors, writers, musicians, dreamers, and a gay world of geniuses, all of them taking me into to their lives, their confidence, their visions, and creating mine. They are the fuel that propelled me to unforeseen adventures creating a life of unexpected encounters and spectacular opportunities.

But I learned that nothing about this way is easy. They fought for it, lived for every minute of it, and many died for it.

I will take you there with me. Caution, though: It's a world of extremes. But underlying the crazy fun of it, the ecstasy of dreams realized and the survival of horrific losses is the most empowering force, a monumental love affair.

We may never meet, but my hope is to inspire and entertain you, and also to pass along some hard learned tips on how to deal with the unimaginable.

The Heartbreak of Static Cling is both hilarious and tragic, as the life I've lived.

And isn't every one's life just that?

SOMETHING MORLEY

1969—The world is more nuts than ever and I'm nearing the end of my fourth year at the School of Visual Arts. Four years of Pop Art, Op Art, Conceptual Art, Performance Art, the Art of Speed, Psychedelics, Sex, Warhol, Max's Kansas City and New York City at the height of its Plastic Exploding Inevitable Sixties.

    The student lounge is packed with young artists determined to create themselves. Marvin Gaye's "What's Going On" nails it on the jukebox and I spot Ronnie Cutrone speeding away racing out of the Lounge to visit his fire hydrant friends; he names them. I'm introduced to his new friends every time we take a walk. Yesterday we discovered a three headed beauty on Canal Street.

Something Morley   4

"Hey Ronnie, wait up."

"I got to go. "

"You seen Malcolm?"

"Malcolm?"

"Morley, I'm supposed to meet him here."

"No, I'm taking pictures of Moe, Larry, and Curley."

"Wait a minute, Ronnie, I need a favor. You got any pills? I haven't slept in a week."

He reaches deep into his overall pockets and pulls out a small baggie of pills, he opens it and hands me two. "You're in luck."

"Wow, Tuinals! Give my regards to the tripleheaders."

Ronnie's the one who brought me to the Factory to meet Andy when I was in my first year at SVA. He helps Warhol print silk screens.

What's up with Malcolm? He was so mysterious on the phone, like he has some big news he needs to tell me in person, and now he's a no show?

Malcolm's paintings are astounding, creating a whole new category called Photorealism. He was my instructor last year and we've since become close friends outside of SVA. Malcolm has this infectious rebellious mischievous energy about him. I spend many hours with him at his studio loft on the Bowery and at Max's where I introduced him to a strange creature friend of mine who calls himself Wahundra, an ethereal beauty with honey blonde waist long silk hair, I like looking at him so does

5   The Heartbreak of Static Cling

Malcolm. Wahundra seldom talks much but that doesn't matter. The three of us actually find ourselves in bed together one night at Malcolm's loft, no heavy sex just curious Malcolm.

I've had enough waiting for him, my classes are over for the day and I really need to crash and go home to my small place on 21st Street just two blocks from SVA. The pills are kicking in and I'm in bed but the Malcolm question keeps nagging me. I pick up the phone and call him. "Hi, I was looking for you... Oh... okay I'll see you then at Max's." I hang up and pass out.

Before I know it the damn alarm clock sounds off and I pull on my jeans and t-shirt, grab my beat-up leather jacket and split.

The back room of Max's Kansas City is ground zero for New York's underground. It heats up after midnight. Warhol and his Superstars, Wannabe Superstars, Movie Stars, Rock Stars, Artists and Major Crackpots perform for each other nightly. I've become one of them.

It's early and Max's is mostly empty, good for a quiet conversation. I find my favorite corner booth under a red fluorescent glow of the Dan Flavin sculpture hanging from above. Starving, I order my usual one meal a day, chopped liver and a big pitcher of white wine.

I'm on my third glass when Malcolm appears and sits opposite me. Before I can say anything he begins, "Robert, I have a commission to paint a portrait of Harold Wilson."

I pour him a glass. "Who's Harold Wilson?"

"He's the Prime Minister of England."

"Oh, wow."

"Here's a proposal for you, I'll be in London for several months, would you like to come with me? I need an assistant."

"What?"

"I rented a nice house in Chelsea, there's plenty of room for you to stay. I'll pay your air fare and take care of your expenses. We need to be there mid-June."

I'm trying to respond but I can't get my mouth to work. Finally, "What kind of assisting do you need?"

"Pack and ship my pre-mixed paints and all my equipment and personal things. Jasper Johns wants me to take one of his paintings to the Tate, it needs to be crated and shipped. Once we're there I'll need you to deal with organizing appointments and help me set up the studio. The rest is just doing the day to day things I can't think about when I'm working. Why don't you ask Wahundra if he would like to come with us, he could keep you company."

Wahundra? That's interesting. "I'll ask him."

"So do you agree?"

"Jesus Malcolm, let me think about it for a hot second. Do I agree to be your assistant in London? Holy shit what a fucking question... well... I don't think I have anything better to do!"

"Good, I got to go, call you tomorrow." He leaves and I immediately order another pitcher of wine.

7   The Heartbreak of Static Cling

I'm playing our conversation over again in my head, was I tripping? This is sinking in and I feel my life about to take a sharp turn at a hundred miles an hour and there's no seat belt and I don't give a shit.

I turn twenty-one on May 21st and soon after I graduate SVA and get to continue my education in Europe, I just might never come back.

The back room is filling up with the unusual suspects I'm not into now, there's more to think about like giving up my apartment, telling my folks, calling Wahundra and starting my job at Malcolm's loft preparing for our adventure. I down my last glass and head home.

I'm in bed staring at the ceiling becoming a movie screen projecting images of things to come, all sorts of visions but not of Europe, just all the stuff I have to do in order to take those steps onto that plane. Finally I fall into a deep sleep.

Dealing with my folks is my first priority today. They sure have been exposed to a lot of my surprises, especially my debauchery at SVA. They rescued me when I had hepatitis from drug abuse a year ago. Zelda is the definition of unconditional motherly love; my relationship with my dad Ted is more complicated.

I don't need their approval, I just want it. They seem excited about this but insist on meeting Malcolm. We'll see.

Wahundra, how odd Malcolm would include him. It would be good to have a companion but Wahundra? I was sure he would jump at this but for whatever unexplained reasoning he declines the invitation. I'm surprised but not disappointed. Wahundra's other worldliness would drive me nuts on a daily basis. I tell Malcolm and he seems not to care. Good.

I need to get some air, clear my head and try to organize a list of things I need to do. I get downstairs and check my mailbox. And there it is a terrifying love letter from the Army, a fucking draft notice!

I'm required to report to the Fort Hamilton Army Base in Brooklyn at 9 AM five days from now for my physical and written test. Seething I read this again and again. Holy goddamn fucking *shit*! There's no way in Hell I'm going to Viet Nam to be returned in a box, and for what? Motherfucking Nixon.

The breaks have just slammed down hard on my life—I can't blow this off. I have to show up or any chance of beating this shit show will be a lot worse. There's no way I can go to London, I would be stopped at the airport. Damn it.

I come up with a plan quick and call Katrina, one of Andy's original Superstars and my partner in crime. I make sure she can shoot me up for the next few days; I need obvious track marks on both arms. And I'm determined to shove whatever I can get up my ass, they love bending you over to examine your asshole. Fuck them.

There's no way I'll be able to make it to Fort Hamilton in the morning from my apartment zonked out

9   The Heartbreak of Static Cling

of my head, I'll have to stay overnight at my folks' place in Brooklyn. My dad agrees to drive me to the army base, Zelda is horrified. Ted doesn't dare add his two cents and suffer my mother's wrath. He's a WWII vet and thinks the Army will make a man out of me—yeah, Dad, a dead man.

If my plan doesn't work, I'm heading straight to Canada and nobody can stop me.

Katrina comes through and my arms are a junky's roadmap. I'm wasted on speed and determined to show up for my physical a haggard strung out mess. I watch the nightly coverage of Napalm, Agent Orange, and mass murder brought to you live from Viet Nam. The news covers the parade of cadavers in coffins rolling out of Army cargo planes daily, something to look forward to.

It's time to drag myself onto the F Train to Brooklyn. I'm struggling to control my demented state and keep my parents calm. I crash in my teenage bedroom but I'm awake most of the night in horror of what I have to face tomorrow.

Shockingly it's daylight and my dad is knocking on the door yelling it's time to get out of bed. After a quick breakfast I can't eat, it's showtime. I get into Ted's '64 Dodge and we don't say a word except when we get there he tells me he'll wait for me in his car.

My knees buckle as I walk into that door. I hand my draft notice to an officer who directs me to what looks like a classroom. It's filled with boys facing their destiny. Some are so stoned they're falling out of their seats.

Multiple choice exams and pencils are distributed on each desk.

I stare at the questions for a minute and begin to fill in the dots.

Are you a consciences objector?—Yes.
Do you use illegal drugs?—Yes.
Are you homosexual?—Yes.

Those are my favorite questions. The rest is just bullshit.

The kid next to me nods out and drops his pencil. The officer picks the kid's head up off the desk and puts the pencil back in his hand. The kid nods out again and the officer takes his hand controls the pencil and fills in dots. Not a good sign, the Army is under pressure to quickly ship out as many boys as possible, they actually shortened basic training time. It's 1969 and this is the Viet Nam express.

Do you want to get the fuck out of here and go to Europe? That question wasn't on the exam. I fill in more dots of more lame questions and sign my name testifying I've told the truth. The exams are collected and we're marched to a locker room and instructed to strip down to our underwear. Then we're taken to an examination room and lined up side by side.

The Army doctor arrives with his clipboard, stethoscope around his neck and a small flashlight clipped to his pocket. Methodically he examines one kid at a time and now me. First the eyes, tongue, pulse and

11 The Heartbreak of Static Cling

heart and then I'm told to drop my drop my Jockey's. I do so in a way he can't help seeing the tracks on my arms. He squeezes my balls, turns me around and tells me to bend over spread my cheeks and he uses his flashlight to examine my asshole. That done he makes notes and tells me to pull up my underwear.

I join a line of guys in a corridor leading to an open door office. We're waiting for our turn to be grilled by a thick-necked Bulldog Officer seated at his desk. Finally I'm standing in front of him and scratch myself like a junky adjusting my balls. Grimacing, he eyes me head to toe then turns his attention to the papers in front of him quickly scanning the results of my exam and doctor's notes.

He slowly puts the papers in a folder on his desk. And with a drill Sergeant's bellow loud enough to be heard by at least thirty guys behind me he yells, "So you're a homosexual, huh?!"

I'm stunned silent.

He yells even louder, "Answer me, are you a *homosexual?*"

I consider asking him to repeat the question but I just reply, "Yes Sir."

Gritting his teeth he hisses, "Do you have a specific lover?"

Shocked by this insane question, my mind races for an answer my life depends on. I really want to say, "Why, are you interested?" But a big caution sign flashes in my head. I take a deep breath and finally say, "No sir, just anybody who comes along."

The Sergeant's fat neck turns a bright shade of crimson and now he's a rabid Bulldog seething. I blurt out, "I want to see the psychiatrist." The hulk slams his big fist down hard on his desk. "Get your clothes on, you're 4F."

I want to jump for joy and pinch the bulldog's adorable jowls, but I control myself with a quick about face and march out of his office, run down the corridor to the locker room, throw my clothes on, sprint out the front door, dash across the parking lot and jump into my dad's Dodge. "Floor it, let's get the hell out of here, I'm 4F. Hallelujah!"

Dad doesn't ask anything and we speed away.

I never felt I had to have the "I'm gay" conversation with him. Actually, I felt his disappointment with me long ago. That contributed to my miserable childhood. I was disappointed as well by his disgust. I was horribly uncomfortable in my chubby skin. I wanted to be a happy athletic beautiful carefree child like the ones I watched in the playground with amorous envy. I had to wait till I was well into my teens to shed this suffocating self-loathing. Oh well, now I'm going to Europe!

Mom is thrilled I escaped the Army. Now they both again insist on meeting Malcolm. I tell them I'll arrange it and I pack my overnight bag and head back to the City.

Only two weeks to get my shit together, I start

13 The Heartbreak of Static Cling

getting rid of most of the junk in my apartment, I have to give up the lease. Malcolm calls, he wants me to come by and help him with the Jasper Johns painting and start organizing all the freight labels for shipping.

Jasper Johns' studio is also on the Bowery, practically across the street from Malcolm's loft. We go over there and I'm overwhelmed by John's presence and incredible work. The painting we need to ship is about forty by sixty inches and it's already packed in a wooden crate. After a few drinks, Malcolm and I carry the painting back to his loft which is filled with more large crates and trunks for everything he'll need in London. He decided to use Japan Airlines Freight. I also discover he booked us on Japan Airlines to London. Japan Airlines? Strange choice, he just says he likes them. He shows me how to fill out the packing labels and insurance forms and my job begins. I'm determined to be meticulous with every task for Malcolm, that's the least I can do for this chance of a lifetime.

I tell him my folk's request. He's glad to meet them but it'll have to be at the airport as he has much to do and can't set aside time before we leave. I'll work that out.

It's hard to believe this is happening soon. Excitement is kicked up a notch each day we get closer to takeoff. Who knows what I'm getting myself into and who cares, my life is now on fast forward.

We get to Kennedy early for Malcolm to meet Ted and Zelda. She falls in love with him instantly. Ted's skeptical of course, but fifteen minutes into the conversation he's impressed and wishes us Bon Voyage. I promise I'll write often. Big hugs and kisses and we go to the gate.

I might as well be boarding a spaceship to Mars, that's the feeling I have stepping onto that jet.

Watching America disappear below me is thrilling. I settle in exhausted by all the shit I had to go through to get here. We both doze off to the hum of the plane.

I'm awakened by Malcolm fighting something in his sleep. I decide to interrupt his agitation. "Malcolm, you okay?"

He jerks awake. "Sorry, did I disturb you?"

"Bad dream?"

"No, "It's nothing. You know this is the first time I'll be back in the UK since being thrown out of the Royal College of Art."

"Thrown out?"

"I had one too many disagreements with their attitude."

I decide to leave this alone. "Good for you."

Malcolm was what they call a Borstal Boy. Borstal is England's version of Juvenile Jail. He was locked up for two years in his teens for theft. The class system in London is oppressive. Malcolm being from the wrong side of the tracks compounds his rebellious nature and I can imagine the conflicts he's had once he was accepted and admitted to the Royal College of Art. I'm sure there's

15 The Heartbreak of Static Cling

a good amount of revenge being commissioned to paint a portrait of the Prime Minister.

Food is served and it's time for drinks. I'm celebrating and so is Malcolm.

The flight is long, our conversation light and minimal, both of us caught up in our own thoughts until the Captain announces we're fifteen minutes from Heathrow. Malcolm gets up and rifles through his bag in the overhead compartment. He returns to his seat and pops open a pill bottle. "Do you like Magic Mushrooms?"

As if this situation isn't psychedelic enough, I think about it for a second. "Sure."

We both down the mushrooms with wine, how gourmet!

The plane lands and I take off. Everything is through the looking glass and in the opposite direction, sometimes sideways. This movie continues as Malcolm navigates us through Heathrow to a cartoon London cab. The wrong side of the narrow road takes us to some strange shabby neighborhood. Malcolm explains it's just for one night; the house in Chelsea will be ready for us tomorrow. I barely make any sense of that, I can barely make sense of anything but I'm having fun. I'm in London!

I can't feel my feet but I know I'm climbing stairs behind Malcolm. He opens the door of a flat from another century. I find a room with a bed and collapse with my first impressions of London hallucinating and finally lights out.

Something Morley 16

Woke up and it's a Chelsea morning. Our taxi winds down narrow streets to The Kings Road where pubs, boutiques, small trendy shops with Mod Rockers hanging out appear a blur as we make our way to Glebe Place just off the Kings Road. No. 15 Glebe Place is our home, one of the ancient row houses lining this beautiful street equally distant between Kings Road and the river Thames.

We climb the front steps and Malcolm opens the door. I expect a traditional quaint English house but instead this place is actually set up as a perfect modern art studio. The parlor floor is a vast open space with very high ceilings and tall windows. Several large crates and trunks have arrived and are stacked ready to be unpacked. Upstairs is Malcolm's lair, his bedroom contains a sitting room and huge bath. Another flight up I find my space, a comfortable bedroom and bath. A large fully stocked English kitchen and dining room is ground level leading to a bucolic back garden. What a contrast to Coney Island where I grew up.

We unpack our suitcases and head out for some food. I'm in love with Chelsea, especially Kings Road. We find a small restaurant. "Let's take it easy today and settle in. We can attack the crates tomorrow." After brunch I decide to explore the neighborhood and Malcolm goes back to the house.

My first outing in wonderland and the faces, bodies, clothing, hangouts and the whole English trip seems to congregate on Kings Road. A whacked out

17 The Heartbreak of Static Cling

boutique catches my attention, I buy something of the moment to wear and continue my walk discovering stately massive stone mansions, probably built in the 1700s. Funny how a New Yorker thinks a pre-war building is old world. These magnificent semicircular streets lead me to Cheyne Walk by the river. I'm mesmerized by the view of life on the Thames.

    I find my way back to Glebe Place and wave to Malcolm who's in an intense conversation on the phone. I go upstairs to write my folks a letter. Malcolm calls out to me, "Robert, we're invited for dinner this evening at David Hockney's house, are you up for that?"

    Trying to be cool, "Sure, sounds like fun." Hockney is one of my favorite artists and I can't wait to meet him.

    And here I am with Malcolm Morley going to visit David Hockney at his home for dinner... just a typical evening in London.

    A handsome young guy answers the door and stares at me and smiles. He's Hockney's lover and muse, the subject of many Hockney drawings and paintings. Peter Schlesinger is my age, and there's an instant attraction. Hockney is wonderful, warm welcoming and obviously a good old friend of Malcolm's. They have a lot of catching up to do and Peter takes me on a tour of the house. It's thrilling to see Hockney's paintings and his works in progress up close.

    Peter takes me to his room, we sit on his bed and his eyes examine my face. "Robert, I'd like to photograph you."

Well, this is unexpected, I'm taken aback and very flattered. "Sure, that would be great."

We make arrangements to meet tomorrow morning and Peter plans the photo shoot at Kew Gardens, The Royal Botanic Gardens. We talk and talk. Peter's originally from California, he's lived in New York and tells me David Croland is here in London, and tomorrow we'll drop by his place to get his help with wardrobe.

I haven't seen Croland in years. I met him through my friend Richard Bernstein who illustrates most of Warhol's Interview Magazine Covers. David was a model and Robert Mapplethorpe's first male lover. Now he's a fashion illustrator.

We rejoin Malcolm and Hockney and enjoy a great dinner. What a night.

On our way home I tell Malcolm my plans with Peter and he's happy I have a new friend in London. He tells me he'll start the unpacking himself and wishes me a great day at Kew Gardens.

Peter arrives early morning and approves the get up I'm wearing. Looking in a mirror I'm an English rocker, long hair, mustache, my newly acquired skinny deep purple crushed velvet pants and an unbuttoned collarless black crepe shirt. We grab a cab to visit David for accessories.

It's been a few years since I've seen David. He hasn't changed much, still the lithe elegant fashion

19 The Heartbreak of Static Cling

forward gentleman. I receive a warm welcome and David's critical eye. "The Frye boots got to go." He rifles through his large closet and presents me with a pair of Python platform boots adding another inch to my height, they're almost my size but manageable. Then he ties a long vintage silk scarf around my neck, Mick Jagger style. And his last addition is a spectacular vintage English Officer's coat, now the look is complete. Thankful hugs and we rush to catch the train to Sussex and Kew Gardens.

The train is from another era with wood framed windows. It's perfect for photography, also perfect transportation back in time to the Royal Botanic Gardens which were established in 1759.

Nothing I imagined could match the magnificence of this place. Miles and miles of fantasy paradise, nature's brilliance accentuated with huge majestic Victorian ornate glass pavilions and ponds of Swans.

Peter captures the contrast of my 1969 figure juxtaposed to this regal landscape. What a great day, I could spend weeks here. I remember my dismal childhood brightened when my mom left me alone with my sketchpad in the Japanese landscape section of Brooklyn's Botanical Gardens. That rare peace and tranquility covers me again here.

The day comes to an end and we head back to London, we return the wardrobe to David and I go back to Chelsea.

I barely get in the door and I'm greeted by a black stranger. She tells me in a thick Cockney accent her name is BJ and Malcolm's not in a good mood. "It's something about the shipments."

I notice a new delivery of several more trunks and crates. "Where's Malcolm?"

"He's taking a nap."

I run up to his bedroom and quietly open the door. Malcolm's asleep. I return to BJ, "What the hell is going on?"

"He said something about Jasper Johns."

"Oh God, no." I check the newly arrived crates, "Shit shit *shit*!" The Jasper Johns painting is missing!

I riffle through all my papers in my room, get all the shipping documents from my folder and call Japan Air Freight. They tell me they are aware of the situation and investigating. "Investigating? Investigating! Was it stolen?"

"There's no evidence of that, be assured we will track it down and deliver it as soon as possible."

"How can I be assured of that?"

"Please be patient, things like this do happen occasionally and we resolve these issues quickly."

"I'm not patient. I need direct numbers of those investigating this." After a bit of an argument and back and forth I get the phone numbers I need and hang up. I'm determined to call them morning and night every day until this is resolved.

I hear some conversation and run downstairs.

21 The Heartbreak of Static Cling

Malcolm is embracing BJ, and he doesn't look to disturbed. "How was Kew Gardens?"

"Malcolm, I just called the freight company."

"It's okay I spoke to them earlier, they'll find it. Don't worry about it, it's not your fault."

I'm relieved he said that but it is my responsibility. "I've got their direct numbers."

"Calm down, it's okay, did you meet BJ?"

"Yeah."

"We're going out for awhile. There's plenty in the fridge, see you later." They leave and I'm glad he's not freaking out like I am. And who is BJ? He never mentioned her; I wonder where and when they met.

My stomach is turning about the painting. Sure there's insurance but not anything near its real value Goddamn it!

I can't let this get me crazy, at least Malcolm's being good about it. I grab a bottle of white wine from the fridge and finish it in my room and I'm finally calmed enough to sleep.

Suddenly screams jolt me and out of bed, it sounds like murder. I cautiously walk out of my room and freeze at the top of the stairs. The commotion escalates and I hear Malcolm grunting. I'm relieved; he's just fucking the shit out of BJ and she's screaming her guts out. I return to bed with an extra pillow over my head.

Morning comes with a bit of a hangover and I rush downstairs lured by the smell of fresh coffee. BJ is leaving the house and she waves a carefree, "Tata!" I'm amazed she can walk.

    Malcolm joins me in the kitchen. I stay away from talking about last night's commotion. I tell him my plans to unpack the remaining crates and begin setting up the studio, no talk of the missing painting. Malcolm has meetings all day and leaves the house.

    It's a nonstop marathon organizing everything. I finally take a break and call the freight company to bug them, but still no news. Then I call Peter—I'm looking for a gay bar and London so far seems so closeted. I need to go out tonight in case BJ returns for round two.

    I finally quit. It's early evening and I have only one smaller crate left to tackle. Malcolm's not home yet and I'm not waiting for him. I take a quick shower and get dressed for the night, black jeans black T-Shirt and a jean jacket, my New York gear. I go for a long walk before getting into a cab to that bar Peter told me about.

    There's a distance happening between me and Malcolm, I can feel it, I wonder if my stay with him in this house will become unnecessary. I'm sure the missing painting fuckup is causing a lot of anxiety, even though he won't admit it.

    Malcolm's return to London is bringing up old demons and wounds. I guess BJ is good for him. He needs the release.

    I want to explore Europe on my own but I've made a commitment and I'll stick with Malcolm for as long as he needs me here.

23 The Heartbreak of Static Cling

The Black Hat is a long narrow crowded pub. I manage to get a seat at the bar and inspect the crowd. What is it with English gay men? They look like flight attendants who don't wear deodorant because they have no body odor. Some are cuter than others but there's no animal attraction here. I pick up on a conversation about of all things the Stonewall on Christopher Street! I've avoided newspapers and TV and have no idea why this is a topic of conversation, until I learn about the uprising. How fabulous, New York drag queens proving they have bigger balls than the cops! Hopefully Stonewall will inspire these guys to do something here.

They're buying me drinks and I'm having fun decompressing from Malcolm's drama. I decide to stay till closing time.

It's nearly 3 AM, the house is dark and quiet and just as I lay my drunken head down it starts again! He's plowing BJ with a vengeance and she's making her orgasms known to everyone on the block. I don't know how much more of this I can stomach. I come really close to running downstairs and shutting her up, but thankfully I'm too stoned... Those flight attendants at the bar had great Opium and Hash.

I get cotton balls from the medicine cabinet and stuff my ears. It helps a bit and I pass out.

Another hung over morning; this can't become a routine. I won't mention the racket last night, I'll just let it slide. Malcolm's having his coffee. "Hi Robert, did you have fun last night?"

I hesitate for a minute, then, "Not as much as you apparently."

He brushes me off with a sly devilish laugh. "You did great yesterday, we're almost all settled in."

"Yeah, I'll attack the last of it today, anything else I can help you with?

"No, take a break, do some sightseeing."

"Okay Malcolm, sure..."

He finishes his scone and tells me he won't be home till late evening.

I feel trapped, I love Malcolm and want to help him but it's more apparent he doesn't really need my help. I don't know how much longer I can be here.

Putting it all out of my mind I complete the unpacking and finish organizing his studio. By late afternoon I'm done and the place is ready for Malcolm to get to work.

I go out to find a place where I can make copies of the shipping documents I'll take with me when I eventually leave. Wherever in Europe I find myself I'll continue to drive the shipping company nuts calling them every day until they find that fucking painting.

I get back home and Peter calls. We make a date to get together later tonight.

Peter leads me to a room of flat files and pulls out a box containing prints he made of our day, and the photographs are really good. I'm oddly drawn to the portrait of me on the train headed to Kew Gardens. He captured something I haven't seen before... an unusual

25 The Heartbreak of Static Cling

expression, a sense of knowing. About what, I wonder? Seeing how moved I am at this, he gives me that photograph.

I open up about my problems with Malcolm. It's good to talk about it. Peter agrees I have to leave Malcolm. But when is the question. He listens long enough for the answer to become clear: I have to wait until Malcolm is immersed in his painting. Once he's in his world, the right time to leave will present itself.

Peter suggests distractions and mentions people I might know from New York who are now living here. Astonishingly he names Samantha Grubbs. Peter tells me she's working at a pretty good gallery and that's how he knows her. She's a lot of fun from what I can remember. Samantha dropped out of SVA and my life awhile ago. Yep, she could be a good distraction.

I tell Peter how grateful I am for our friendship and his advice. Now I can go back to Glebe Place with more patience and a plan.

File 9-South London Gallery—The trendy small gallery is exhibiting some terrific work, but that's not my focus right now. I spot Sam appearing from a back room walking to her desk in the gallery.

Hippie chick turned gallery chic, thigh high white glossy vinyl boots, shocking lime mini skirt, and a tight black boat neck, that's mad Mod Samantha! I walk over to her but she's involved with paperwork and pays no attention.

I just stand in front of her breathing heavily and

she glances up and immediately returns to her papers. I whisper, "Sam."

And she jerks up out of her seat. "Robert?... Robert fucking Starr, you gorgeous thing!" Now she has an English accent. "I'm going to have a massive attack, I was thinking of you just yesterday! Hang on, I have to tell them I'm leaving for the day. Let's get a drink, I need one, darling." She darts into the back room and returns carrying an enormous bright red shoulder bag, the same color of her hair. She grabs my arm and we dash out to a local dive bar. Sam is fun!

Sam orders double whiskey sours and tells me she's living in a large flat off the Old Marylebone Road with her Brazilian boy toy, Mario. "Can't wait for you to meet him, you'll be gobsmacked! But hands off, he's mine." She downs her drink and orders another round. I try to tell her why I'm here in London, but she interrupts. "You're coming home with me, we need to catch up, it's too loud here, drink up darling!"

We kill our third round and fly out of the bar. Sam puts two fingers in her mouth and produces an earsplitting whistle—one of her trademarks back in NYC—and a cabby stands on his breaks.

Oxford and Cambridge Mansions off the Old Marylebone Road is a large vintage six story stately row of buildings. We get up to her flat and there he is, the Brazilian boy toy Mario, wow! He's short and sexy, with creamy light skin, honey blonde long hair, and a body you want to touch, especially that huge lump at the

27 The Heartbreak of Static Cling

crotch of his white jeans. He's sweet, adorable, and he's hers.

We spend the night with drinks and pizza reminiscing our SVA days and Sam's adventures in London. I finally fill her in on my situation. She remembers Malcolm from SVA and has followed his impressive career. She's sympathetic to my need to spread my wings. "There's so much you need to see here in London before you explore Europe. We'll be your guide and if you need to leave Glebe Place you can stay here with us until you get London out of your system." Just what I needed to hear. I know I'm going to take her up on this.

Sam makes arrangements for us to see The Jimi Hendrix Experience at the Royal Albert Hall. She has back stage passes of course. It's tomorrow night and I'm thrilled.

And in a few weeks I'm determined to go The Isle of Wight, England's answer to Woodstock. Bob Dylan, The Band, The Who, Joe Cocker, The Moody Blues, and after that it could be bye-bye London. I can taste the freedom but I can't rush anything, I owe Malcolm a lot.

The weeks leading up to The Isle of Wight are filled with sights and scenes with Sam, Mario, and friends experiencing more life in London, but I'm feeling like an intruder at Glebe Place. BJ and Malcolm are still a nightly sex fest but thankfully BJ quieted down a bit. Malcolm is consumed with his work and whatever it is that he is silently struggling with. I'm here for Malcolm but our seldom short conversations seem distant. He's having a problem with something he won't talk about.

I finally decide it's time for me to leave and get a chance and tell Malcolm my plans. He's genuinely happy for me and tells me how much he appreciates all I did for him. It's hard to hold back my emotions, I'm so grateful for our friendship and this gift of Europe.

I pack my bag and leave Malcolm. We'll meet again.

The Isle of Wight is a week away and I'm staying with Sam and Mario temporarily. Sam's a seasoned traveler; she makes a list of Pensiones in Paris and Italy for me and explains the wonders of the cheap Eurail Pass that will get me there. My European adventure on a very tight budget is now set.

I plan on camping out overnight to get the full Isle of Wight experience. Sam can't break away from her job, but Mario is free and dying to go. I make a solemn promise to behave and Sam finally agrees to let Mario come with me, great!

The Isle of Wight event is spectacular, tons of kids from all over Europe, there's even a San Francisco love child contingency as well. There's plenty of space to breathe and get off on the greatest artists doing their greatest on stage.

Mario and I are kind of an attraction and we get invited into the California kid's tent, they have a water pipe and great Hash waiting for us. One of the gorgeous hippies puts the make on Mario. Clever Mario pulls me to him and kisses me passionately and then he tells the hippie we're monogamous, smart boy! Our one kiss will not go any further. I did make a promise, damn it.

We're great buddies having a Rock'n'Roll blast, I'm so glad he's here with me. We get back home and tell Sam all—well, almost all—about it.

The time has come for me to pack up my stuff and head out on my own for my big exciting terrifying fabulous trip.

Mario and Samantha wave and blow kisses. I'm sitting in the bus to Victoria Station for the boat train to Paris. I press my lips to the window and wave back as they grow smaller in the distance.

My budget won't allow me to stay long in Paris. I just need to meet Mona and the masterpieces close up and personal at the Louvre. And I'll hang out at a café, go to a club or two and leave Paris for another time when I can afford to explore this city.

I follow a strong pull to Italy and my trusty Eurail Pass takes me to Venice. I couldn't resist Venice just for two nights before I land in Florence, then finally Rome till money runs out.

My tiny room has a view of a brick wall. An ancient brick wall but who cares? I'm in Venice, what a jewel. I'm an unabashed tourist with little time using every hour to explore. I wind up at the infamous Harry's Bar for a drink, or two. No dinner here, can't afford it.

I'm sitting at the bar trying to ask the bartender for the lowdown on this hangout in my lousy Italian and his hysterical laugh catches everyone's attention. Finally he composes himself and speaks good enough English to fill me in. Since 1931 this watering hole has seen the likes of Barbara Hutton, Katherine Hepburn, Gary Cooper, Peggy Guggenheim, Orson Wells, Frank Lloyd Wright, Joe DiMaggio, Truman Capote, Ernest Hemingway to name a few, and now me. I wiggle my ass on the barstool trying to pick up some vibes.

I'm sipping my martini aware of a very stylish woman at the end of the bar staring a hole in my head. I smile at her wondering why women are attracted to me more than men. Maybe it's because I'm not interested.

She walks over to me and takes a seat by my side. She's gorgeous, sexy, dressed in chic black and wearing some very expensive jewels.

In a thick Italian accent she begins, "You're American, yes?"

"New York."

She reaches into her Gucci bag and presents her card. It reads, Donna D'Amelio—Milan.

"Hello Donna, I'm Robert Starr."

"What are you doing in Venice?"

"It's just a brief stopover, I'm headed to Florence then Rome, this is my first trip to Italy."

"Would you please stand up for me?"

Okay, this is getting weird. I slide off my stool and stand in front of her.

She sizes me up and, "Could you please turn around?"

What the fuck?! Okay, I turn around and return to my barstool.

She's all smiles. "What would you think of a small stop in Milan? I'm putting together a catalogue for my new men's knitwear. Would you be interested to model?"

This has got to be some kind of a joke. "Thanks, I'm not a model."

"Exactly, I don't want models, I want characters. You are a New York character."

Okay, lady. "Thanks for noticing."

"We'll be shooting in Milan next week, would you come?"

"Thanks for the offer Donna, but Milan's not on my agenda, I'm on a tight budget."

"No problem, we will take care of your travel expenses to Milan and put you up for a night, plus you will be paid for the one day shoot. Interested?"

I try my best to contain myself appearing to be just pleasantly pleased. "This could be interesting, are you sure you want me for your catalogue?"

"Absolutely, you'll be one of four models I've booked."

This is beginning to seam real. "Okay then, thank you Donna!"

She stands up and bends close to my ear. "Call my studio and they will arrange it all. I have to be back there tomorrow. See you Robert, in Milan." She turns and walks to the door, plants a kiss on the cheek of the maitre d and waves, "Ciao."

And a much needed nightcap ends my first night in Venice.

The encounter at Harry's keeps me awake invoking the forces of fate, I'm wishing to have a serious talk.

First thing this morning I call Japan Airlines Freight and bug them again. I get the same runaround, still investigating... Will the ever find that painting?

And then I call Milan and Donna's assistant answers. She knows the whole story and gives me my itinerary. This is real, I leave for Milan tomorrow. Holy shit!

My last day in Venice is even more of a daydream. I spot a beautiful gondola, sleek black with a deep red plush interior and Sergio the gondolier is gorgeous. I make arrangements to meet him at the Rialto Bridge at midnight for a tour of the small canals.

I do my tourist thing all day taking in as much in as I can. By late afternoon I return to my room and collapse.

A few hours later, it's dark, from what I can tell from my window. I quickly throw on my jeans, white shirt and black blazer. Why not? That look worked last night.

A take a short walk to dazzling Piazza San Marco and find a small table at an outdoor café and watch enchanted strollers part hundreds of pigeons to the accompaniment of a string orchestra. A waiter presents the bottle of Pinot Grigio I've ordered to celebrate my

33 The Heartbreak of Static Cling

upcoming Milano adventure.

I'm halfway into my second bottle when suddenly a hand is placed on my shoulder from behind. I snap around and find the embodiment of a woman from somewhere in Ohio. She asks me for a light and introduces herself as Shirley, a schoolteacher from the suburbs of Chicago on a solo whirlwind tour of Venice. I invite her to join me for some wine. She's in her fifties and hot to trot. What is it that attracts them to me?

I'm loaded and so is Shirley, she started her boozing earlier. She's bizarre enough for me to really enjoy her company. It's getting close to midnight. I think about it for a minute and tell Shirley we have a gondola waiting for us at the Rialto Bridge.

We wobble over to the bridge and there he is: glorious Sergio and his glamorous gondola. How I wish Shirley was at the helm and Sergio was snuggled with me. Oh well. Somehow we manage to get on board and settle in.

Sergio pushes off drifting us along a dark narrow winding canal. Shirley moves closer to me and puts her head on my shoulder. I let her, it's Venice and it's her fantasy. I make believe it's Sergio.

The canal bends gently and we're in the wonder of it. Suddenly, Shirley becomes animated and attacks my shirt ripping off buttons and groping my crotch. She's in heat and I'm trapped! I tear her off of me and stand up and yell, "Sergio, pull over!" I step out of the gondola and plunge into the canal and my heavy Frye boots pull me under. Shirley's shrieks pierce the darkness. I get to the surface gasping for air and Sergio finally manages to pull me up like a dead fish into the gondola. He finds the nearest dock and gets rid of both of us.

We're hysterically laughing and blowing kisses to Sergio. I give her a big hug and now she's also soaking wet and in heaven. She certainly has something to tell her fellow schoolteachers back home! And I have the perfect ending to my "romantic" encounters in Venice. The canal plunge sobered me enough to find our way back to her hotel and say good night to Shirley. I head back to my pensione.

It's not easy getting up at the crack of dawn after swimming in Pinot Grigio and the canal, but I stuff my duffle bag, check to be sure I have all my papers, passport, and the important info about Milan. By some miracle I get the train station in time.

I manage to drift off to dream world on the train.

At the station in Milan I'm met by a young guy holding a sign with my name handwritten in thick black marker. He greets me in Italian and takes me to his little car. It's a short drive to the photographer's studio.

The assistant tells me Donna will be here later and she brings me into the studio and introduces me to the stylist and three striking guys in sweaters. They're astounding. The tallest is black, bald, and beautiful; he looks like he's carved out of ebony. The China doll is porcelain by contrast, and there's is a fabulously freckled redhead with a giant Orange Afro. They're characters all right, but they're also definitely models, for sure. I'm feeling a bit insecure but I have to trust Donna knows what she's doing.

The guys try on sweaters chosen from a large table organized in rows of different color ranges. The stylist snaps Polaroid's of each change of outfit. No sign of the photographer. She hands me a white t-Shirt and a bold blue gray and yellow plaid V neck. I take one feel of it and realize it's thick cashmere. The label is a well designed, DD Milan.

The stylist takes the Polaroid and pins it on a large display board with the rest of the shots and efficiently returns with another sweater and it's the same routine taking turns with the other guys for the rest of the day. I stopped counting how many crew necks, V necks, sweater jackets, and hooded zippered creations I've tried on, but for sure each of them is spectacularly inventive unique and the finest Italian cashmere. Donna doesn't fool around.

It's late afternoon and I'm told to go to the hotel and rest. The shoot starts early and I have to be ready before sunrise.

The kid who met me at the train drives me a few a blocks to a small hotel. It's nothing fancy but for me it's the Ritz compared to my typical accommodations. And there's room service!

It's 4:30 AM and I realize I slept in my clothes. I jump in the shower and run downstairs. The guy with the car is parked in front of the hotel and we drive to an enormous outdoor market place. The stylist set up a large table and clothing racks. The "characters" are there and so is the photographer, a very handsome white haired man who could be a model himself. He's going through pages of edited Polaroids from yesterday. Donna is next to him looking spectacular in tight black jeans, t-shirt, and red high heels. She rushes to me, we embrace and she introduces me to Gianni. He's intensely organizing today's shoot but even so, he's very warm and welcoming. The stylist grabs me and selects my first wardrobe and we're off!

The shoot is run like clockwork. It's like doing a film and Donna is directing. We're buying fruits, examining vegetables, juggling melons, arguing with the butcher, smelling the fish, carrying groceries, buying massive bunches of flowers, hopping on and off motor scooters... *Action, action, action*! All this with constant sweater changes. And then close ups, details of the sweaters. Lastly, Donna directs us to "play" with the crowd of onlookers and I take cues from the guys and we get great reaction shots. This is no stilted catalogue shoot.

It all seems a blur at the end of the day. What a blast! Donna and Gianni are very pleased with the shoot and invite us "characters" to the studio for dinner.

I'm sitting next to Donna at a big table beautifully laid out with tons of delicious foods. I've fallen in love with her. She is a magnificent woman, extremely talented with great style and beauty. And who could imagine, we have friends in common? This becomes apparent as I fill her in on my Max's/Warhol background. She tells me Donyale Luna is in Fellini's Satyricon, filming now in Rome. And my favorite crazy witch, Orion de Winter, is living in Trastevere, a neighborhood in Rome filled with my kind of people. She gives me Orion's number. What an amazing experience and twist of fate.

Kisses and hugs to everyone and I say farewell to my new fabulous friend, Donna.

I get back to the hotel and the concierge hands me a large envelope from Donna. I open it in my room and find a beautiful note thanking me and wishing me well. And there's another envelope containing a wad of cash. Wow! And it's good bye to Milan.

On the train to Florence I dream about what is waiting for me. My brief time in Florence can only be about him and his creator.

He's seventeen feet tall and I'm fallen to my knees looking up at this miracle. God created him by creating the gay genius, Michelangelo. David stands magnificently composed, prepared to confront his monstrous oppressor Goliath.

A myriad of emotions overwhelm me and I pray to somehow find his strength and overcome my demons.

Many Michelangelo masterpieces are now experienced and my brief time in Florence comes to an end.

I'm in Rome and Jesus Christ, Roman men are spectacularly sexy and so is this city. Oh God, how I love Italy.

Something Morley 38

My small hotel is near the Spanish Steps, a big hangout for people watching. Even better and sexier is a café at night on the Via Veneto. It's La Dolce Vita and I'm in heaven.

It's time to reconnect with old friends. I call Orion de Winter. The phone rings and rings, I wonder if she... and she does! That deep-throated voice full of magic and craziness warms my heart. She gives me instructions how to get to her place in Trastevere.

The carnival of crackpots, the menagerie of maniacs, the outrageous outlaws, the divinely demented and newly invented, all gather at Orion de Winter's lair and are my partners in glorious crimes of passion and commotion in Rome. It's Max's, Fellini style. I couldn't find a better place in the world to complete my stay in Europe.

I'm luxuriating in Orion's bathtub filled with Mr. Bubble and rubber ducks on Opium and heavenly Hash. Orion makes an entrance in a Chinese silk robe on Acid. She abandons her garment and plunges into the tub opposite me. Gazing at me like the glamorous madwoman witch that she is, she slowly begins her incantation: "Cock, cunt. Cock, cunt! Cock, cunt!

She's very amusing but I have to make a phone call. Her chanting will be a perfect background for this call. I reach over to a pedestal with drugs and a phone. I first do the drugs then I do the phone, I know that fucking number by heart.

It's ringing and Orion is getting faster and

louder. "Hello again, this is Robert Starr calling Mr. Thompson... Where is he?... Well, who can help me regarding case number 11715? Thompson is my contact... That's the radio, just a minute. Orion, shut up! Okay, lady, is there anyone who knows about this? I need an update... I'll wait, thank you... Hello, hello who is this?... Say what?... *What?*... Japan? Japan! Holy fucking shit!" I drop the phone in the bathtub.

"They found it! Orion, they found the Jasper Johns in fucking Tokyo!"

"Cock cunt, cock cunt!"

And with that I plunge under Mr. Bubbles in ecstatic relief. The missing painting drama is resolved and my first European adventure comes to a close.

Man, what a trip.

CAPTURED BY THE CULT

BACK IN BROOKLYN, broke, and living with my parents. What an adjustment.

When I was in Rome, my dear friend Carol picked up my portfolio from my folks and presented my work to the agency she works for. They create print ads and trailers for feature films. I get an interview and I'm hired, but at this salary it'll take forever to move back to the City.

It's Thursday night and I'm back at Max's. It's changed, it seems over in way. Some are dead, some are just staying away. Max's is lonely tonight.

Sitting at a table in the back room I'm hoping for

41 The Heartbreak of Static Cling

a familiar face to appear. And boy does that happen, it's Michelangelo Antonioni's discovery, Mark Frechette.

Michelangelo Antonioni, Director of Blow Up and now Zabriski Point, conducted a massive search for the lead in his new film. It's been widely covered by the US and European press for months. And here he is, Mark Frechette, now starring in Zabriski Point and on the cover of every magazine. Mark is billed as the most beautiful new face in pictures.

Mark pauses at the entrance to the back room looking like he's searching for somebody and then he heads directly to my table and sits down. I manage to catch my breath and break the ice. "Well hello, you must know me. I've seen you in the movies."

He flashes a smile and his spectacular face lights up. "I'm Mark." As if I didn't know.

"I'm Robert." Things just happen to me but I'll never get used to it.

Daria Halprin, the other new discovery co-stars with Mark in Zabriski Point. She's also an impossible beauty. Their love affair was well publicized and true. Mark is straight and why is he alone and why is he sitting here with me?

I find it almost impossible to look at him, he's that kind of startling. Our conversation is casual and he seems genuinely interested to find out more about me. Why, I wonder? Mark asks me what I do and I tell him I'm an Art Director. He tells me he's living with people who are creating a magazine and they're looking for an Art

Director. The name of the magazine is Pluto—it's astrology based.

"That's interesting but I have a job."

He moves closer to me. "You could work on the magazine part time and,"—here's the kicker—"if you want to work on it, you can live with us. We have a townhouse on 13th Street."

I immediately order more white wine.

Questions about who's "we" and "us" for some reason doesn't cross my mind. I only hear, "You can live with us... we have a townhouse on West 13th Street." Could this be my escape from Brooklyn... with Mark Frechette?

He invites me to come to the house and meet the people working on the magazine. I tell him I'll bring my portfolio, thinking this is a job interview. We set a time tomorrow for the meeting, Mark splits, and my head is spinning.

I'm now the center of attention of the onlookers in the back room as I recover from this encounter with the help of much wine before I get on the F Train back to Brooklyn.

Tomorrow comes quickly and I'm looking for the address on this tree-lined street and gasp when I find the Georgian townhouse. A pleasant woman, Sophie, greets me at the door. She brings me into a comfortable living room and introduces me to five people who know my name and are very happy to see me. I notice two women in the kitchen cooking and caring for children.

43   The Heartbreak of Static Cling

The scene is a combination of Father Knows Best and Little House on the Prairie. Some of the guys look like they work at a law firm; others look like carpenters or accountants. The women are suburban housewives from another era. All of them are ultra-conservative, unusual, and interesting, like Sons and Daughters of the Revolution. I can't help being attracted to the weird and strange.

The house is just a lived-in home as bizarre as its occupants, dressed by Ethan Allen and furnished by Sears.

Sophie gathers two guys, Owen and Seth, and another housewife, Sarah. We move into the dining room table and I present my portfolio. They're fascinated and tell me Pluto's production office is just a block away on 14th Street. As far as they're concerned, I have the job, but they see my hesitance. Sarah takes over and brings me upstairs and shows me what would be my room if I decide to join them. The bedroom is large at the front of the house with three tall windows overlooking trees and there's a wonderful original carved marble fireplace.

What is happening? Why am I being treated this way? Is it because I came to them by way of Mark Frechette? Where is he?

Sarah tells me he's on the Hill.

"What's the Hill?" I ask.

She just says, "Boston."

We rejoin the group downstairs and I pack up my portfolio. I tell them I'm very interested, but need some time to make a decision. Then they inform me more of their arrangement. They all give half their salaries to the house each month. This way, expenses are met and food and board can be provided. Well, my pay is not much now, certainly not enough to rent a livable rat trap in Manhattan. This arrangement is compelling even though it's as weird as all the rest. I tell them I'll call tomorrow.

And just as I'm walking out the front door, I notice a framed photo of Charles Manson hanging on the foyer wall. I brush it off as an absurd Pop Art statement. Maybe they have a sense of humor?

Next day and my mind's made up, I'm doing it. I tell my folks about this fantastic opportunity and don't mention the salary thing or the portrait of Manson. I call the house and they seem very happy. I move in this evening.

I get there around 7 PM. They're all seated at the dining table and have a place set for me. The Norman Rockwell dinner is delicious. Owen plans to take me to the Pluto office tomorrow morning.

After dinner, conversation turns to a football game they're excited to watch together tonight. To their strong disappointment, I make every excuse not to join them. "I just want to unpack and settle in, I'm exhausted."

They shoot piercing looks at each other like they have a plan.

I'm upstairs in my room lying on the bed about to drift off and there's a knock on the door. It's Owen with

The Heartbreak of Static Cling

a small portable TV. He walks over to my bedside table and he sets it up so I can watch the game.

How thoughtful. "Thanks a lot."

Maybe I can find an old movie, but I'm sure this TV only broadcasts ball games. Father Knows Best meets The Twilight Zone.

Early morning and Owen is again at my bedroom door. "Grab some breakfast and I'll take you to Pluto." I throw on my spacesuit and go downstairs.

I take an egg sandwich and coffee from the table laid out buffet-style. Most of the others have already left for their day. Owen is in a rush and we dash out the door for a quick walk to the 14th Street subway station.

"I thought the office is on 14th Street?"

Owen descends the subway steps and shouts," It is, follow me."

Down a few flights and instead of going through the turnstile, Owen makes a sharp turn to a door at the end of a dim corridor. And there an office like no other, in the subway! It's a large room, three other guys are there working behind long tables near a window overlooking the tunnels subway tracks just a few feet away. Several trains scream by crossing each other in opposite directions, the room shakes. I'm in surreal heaven; this bizarre office is an underground art installation!

Pluto is in its infancy and has no graphic identity. I make a suggestion for the masthead, a three dimensional logo that can be photographed and lit differently for each issue. It's accepted and Seth, a carpenter, will follow up using the font I've chosen and create the logo from a block of wood. Perfect.

Next day back at my day job and I tell Carol my new address on West 13th Street. She lives just across town on University Place with her roommate, Marcia.

I'm assigned a confusing sci-fi cowboy time-jumping script. The film's name is Zachariah. It's currently in production and there are no production stills I can pull from. I invent an image of a cowboy plugging his headphones into his gun and this becomes the kickoff of the campaign. Another more interesting script with production stills are handed to me—it's Midnight Cowboy.

I'm now settled into my routine. It's good I have my job during the week and not spending much time at the house. Weekends are work at the subway office and back at the house on the prairie for dinner.

The strange becomes stranger. They have their own language, some of it is based on astrology and the rest is rhetoric about their devotion to their leader, Mel. Emotions swing from euphoric to high-drama with disturbing flash conflicts.

I stay a neutral observer. Rules are set and adhered to beginning at the front doorstep—no shoes allowed in the house. I tolerate the small stuff and try to comply with the rest. I'm even adapting to some of their catch phrases. They haven't focused their venom on me as of yet—I'm still on honeymoon.

47   The Heartbreak of Static Cling

As I was rushing to leave for work, I discover my favorite boots have disappeared—gone from their spot at the front foyer. Sarah flashes a deadly wide-eyed stare and declares the boots were evil and unacceptable and she's thrown them out. I'm stunned as she goes on about giving up what's not needed. I want to belt her but just leave it alone.

Just under that ultra-normal middle Americana façade lurks a monstrous, manipulative power, determined to make you worship and obey their Avatar.

I'm able to hold off avoiding conflicts and fascinated by their hidden truths exposed in stages. I'm here as an observer and that's all.

Weeks pass with just a few bumps in the road. My salary and work on Pluto are too valuable for them to release their full force to break me down and rebuild me in their image. So far, they continue to handle me gently.

Late one night, Sarah knocks on my bedroom door. She needs to have a talk with me and wants that to happen in her room. I follow her down the hall to her bedroom thinking she has some dramatic revelation, maybe instructions to lay down the law about some unknown beef. Okay, whatever it is, I can handle it.

Sarah pulls me into her room and onto her bed. She desperately wants me to fuck her and sticks her tongue down my throat. No way, baby! Now she's full-tilt furious and throws me out of her room with the force of a linebacker. She proved to herself and will make it clear to the "family" that I'm gay—not acceptable, just like my boots, not in this twisted culture.

Now they have more reason to tear me down and they savor the challenge. Tough shit, just try it.

I'm more guarded and they're more determined. It becomes more awkward every day and I tolerate it but I can feel their impatience growing.

I'm in my room almost asleep and suddenly I'm jolted by loud crashing furniture being overturned and violent screams. I'm shocked out of bed and pad to the top of the stairs where I have a partial view of the living room below.

I see Owen throw a lamp at a girl in her twenties. He slaps her face hard and shakes her shoulders, yelling, "This is real! You're not real, this is real!" He throws her to the floor and she hits her head on a side table and seems unconscious.

I want to run downstairs but I stop myself. I'm overpowered.

I hear Sarah add her vitriol, "She's just a privileged spoiled brat wanting to escape her bullshit cushy life. She wanted to drop acid and get the shit kicked out of her and that's exactly what she needs."

And I hear muffled whispers, but no more punishment.

This level of violence is new to me and right then I realize I'm out of here. I quietly pack my bag and wait. Three hours pass, it's 3:30AM and the coast is clear. Holding my breath I take one cautious step at a time and I get myself downstairs. Everything is meticulously put

The Heartbreak of Static Cling

back in its place like nothing happened, except for some bloodstains on the carpet.

Finally I'm out the door and run to 14th Street find a pay phone and call Carol. I tell her I need to see her right away. I figure the less she knows the better.

I get to Carol's place and spare the details, I just ask if I can hold up at her place for a few days and she agrees.

Most of today is spent detoxing from last night and trying to plan my next move. Carol comes home from work early with food. We're having a quiet dinner and not talking much. I'm obviously still on edge.

The intercom buzzes and I jump to my feet. Carol presses the button and I hear, "Tell Robert to come down, Mel wants to talk to him."

"That's Owen's voice! How the hell? Goddamn it!" I have no choice, I have to go; I can't let them anywhere near Carol. I guess the only way to really end this is to have a talk with Mel.

I get downstairs and see Owen at the front door. Seth is sitting in his car parked in front. Owen opens the back door and I get in, thinking Mel has come to 13th Street for one of his stealth visits and we're just driving across town to the house.

Owen speeds off and before I know it we're on the East River Drive. "Where are you going Owen?"

"The Hill." Motherfucker, I'm trapped and being kidnapped to Boston!

Can I trust him? Are we really going to Boston, or

what? I erase these thoughts and grab the door handle but if I could open the locked car door it would be suicide. I'm trying to breathe normally I know I can't talk my way out of this. My only hope is if we get to the Hill somehow I'll be able to convince Mel to let me go.

It's dark and I don't know where the hell we are, I've never been to Boston. We arrive at a chain link fence and an armed guard lets us in. The Hill is surrounded by the most dangerous ghetto in Boston, Roxbury. We ascend a long driveway revealing a compound of several old small houses in different stages of construction. I'm released from the car and led to one semi-completed structure with *bunk* beds.

I stop in my tracks and turn to Owen and Seth. "Where's Mel?" No answer and the two of them just leave.

There is no way out. I do everything I can to stay positive, thinking once I get to meet with Mel, this nightmare will be over. I have to believe this. And maybe if Mark's here, he can help.

I pull the blanket over my head and try to escape this nightmare.

Hammering and buzz saws at day break. Where am I? Oh, shit, Owens at the foot of my bunk. "Get up, you got work to do."

"Where's Mel?" Again, no answer.

I follow him outside and he leads me to a table with some sandwiches. "Is Frechette here?"

Owen points to a construction site. "You'll be

working with him building our recording studio."

What the fuck, slave labor?! I'm a kidnapped construction worker!? The absurdity kicks in and I bust into convulsive laughter, I might as well try to enjoy myself!

Owen yanks me to the construction site and takes off. I spot Mark, bare-chested drenched in sweat wielding a sledge hammer, very erotic. I approach him but he seems not to recognize me, he just keeps banging away like I'm not there. My heart sinks.

Another robotic worker hands me a saw and points me to planks of wood on a worktable. This is much worse than being forced to watch a football game, I'd like to take this saw and cut his head off.

My attempts to use a saw are obviously useless. I try again to get through to Mark but he seems to be in a trance. I just give up on him and the saw and run outside where I'm stopped by yet another robot. I'm yelling, "Where's Mel, he wants to talk to me!"

The robot replies, "Mel isn't here."

The wind is knocked out of me and I collapse to the ground. Several emotionless worker robots surround me. Owen breaks into the circle and pulls me up to my feet and drags me back into the bunkhouse. "You're useless here. Mel is in New York. You'll be taken to him tonight."

I'm an emotional mess crumpled up on the bunk and pass out.

It's dark and cold and there's a figure looming

over me. Again, it's Owen. He pulls me out of the bunkhouse and shoves me across the compound to his car. Horrible thoughts are nonstop but I force myself to shut down my fear and somehow believe he's actually taking me back to New York.

We're driving through Roxbury, streets are on fire and there's occasional gunshots punctuating the darkness. Owen speeds through the ghetto and gets onto a highway. I decide to keep my mouth shut, knowing I won't get anything from Owen. I have no idea where we are or what direction we're travelling. I try to get clues from road signs but I can't make sense of them. He takes an off ramp and I hold my breath until I see he's headed to the entrance of another highway heading south. As long as we stay on highways I feel safe.

Finally things start to look familiar and a whole new set of craziness fills my head. Who the fuck knows what Mel has in store for me and how can I handle it?

And here we are on lovely West 13th Street in front of that pleasant looking townhouse. Owen parks and gets me out of the car. He grabs my arm and walks me up the steps and into the house. No one's here, what? Are they hiding? He leads me to a door at the end of the foyer and opens it. I thought it was a closet but it's a staircase leading downstairs to Mel's private apartment.

And there he is in the flesh, the impish frail figure with smiling eyes, Mel.

I'm furious but showing any emotion is sure to backfire. I just have to stick to the script I

53   The Heartbreak of Static Cling

silently prepared.

"Hello Robert."

"Mel, hello, I'm so glad to be here."

"You were on the Hill!"

"Mel, it's really amazing, what a great compound. It's terrific to see all that great work being done."

"We're building recording studios, film studios and much more."

"Wow, that is so great! ...Mel, I need to tell you how much I care about you and everyone here. It's been really wonderful working on Pluto and it's shaping up to be a beautiful magazine. Mel, you're an artist. I'm sure you understand that I also am an artist. And Mel, that means even though I feel so connected to you and the family, I have to fulfill my purpose and in order to do so, I must leave and be on my own trip now."

Wow, I hope he swallows this bullshit. He stares at me and replies, "Robert, you're valued here, we care very much about you. I see you and I feel you. I know you have to find your own path. Realize we are here for you when you come clear and decide to return."

"Mel, thank you."

It fucking worked. With my elation disguised I soulfully hug Mel good bye. And I leave this house for good.

I crash at Carol's place. Even though ties have been cut, I'm still skeptical and I don't want them coming anywhere near Carol again. I've got to move.

In the morning I call a number I've kept in my

wallet for awhile—a guy at the ad agency gave it to me. Jean-Jacques answers and tells me he's still looking for a roommate.

I head uptown to his place as far from the cult as I can get.

SAINT BROADWAY

THE FLAMING DUTCHMAN lives in a Bauhaus townhouse apartment on East 72nd Street. Jean-Jacques Blooms is the premier adored florist for the mega rich Upper East Side society gala gals.

Jean-Jacques is in his late thirties, blonde, tall, and almost handsome. I suspect he's looking for more than a roommate. I'm so distracted by the fabulous apartment that I initially miss his outfit, black leather hot pants, tank top, and Dutch wooden clogs. And to think just when I've almost gotten used to the Gingham Prairie Frontier Pioneer look, now this!

The slick ground floor apartment has a giant wall of glass doors opening to a sumptuous garden and backyard. Everything is upholstered in raw silk, even the huge bed. But here's the catch, there's only one bedroom and we'd have to share that bed... Oh, really, mister hot pants?

I'm anxious to move in quickly but even so I make it very clear, I'll share that bed to sleep only. He agrees, we'll see. Tolerating Jean-Jacques will be nothing compared to the cult.

Life on the Upper East Side is also surreal, how I love the surreal! I'm at home, feeling obligated to dress up to take the garbage out. The Dutchman's friends are not at all amusing or interesting but easy to disregard.

My Max's/Warhol friends love this place, especially when Jean-Jacques isn't around.

Dutch is not a pretty language—putting it mildly—but when it's an opera, it's absolutely unbearable. I put my foot down and he relents, promising not to blast that guttural screeching when I'm home.

I wear pajamas to bed and keep hands off. And of course an attempt was made and again I have to make it very clear, there's no way. He now keeps his distance.

Two of his friends visit. Both look a little too slick in black leather jackets and Upper East Side tailoring.

The better looking one approaches me. "Do you like older men?"

I take a moment and reply, "Sure I like older men, younger men, women, and strange people," an answer from my hippie days.

He continues, "There's an older man, he's very rich, I can set you up with him."

"Set me up?"

"I'll make arrangements for you to have dinner with him but you have to agree that we get ten percent of everything you get from him." Wow, these guys are pimps! Well, I've never been pimped out before.

Would I like to meet a very rich old man? Who can he be? How did he get his fortune? Could this be interesting, could this be fun? But they're not getting anything from me, I'm no hustler and I won't take a dime from this old man. "What's his name?"

The pimp replies, "Saint."

"Saint? Is he clergy? Saint what?"

"Saint, that's all you need to know." He scribbles the address on a piece of paper and hands it to me. 17 West 64th Street.

"What's the apartment number?"

"It's a private house, be there tomorrow night at 8 PM sharp."

Saint's home stands among the mansion townhouses of 64th Street, discrete and stately. I arrive ten minutes early, time enough to study the chic limestone and brick exterior and that highly lacquered black door just within my reach.

My finger is on the brass doorbell wondering what waits. Finally I press it and hear a muffled chime. The door remains quiet for a moment and then a Chinese houseboy greets me looking me over head to toe. He leads me through a gallery entry foyer lined with giant framed posters. That's odd. I would expect fine paintings on these walls. The posters are all Neil Simon Broadway hits: Dark at the Top of the Stairs, Barefoot in the Park, The Odd Couple, The Star-Spangled Girl, Last of the Red Hot Lovers, Plaza Suite, The Gingerbread Lady, The Prisoner of Second Avenue. And then I realize what's printed on every poster in bold lettering–PRODUCED BY SAINT SUBBER.

Holy shit! That's who he is... He's Saint Broadway!

The houseboy brings me to a cozy den. "Saint will be down in a minute." He turns away and disappears into the elevator.

I'm not a major Broadway fan, but every single Neil Simon smash hit is produced by this Saint, Saint Subber! I sit there imagining the wealth of experience I'm about to meet.

Saint emerges from the elevator and I stand up to greet this frail, aged figure approaching. "Hello Saint, I'm Robert."

He takes my hand and studies my eyes and says, "It's great to meet you. I thought we'd have a nice dinner here, I have some steaks." He walks me to the kitchen. "Would you like to cook?"

"Doesn't your houseboy cook? I'm really not good at that."

He smiles. "That's okay, I'll do it."

I never thought he'd be cooking me dinner. I'm

watching him negotiate the kitchen, thinking there's no way this will ever be a physical relationship. But this just might be the beginning of a friendship, odd, fabulous, and unexpected. That's if he's not too upset I'm not a sex date.

Saint introduces me to his world and I bring him into mine. Our time together is filled with chic lunches and dinners at Le Cirque, La Grenouille, 21, Orso, Elaine's, and on and on. But it isn't the fanciness or the spectacular food, it's the candor, the warmth and humor and Saint sharing backstage secrets with me. Eye-opening stories of his close friends like Monty Clift, Truman Capote, Otto Preminger.

We're enjoying each other's company. I share my love for experimental theater at La Mamma, stories of Warhol, Candy Darling, Holly Woodlawn, Jackie Curtis, Eric Emerson, Elda Stiletto, Andrea "Whips" Warhol, Viva, Nico, Katrina, Ultra Violet, Lou Reed, The Velvet Underground, and the most outrageous performances happening nightly in the back room of Max's Kansas City.

One night after an unusually stuffy—if not delicious—dinner at La Grenouille, I just had enough of the Upper East Side and I drag Saint to Max's. And that night we're privileged to witness an encore performance by Andrea climbing on top of a table in the back room with an ice cream fantasy called 'The Snowball' screaming, "A little Acid, a little Carbona, some ups, some downs, some Methedrine, you mix it all up, you drink it all down!" And she breaks into her signature song, "Look what they did to my brains, Ma... Look what they did to my brains!"

Now that's what I call theater.

Mickey Ruskin runs into the back room and grabs Andrea off the table and carries her out, with Snowball still intact. Saint is impressed.

Magical weekend afternoon picnics begin. Saint gives me the keys to his delicious big chocolate brown Benz convertible and guides us across the George Washington Bridge to the Jersey Palisades where we find our spot and have wine and cheese and other goodies enjoying the view of the Hudson below and skyline across the river.

He tells me the story of a Thomas Mann novel entitled *The Transposed Heads*. It explores a couple's relationship between the spirit, body, and mind. Inspired by an ancient Hindu legend, Mann writes about two Indian friends, Shridaman and Nanda, one very physical, and the other all intellect. They decide to decapitate themselves. They awaken to find their heads restored to the wrong body. Now, Sita, the wife of Shridaman must determine the true meaning of identity as she navigates her own feelings as to which representation is her actual husband. As the love triangle carries on Mann shows just how entwined our mind, body and spirit are.

Saint wants to produce this not as a play but a film, a musical! And he wants me to create the key visuals, a storyboard illustrating the film. What an opportunity, what an amazing project!

    My birthday is coming up and though things are edgy between me and the Dutchman, I decide to throw a party. I know living with the flaming florist is coming to an end and this is my last chance to celebrate in that great apartment. He's cordial enough to bring home an over the top enormous floral centerpiece creation for the occasion, nice gesture. Could be he's celebrating my imminent departure. He tries not to reveal his frustration about our nonsexual relationship and the lack of any information whatsoever regarding Saint and he decides not to be home for the party. Good.

    It's a festive soirée and the underground goes uptown. As a parting party favor I instruct my debauched guests to grab some flowers and take them with them, a major faux pas.

    I'm having sex with a guest whom I haven't met before on the raw silk sofa near the wall of glass for the amusement of our posh neighbors and Jean-Jacques arrives back home in time to catch the action.

    I don't know which indiscretion is greater, having sex in full view of his neighbors or corrupting his precious floral arrangement. But whatever, it's the end of me and the flaming Dutchman of 72nd Street.

    Desperately needing a place to crash I call Carol and she again agrees to let me stay at her place as long as I need to, bless her. I pack up my things and split.

    Marcia, Carol's roommate, tolerates me sleeping

on the couch. My contribution to the rent helps and all is good for the time being. I'm filling Carol in on the details of the Dutchman's story when the phone rings. Carol answers and hands me the phone, It's Saint. He asks me if I want to go to the movies. That's new—we never go to the movies. He tells me he'll pick me up in an hour. That's even stranger. I usually go to his garage and get the car.

I'm waiting in front of the building and Saint's big Benz pulls up with the top down and someone is sitting low in the passenger seat.

I approach the car and the passenger extends a limp hand. Truman Capote says, "Hello."

Truman Capote opens the door and scoots forward to let me get into the back seat. All I can muster is, "Truman, great to meet you." He waves his little hand and replies, "You too."

In shock, I manage, "So... Where are we going?"

Truman replies, "Time Square."

I take a deep breath. "Great! Reminds me of Coney Island, especially the greasy alleyways lined with freak shows, spook houses and toothless hookers. I grew up there." Truman turns around to look at me and I continue, "I love Alligator Boy, but my favorite is Pin Head, she's always so happy!" I'm thinking, did I take acid fifteen minutes ago? "What movie are we seeing?"

Saint replies, "Willard."

I ask him, "The rat movie?"

He nods his head. "Yep."

The Heartbreak of Static Cling

"Truman, you like rats?"

"I've known a lot of rats, some of them I've gotten to like very much."

"What about the ones you hate?"

"I set traps." He turns around and lets out a little giggle. At this point I better shut up and enjoy the ride; I'm in a car with Saint Subber and Truman Capote going to sleazy Time Square to see a rat movie!

I finally settle into the fact this is really is happening and I can talk again. "I feel a kinship to rats, rats is my last name backwards."

Truman chuckles. "Oh, how glamorous." He sounds just like Andy Warhol... I must have taken that acid with my grapefruit juice this morning.

Saint pulls into a parking lot on 42nd Street and parks. We get out of the car and make our way through piles of garbage and shady characters living on the streets of Time Square. And there it is in broken letters on the marquis of a fleabag theater: WILLARD.

Saint buys three balcony tickets. My sneakers slide on the greased carpeted stairs up to our seats. I sit between Saint and Truman. It's stadium seating up here and as we settle in a rough looking guy sits himself one row below us right in front of Truman. The guy's bald tattooed head is level with Truman's knees.

The lights dim and Truman squirms in his seat with excitement. Willard begins and it's taking shape to be especially good featuring Saint and Truman's old friend, Elsa Lanchester.

We get to a scene with hoards of angry rats and Truman sinks down in his seat and disappears. Suddenly I hear weird squeaking rat noises at my feet and my ankles are attacked! "What the hell?"

Truman Rat is on his hands and knees biting my ankles! I swat his head. "Stop that, Truman. Stop!"

He scurries away and attacks Saint's ankle and Saint lets out a loud yell. The bald head in front turns around to see what the commotion is about.

I smile at him as I grab Truman and put him back in his seat like a good boy. He continues making rat noises throughout the remainder of the film.

Willard comes to the end and lights go on and the thug springs to his feet and turns quickly facing Truman. Well, here it comes, Truman is going to get a fist in his face! The thug barks, "Hey you!"

Truman recoils.

The thug continues, "Are you Truman Capote?"

Truman meekly answers, "Why yes."

The tattooed headed thug replies, "I wanna shake your hand, you're the greatest!"

Truman extends his little hand. I'm doubled over hysterically laughing, struggling for breath. That was the best scene of this movie!

And that's the end of my play date with Truman and also the beginning of a turning point between me and Saint. Nothing to do with our time with Truman, it's about my long distance relationship with someone I've met and fallen deeply in love with, Don Hall.

The Heartbreak of Static Cling

I've let Saint into very personal parts of my life including how much I'm anticipating Don's return and beginning our lives together and this information changed Saint. I believe he feels our friendship has gone as far as it will and time has come to let go. With gratitude and sadness I feel the same way.

The amazing key visual illustrations of *The Transposed Heads* are completed and I give him the drawings as a parting gift.

UNIVERSITY PLACE

THE SMALL AD AGENCY Carol and I work for is becoming a dead end. More film studios are creating their own in-house advertising and our agency is hurting for business. I'm hounding headhunters for interviews with as many ad agencies as possible. Pounding the pavement is my new occupation. Carol is searching for free lance design work to ease the pain of the inevitable collapse of the agency.

Landing my dream job seems hopeless. I fast walk city blocks with my portfolio from one interview to another with agencies I'm really not interested in mostly every day, it helps me blow off steam.

My headhunter, Mitzy Morris, is getting sick of

The Heartbreak of Static Cling

my constant calls. I've pushed her to her limit and she's been setting up appointments for weeks. But the meetings are rehearsals for the interview I really want at DDB, if I can get one.

Doyle Dane Bernbach is very difficult to crack. There's a line around the block of very talented candidates competing for a chance to get a foot in the door of the most acclaimed creative advertising agency in the world, DDB.

I've got to figure out a way that will get me there.

Carol and I reminisce about how our lives were changed by the legendary Mr. Leon Friend who created a world like no other long ago at Abraham Lincoln High School in Brooklyn. We were among the last very lucky ones to benefit from his mentorship. Mr. Friend created an art department in a public High School in Brooklyn rivaling most art colleges and universities. We had four years with him opening worlds of the Bauhaus, typography, graphic design, print making, editorial design, illustration, art history, and so much more. He would inspire us with news of his former students who've become giants in all fields of art, design, and advertising.

I knew of Mr. Friend even before I was old enough to go to High School. My uncle Morris was one of his students long ago, he told me about the miracle of Mr. Friend when he discovered I had a passion for art.

Uncle Moe, as I call him, is a great painter and also the founder of a successful advertising agency. He and his elegant wife Francis have three sons, Ronnie,

Howard, and Eric, all beautiful. As a kid I felt their lives were a dream fantasy, living in great home on Long Island. Uncle Moe had a Harley Davidson, loved flying, piloted a Cessna, and restored a vintage yacht. He has always been my inspiration.

When he heard I was about to attend Lincoln High School, he wrote a letter of introduction for me to present to Mr. Friend.

This conversation with Carol suddenly sparks a strategy and I begin investigating Creative Directors currently working at DDB. And there they are, Lester Feldman, and William Taubin. Both are Mr. Friend's alumnae. They were at Lincoln around the same time as Uncle Moe.

I've had it with head hunters endless interviews and phone calls, now that I have a different plan in place.

More research reveals Taubin is about to retire, but Lester Feldman is still going strong. Bingo! And my calls to Lester Feldman's office cracks the door open enough for me to get an appointment with him at DDB.

I'll do anything to work here no matter how menial, no matter the salary. I would pay them for the opportunity and that's exactly what I tell Lester. It's easy to talk to him, like we're old friends with something very important in common. I have a good portfolio, but wish it was stronger. I hope he sees potential.

But weeks pass and nothing and no word. I have too much respect to hound him. I sink with the realization that I'll have settle for less and just get a job,

69   The Heartbreak of Static Cling

any job. So it's back to pounding the pavement.

It's been a month since my meeting with Lester, still no job and the phone rings and I can hardly believe it. I'm offered a position as an Assistant Art Director at DDB and my career officially begins.

I wish my Uncle Moe was alive to see this. He was just forty-four when Lymphoma took his life. The ad agency he created couldn't sustain his loss and my dream of being a part of that ended.

DDB is situated on several floors of a prewar office tower on 5th Avenue and Forty Second Street. My small office is adjacent to Lester's. It has a big south facing window with a view of the downtown skyline.

My first assignments are simple tasks, paste ups and mechanicals. Nothing creative, just the nuts and bolts of Lester's GTE account which is in the midst of a long standing print and TV campaign. Lester is a master at typography and conceptually his campaign is pretty great, I have a lot to learn from him. He's upgraded GTE's image giving that company new life and a unique personality, inventively along the same lines of how DDB took an odd looking underpowered small unpopular German car and created VW Beetle mania.

The creative energy here is palpable and yes, this is the place where I can do it.

And another really important beginning is about to happen. Don and I will be together again very soon.

The search is for an apartment for us is no easy task. My salary isn't much now and Don doesn't have anything lined up. Even if we had the money, apartment hunting is just as awful as job hunting.

I scour rental listings in the Times and Village Voice and make dozens of calls to realtors and I go to lots of showings of unlivable expensive crap. Weekends, I just walk the streets, hoping to find a "For Rent" sign that doesn't exist in New York.

Time is running out and there's little chance of finding something quickly. But Carol comes to the rescue, she tells me her roommate Marcia is moving to Vegas, she's aced a dance audition and got a gig there. And Don and I can have her bedroom, how great. This gives us the time needed to finally land our own place.

But I'm concerned the three of us living together, even for a little while, could be awkward. I decide to brush it off and keep it to myself.

How many times has Carol come through for me, I'll always love her.

ALWAYS CAROL

CAROL AND I had just graduated high school and we decide to celebrate by going on a journey before we begin our college days—Carol to Pratt and amazingly my portfolio won me a full four year scholarship to SVA, thank you, Mr. Friend!

It's 1965 and Haight Ashbury, the epicenter of the revolution, is calling us. Our folks are thrilled, believing this will be our prenuptial honeymoon. And that overrides their concern about California hippies, drugs, and rock and roll. They gladly see us off at the airport.

We get to San Francisco and surprisingly we're really put off by the scene in Haight Ashbury. Hippies are overdosing in streets crowded with guided tour busses filled with gawking horrified tourists taking snapshots like visitors at a zoo. Flower power is running out of batteries.

We hitch a ride to who knows where and the guy who picked us up asks what we're into. Of course we tell him, "We're artists" and this gives him a roadmap.

Driving across the Golden Gate Bridge, the fog lifts as soon as we get to Sausalito, spectacularly gorgeous Sausalito. Houseboats line the dock and a completely different creative vibe envelopes us. What a contrast to the ravages in the Haight.

We find a small hotel looking like a Victorian guest house. Casa Madrona offers us a room with a view of the bay and the bridge, Alcatraz and Angel Island and we're thrilled.

It's fish n' chips, galleries and artists everywhere... But that night we need to head back to the city to see something we know we'll always remember, Big Brother and the Holding Company with Janis Joplin at the Avalon Ballroom. Now that's San Francisco!

We return to our hotel filled with passion and we fall into bed. We're in love, but there's been no sex. And if there's a time and a place for sex, it's now. Or is it?

I've always known I'm gay. I didn't think that would stop me but it has, even though it never stopped me from emotionally loving Carol.

Carol remains in bed, sadly understanding, as I throw on some clothes and leave our room to walk down to the dock, crushed.

I'm sitting there with a cigarette, watching moonlight float on the water and I finally come to a resolution. Sex with Carol will never work, but the kind of love we have will work differently and continue for years to come. And to my surprise Carol appears at my side and sits next to me. She has something important to tell me and hands me several small bottles of wine from our room's minibar.

She carefully and affectionately explains how completely alike we are. And then after a long pause, Carol dramatically confesses she's sexually attracted to women.

Well, ain't that a spectacular kick in the head.

We take a good look at each other and suddenly everything becomes so completely hilarious we burst out laughing so hard it hurts. We just can't stop feeling so carefree and gay! Clearly, we're not in high school anymore.

DRELLA

DRELLA IS A NICKNAME coined by Warhol superstar Ondine, a contraction of Dracula and Cinderella. Andy hated it but those close to him use it all the time knowing how appropriate it really is.

Don and I are living with Carol on 13th Street and my concerns about the three of us living together have disappeared. It's great to see Carol and Don become close friends.

It's Saturday afternoon and Carol and Don are out grocery shopping and suddenly there's a banging and yelling at the door. It's Andrea "Whips" Warhol in all her deranged madness. She's carrying a bunch of newspapers that wrote her up as the greatest Andy

75 The Heartbreak of Static Cling

Warhol superstar playing Silvia Miles' daughter in Andy's new movie, *Heat*. Everybody is talking about that and they're also talking about the upcoming Rolling Stones concert at Madison Square Garden and the birthday party for Mick Jagger afterwards on the roof of the Warwick Hotel.

Andrea busts into the apartment yelling, "Andy gave everybody tickets to the Stones concert and the Stones party except me, the biggest superstar that ever hit the silver screen! Look at my reviews! He gave everybody tickets! I want a ticket to the Stones concert, I want to go the Stones party!"

I grab her by her shoulders, "Andrea, calm down, calm down. Let me tell you what we're going to do, calm down!"

She finally shuts up.

"Let's go out for a drink and then we'll go up to the Factory and we'll just ask Andy for tickets, I'm sure this will work, okay?"

Now that we have a plan, Andrea composes herself by flipping through all the newspapers searching for her reviews.

"Come on Andrea, I've seen all that, let's go." I get her out of the apartment and we walk to a bar in the West Village. We have just one drink each and I pull her out of the bar and we head to the Factory to see Drella.

On our way we pass a small storefront toy store. I spot a cap gun and decide to buy it for her, she needs it for protection.

We get to the building on Union Square and I press the buzzer. Andy's secretary, Pat Hackett answers and I just announce, "Hi Pat, it's Robert Starr and Andrea." And after a short pause she lets us in.

When the elevator door opens we see Pat at her front desk and she tells us Andy is in the back. So here we are in the Factory with no one else but Drella and his cohort Paul Morrissey.

Andrea begins somewhat sane, "Andy everybody got tickets to the Stones concert and the Stones party... except me! Give me a ticket to the Stones Party, to the Stones Concert! *Give me a ticket to the Stones concert and the Stones party!*"

Drella stands there deadpan and so does Morrissey. Pat retreats to her front desk and Andy replies, "What do you think, Andrea, I'm made out of tickets?"

Well that did it. Andrea pops open her Bakelite fifties handbag and she retrieves the cap gun and shoots herself in the head three times and keeps shooting. Now this is amusing, Andy's cracked plaster complexion becomes more like blue cheese as he checks to see if he was shot.

Paul Morrissey lunges at Andrea and grabs the "pistol" and takes her by her arms and pulls her out to the elevators. Andrea is in full tilt hysterics screaming, *Give me a ticket to the Stones concert and the Stones party!"* And she opens her handbag again and pulls out a box. *"Here's a present, Andy! It's my music box that plays 'Oh*

77 The Heartbreak of Static Cling

My Papa'!"

Andy grabs it and Paul drags her away. I'm just as deadpan as Drella and he pipes up, "Robert, that was a very bad joke. Go and take care of Andrea."

I get out of the building and Andrea is combusting, laughing and screaming. "Come on, Andrea, we're going to Max's and I'm calling Pat Hackett as soon as we're there."

I'm in the phone booth inside Max's with Andrea at my side. "Pat, what is with him? He gave everybody tickets, what the hell!"

Andrea starts screaming, "I gave him my music box that plays 'Oh My Papa'!"

And Pat tells me, "Andy threw the music box out the window."

"He threw Andrea's music box out the window?!"

Andrea goes ballistic, "He threw my music box that plays 'Oh My Papa' out the window!"

"Now Pat, you get tickets from him right this second and you come to Max's and give them to Andrea or I'm coming back there!"

She puts me on hold and after a pregnant pause, "Okay, I'll be there. " And she hangs up.

"I told you it would work, Andrea, now calm down. Pat will be here any minute you'll see."

It takes about fifteen minutes to calm Andrea and here comes Pat Hackett with an envelope, she hands it to Andrea and leaves.

In that envelope is one ticket to the Stones

concert and an invitation for one to the party.

Andrea puts the tickets back in the envelope and hands it to me. "I'm not going, you go, I don't want to go."

"After all that? Are you sure you don't want to go?"

"Yeah, you go."

A few days pass and tonight's the night. I'm getting ready for the big deal Stones concert and after party, Don is laughing his head off about the scene in the Factory and suddenly *bang bang bang* on the door.

"It's Andrea let me in!"

"Andrea, hi, you change your mind?"

"No! I want to watch it on television with Don!" Don gives her a hug and I continue getting dressed. I'm about to leave and Andrea appears from the kitchen completely naked with a bucket of water and a scrub brush and begins scrubbing the floor. I wish Carol was home to see this. Don is amused, Andrea is happily occupied and I'm out the door.

Madison Square Garden and gang's all here, Drella and his disciples are all sitting in a row behind me and I can feel the daggers coming from Drella. He probably thinks it was all a plot I cooked up to get the tickets from Andrea. I turn to him, blow a kiss, and avoid Drella like a plague the rest of the night.

HALLSTARR

DON AND I are together, nothing else matters and a big change is happening. I'm becoming we and us and me and Don and that's all I want and that's all I need, it's astonishing.

Don lands a job as a photographer for an educational filmstrip company. He's a terrific reportage photographer and enjoys his assignments: children at play, old folks in the park, teens hanging out, and so on. These still shots are put together on film with narration and distributed to schools, corporations, hospitals and the like. He's doing something creative right away even though this has little to do with his passion for music.

I've been promoted again raising my salary significantly. And I'm developing new campaigns for GTE, Polaroid, Atari, Clairol and Bankers Trust and also pitching new business.

I've become more aggressive in the hunt for our own apartment. Newspapers and realtors have proven useless, my new strategy is to find the Supers who live in buildings of interest and have a talk. You've got to get pushy if you want to get anything in this city.

The Gramercy Park neighborhood is my prime target, but it's always been pricey. The park is surrounded with mansion townhouses and landmark co-ops, rentals are few and far between but why not aim high?

THE BIG TIME

TONIGHT Don and Carol are going to the movies but I'm not into it and I decide to check out Max's. I'm in the back room again with the regular crackpots and some newcomers when a guy runs through Max's and into the back room screaming, "Andrea threw herself out the window!"

At first I think this is just a nut auditioning for the crazies in the back room but then horror hits, it's probably true.

I bolt out of Max's and run to Andrea's apartment building on 5th Avenue and 12th Street and I see what's left, just remnants of police tape and a dark, wet, stained sidewalk.

Andrea with a bottle of Coke in one hand and a bible in the other leaped to her death from her 14th floor apartment window. She left a note reading, "This time I'm going all the way, I'm going to hit the big time!"

Spectacularly nuts and vulnerable Andrea, Warhol Superstar, another victim of Drella.

He threw her music box out the window.

FINDING AN IRVING PLACE

IT'S A SIX STORY building on Irving Place just one mansion townhouse away from the Park. Two townhouses were combined and converted into apartments in the fifties but unfortunately their classic facades were lost. Now it's a brick faced building with steel casement windows being the only saving grace. But most importantly, it's a rental building.

I press the button on the intercom marked "Superintendant" and I'm buzzed in. Anne and her husband George are real old time New York Supers. Anne tells me, "George is busy fixin' the Burler and then he gotta go fix a turlit and I gotta mop the lobby." I love

Finding an Irving Place 84

her instantly and I tell her what I'm looking for.

Anne stops mopping for a minute and scratches her head, she tells me a one bedroom on the second floor is coming up. "I ain't sure about the rent, maybe $250?" I want to kiss her but we just met so I give her my card.

She promises she'll call me when it's vacated. I offer her some key money but she refuses. Anne's on the up and up!

Jesus Christ, you can't get a better location unless you're loaded.

Two days pass and if I don't hear from Anne I'll go nuts. I stop myself from bugging her, I'll just wait a little longer.

I'm at work about to go to lunch and Anne calls. I run out of my office grab a cab and here I am at 82 Irving Place. Anne opens up apartment 2C. It's a good size place and the layout's okay. Only one thing, the living room and kitchen face a brick wall. Luckily the windows face south and the place gets some good daylight. The bedroom windows face a rear garden, that's better. I call Don at work and describe the apartment. He agrees we should grab it and we're home!

Life on Irving Place begins and we're shopping for pots and pans. Don is very particular about all that, he's an incredible cook. His dad's Club Café is very popular in Jefferson Texas. It's near the Bayou and Shreveport Louisiana, soul food country.

Big Dolly was the main cook at the Café when Don was a young boy. She showed him what "Vibration

The Heartbreak of Static Cling

Cooking" is, it's all about being in touch with your soul and putting it into your food. And boy is Don in touch; I've never tasted anything like his cooking.

Somehow it feels like we've always been partners. Together we're stronger than New York City and nothing gets in our way. It's fun watching people walking down the street so distracted looking at Don they bump into light poles, he's that good looking.

But the scene happening in New York now is double edged—impossibly magnetic but also dangerous. 1972 New York sex—in blacked out gay bar basements, on rotting piers by the Hudson, inside abandoned trucks, subway toilets, baths, movie theaters and alleyways, the sleazier the better for rebellious anonymous fucking, sucking, and whatever it takes to get your rocks off. And it has nothing to do with friendship or even worse, love.

The danger is part of the draw. Pickpockets, muggings, and occasional torture raise the ante for a good night out. Nobody has a clue this could turn lethal. The biggest horror is at closing time when the pitch dark back room lights flip on and you discover you just did it with someone you know.

We're drawn to the bars, Don loves pinball and I watch guys gawk at him and drool. I get a good laugh at that. The temptation of the back rooms is strong. We give each other the freedom to explore knowing nothing there could get in the way of our relationship.

We have late nights in bed laughing about sordid details of our encounters down in the dark. It's just occasional and meaningless fun.

My job has some annoying aspects I've yet to conquer and I can feel Don's irritation growing about obstacles preventing him from his music. And so our adventures in the dark back rooms distract and ease our mounting frustrations.

Some workdays feel like a week. I finally get home and shed my suit, pull on my jeans and t-shirt, make myself a drink and turn on the TV.

"Eyewitness News reports Mark Frechette and two other members of a cult attempted robbery of The New England Merchant Bank in the Fort Hill section of Roxbury. One of them, Christopher Thein, was killed by the police. Frechette and Sheldon T. Bernard were arrested. They're confined at a state prison in Norfolk Massachusetts."

Armed bank robbery, Mark?! What the fuck for, to build more crap on the Hill? You gave them everything including your soul and now you got a lot of years in prison to thank for that. I hope you use the time to remember who you are.

This is so awful and shocking and sad.

Don gets home and I fill him in on the news and all the details I've held to myself including the kidnapping. He's stunned and asks if I'm sure all ties are cut. I tell him it's definitely ended. We promise to forget about it and move on. We have a whole new life together.

Don's office building is on 5th Avenue just a block away from DDB. He's on the 19th floor facing west and

The Heartbreak of Static Cling

I'm searching for his building from my office window and I call him, "Don, look out your window, look to your right and two buildings from the corner of 42nd Street. Count four floors from the top. Can you see my window? I'm yanking the blinds up and down."

It takes a few minutes. "I see you! Robert wait a minute... Look!"

I spot his window blinds going up and down. "Don... Don!"

We see each other waving like crazy kids and it feels like a miracle. I pull my focus to endless skyscrapers and back again to that window framing Don. I found someone and something so very hard to find in this sea of strangers.

Ann Leonard is the legendary vocal coach of major stars. She is extremely particular and she doesn't work with non-professionals. But Don has been persistent and charming and Ann finally makes an exception and Don gets an audition.

Ann allows Don to bring me with him to her fortress on the upper west side—one of those famous prewar buildings with very thick walls and perfect acoustics. Her concert grand Steinway sits center stage in her enormous living room. Everything about Ann Leonard is of grand scale. She directs me to a chair in a far off corner and shows Don to the piano. Ann settles herself into an armchair facing him and commands, "Begin."

And Don begins with a prelude to the song,

"Everything Must Change." His mastery of the piano is evident and then he sings. This is the first time I realize the enormity of his gift. I'm sitting in the corner of that room astounded.

Ann is expressionless throughout his performance. After a full two minutes of tense silence, Ann Leonard slowly lifts herself to her feet and announces, "We begin next Tuesday at 11 AM." And she pats him on his shoulder.

Don is so startled all he can do is say, "Tuesday at eleven."

Ann almost smiles. "Yes. Now go and take your friend with you."

Don is speechless and elated as we leave Ann's lair and so am I. Ann is exactly what Don needs now.

Back home the electric keyboard he's been struggling to play within these thin walls comes into focus. I hear his song in my head and I know everything must change. I promise myself we'll have a better place for his music and for the both of us soon.

I know what it feels like to have a burning need to fulfill a dream.

FATE

MY FRESH off the press business card reads, 'VP Associate Creative Director.' With this comes more opportunity to produce great work and I've just booked Bill King to photograph my new GTE campaign.

I arrive at his studio early to have some fun with Bill before we get down to business.

King's studio is enormous, minimally chic stark white and pin drop quiet. There's a terrific reason for this unusually hushed atmosphere. Most top photographers keep their studios loud with runway music. Bill keeps his studio dead quiet building tension as much as possible. He whispers instructions to his assistants and models. And when everyone is in position Bill blasts his models with giant fans and assistants spray water into the fans and they go berserk exploding with the kind of crazy energy only Bill can capture on film.

His assistants are quietly setting up for the shoot, Bill should be here soon. I get some coffee and make myself comfortable sitting on a wide ledge of one of the massive windows affording spectacular city views and more impressive views of this fabulous studio.

Bill arrives and rushes to me with a hug. We're about to launch the Phone Mart campaign, Phonetastic! Bill and I will show GTE how to sell phones. This should be a fun shoot with Jerry Hall.

Bill takes me to his private office shuts the door and he slides open a flat file and pulls out some large black and white prints, great photographs of nasty hilarious sex acts. Taking these kinds of shots is one of his late night obsessions. He passes me some coke and a straw. I take a snort and examine the fashion/porno photos wishing I could use them for Clairol.

A knock on the door and it's Bill's assistant telling him he's needed for a lighting check. Bill hurries out and I remain in his office searching through his flat files and find a large black and white photograph he took one fateful night. And I get lost in that image of me and Don in bed together for the first time.

It's Saturday late afternoon, two years ago. Bill and I are walking down Christopher Street and we come across a new small boutique. I follow Bill into the store and my life changes.

The sight of this guy standing behind the counter stops me in my tracks. I study his amazing perfect features framed with black, thick curls. Somehow looking into his impossible blue eyes, I recognize him even though we've never met.

He smiles, kind of shy, and says, "I like your shirt." I detect a slight Texas accent. It's a western cut shirt made with sections of a vintage plaid silk.

"A designer friend made this for me, call me and I'll give you her number, got a pen?" He hands me a scrap of paper and a pen and I scribble my name and number and hand it to him.

"Thanks, Robert. I'm Don."

Bill grabs my arm pulling me to leave he flashes a big grin at Don and tugs me out of the store.

Outside the only thing I can say is, "Wow."

Bill smiles. "Yeah... See you at my place around eight, I'll make dinner."

"Okay."

Bill heads up the block to his place and I walk home wondering if Don will call me and why didn't I get his number?

As soon as I get home the phone rings, could it be?

No, it's Bill. "You are coming over tonight, right?"

"What's up Bill, I told you I'll be there."

"Guess who else will be here."

No, this can't be happening, "Who, Bill?"

"That guy from the store, Don."

"Oh, wow, see you later." I hang up. Shit, shit, shit! Bill doubled back to the store and invited Don, damn it! The last thing in the world I want is Bill luring Don into his craziness with me, drugs, sex, and Instamatics. I cringe but can't do anything about it and I'm not leaving Don alone with Bill. I have to be there. I have to see Don again.

Bill lives at 2 Horatio Street, a coveted pre-war classic building in the West Village. I arrive at eight sharp. Bill opens his door and I spot Don in the living room sitting in a club chair lit by the roaring fireplace.

He smiles at me and all I can say is "Don."

And he just replies, "Hi, Robert," and that did it.

I throw off my jean jacket and fall into the overstuffed sofa. Bill sits in another club chair in front of the coffee table laid out with appetizers, a large mound of powder on a mirror, and a great bottle of white wine. Here we go... I'm in this and there's no turning back. Thanks a lot, Bill.

I pour myself a glass of wine, take a snort, and just let whatever happens, happen.

Don tells us his sublet in Chelsea is just for the summer. He's going back to Texas this fall for his last year at The University of Texas, Austin. And after that he has a few months study planned at a music institute in Vienna. I'm trying to hide my emotions. I want him to stay here and live with me forever. What a crazy fantasy, we just met! What's going on with me?

He's got a lot of plans and needs to do what he needs to do. I can't get in the way of that. Don's a composer, singer-songwriter, and piano is his instrument. Not bad for a kid from small town Jefferson Texas. He's twenty-three, six months younger than me, so open innocent and goodhearted—is it naiveté, or is it an innate wisdom as I suspect?

I avoid going into too many details about myself. I don't want to reveal my New York street smart tough skepticism which now seems so unattractive. He pulls my much better self to surface as we continue to connect.

Don's manner also seems to be rubbing off on Bill, he's actually behaving himself. We're like kids playing and having fun. Bill finds his trusty Kodak Instamatic and snaps away and comes up a with suggestion, "Let's go to Chinatown, I know a great place."

That's a surprise. "Chinatown? I thought you were making dinner? What's this great place called, Hung Fat Dong? That joint's just across the street from The Pearl Necklace Szechuan, right?"

Bill replies, "It's Cantonese."

"Bill, can't on knees? Better on back!" Don cracks up and I love his laugh. We take another hit of Coke and speed outside. Bill grabs a cab, we pile in and Bill keeps snapping away capturing our shenanigans on film as our cab flies through the streets to Chinatown.

Bill orders everything on the menu. Of course we

have no appetite and the platefuls become toys and photo props as we practice our chopstick skills with flying dumplings, springing spring rolls and projectile pot stickers under the fluorescent lights and Bill's flashbulbs. Our waiter is not amused as Bill gets some great pictures of him trying to calm us down. We get our leftovers packed up and split.

We're back at Bill's place, it's three in the morning, and we're stoned and charged with sexual energy. This threesome is exactly what I wanted to avoid but there's no turning back. We rip off our clothes groping, fondling, and laughing our asses off playing with each other. The three of us fall into bed and eventually Don and I embrace and melt together, drifting off.

Hours pass and Bill gets up out of bed and quickly puts his clothes on, grabs his camera and captures a picture of Don and I naked, embracing in bed. And then he quickly leaves his apartment. This is so unlike him, I guess he felt what was happening with me and Don and decided to leave us alone with each other.

I'm lost in the memory of all of that captured in this photograph of our first time in bed together. Bill's assistant knocks on the door snapping me back to today and I quickly stash the photograph back in the flat file.

Jerry Hall was great, Bill was great, and the shots are beyond perfect for the kickoff of the campaign.

I get home and celebrate with Don and go out to a fabulous dinner. Working with Ann has given Don

The Heartbreak of Static Cling

direction and confidence. He's auditioned a lot and landed a lead part in a new off Broadway show, "Jonny Manhattan." We both have so much to be thankful for.

Weeks and weeks of rehearsals and the premier is around the corner. We're both thrilled, and so is my mom. Zelda contacts an old producer friend of hers and invites him to the show. I think about calling Saint, but it's a bit complicated. I decide to wait for the reviews before I do that.

Don was great, the play not so much, it shuts down after just a few performances. That's New York show business. Don is encouraged to continue auditioning but even so, it's hard for him to feel he's really getting anywhere.

And then he gets a call from an old friend.

Don's sitting at the dining table with a serious look on his face. I pull up a chair, "What's going on?"

"I got a call from Mike Ivy."

"Mike Ivy... you went to school with him, right?"

"Yeah, he's in West Virginia and he's starting a band and wants me to go down there and..."

"You want to?"

"Mike's a great musician."

"Are you having some kind of relationship with him?"

"No, he's straight, we're friends."

"West Virginia, Don?"

He seems determined and I can't stand in his way. He has to go to West Virginia, he has to find his music and he has to make a full commitment to this. And I have to encourage him, I can't stop it and it's killing me.

Next day he packs his bags and it's heartbreak for the both of us as he gets into a cab and it pulls away.

I go back upstairs to our apartment and dissolve sobbing. But I want him to go to fucking West Virginia to Mike Ivy and become more successful than our wildest dreams. I want the world to hear his voice.

This hurts all over. I have no choice but to turn the pain of this separation into empowerment and resolve and somehow create a life big enough for both of us.

BEING BOB

AFTER SEQUESTERING my miserable self in bed for a week, I'm back at work as Bob. Bob is stronger than Robert. Bob doesn't have a broken heart. Bob is all ad man and not much else. And Bob Starr sounds powerful when my secretary answers my phone, "Bob Starr's office." Bob means business and he is determined as hell.

The Phone Mart campaign is very successful and receiving notice from the ad world. And now Mickey Mouse enters my life. Of all things, GTE has just created the Mickey Mouse Phone, how's that for Pop Art! Billboards, bus posters, and print ads are needed to introduce Mickey as a phone.

I seize the opportunity to work with the most amazing fashion illustrator, Antonio Lopez. Who in the world would put Mickey Mouse together with Antonio? I would and I did.

I go to Antonio's studio and bring Mickey with me. I had no idea how this would change everything.

It's not accurate to categorize Antonio as just a fashion illustrator, he's way beyond that. His work is sex on paper, brilliant, breathtaking and groundbreaking way beyond the boundaries of fashion.

His studio loft is on 18th and Broadway and there I meet Juan Ramos, also an enormous talent and Antonio's long time collaborator.

I'm a curiosity for them, not like their usual clients such as Vogue, Bazaar, and major fashion designers. This Mickey Mouse project is way out of left field and they love it.

And it's easy to love them, both are gorgeous. Antonio is one of the sexiest men alive and Juan is like a sculpture. But it's who they are, their extraordinary talent, style and magnetic razor sharp wit that sets them apart. An international entourage including top creative talents and beauties are drawn to Antonio and Juan. It's so great to be in their inner circle. Thank you, Mickey!

Antonio's Mickey is a big hit getting great notice and reviews. I'm hanging out at the studio often having a lot of fun with them. Juan can cut you to shreds with his tongue and be hilarious doing so, Paul is Juan's closest confidant and sharp witted, he's also a terrific painter.

The Heartbreak of Static Cling

And of course there's Antonio, whose heart is as big as his talent.

It's been more than a month since Don left for West Virginia. I have Mike Ivy's number but I haven't used it. Don hasn't called me, until now. "Okay Don, what's going on? "

"I'm okay, but—"

"But what Don?"

"It's not so good here, I'll explain later." "Come home."

"I'm going back to Texas for awhile."

"What's in Texas?"

"I'll call you later."

Damn it! Another dream blown, at least he's getting out of there. I don't want to imagine what West Virginia is all about... I'm sure whatever happened with Mike Ivy has taken a toll. Going back to Texas for awhile will be good for Don. Jefferson is a good place for Don to reflect and recoup. He knows I'll always be here for him. Sadly I just have to let time do its thing and turn all my attention to work.

Clairol needs to make a major change and I'm developing a campaign that could hold some interesting possibilities. The TV spots will use original music and lyrics to help define the women we portray. This could prove to be a major opportunity for Don, we'll see.

Creating a thirty second story is similar to producing a movie, just condensed and that's the challenge. Applying this discipline to a feature film would be a very exciting great challenge. I hope one day I'll get the chance.

I'm contacted by an advertising industry magazine. They want to do a feature interview with me and display my work. They also offer the opportunity to design the cover of the magazine giving me total freedom to create whatever I want.

Okay, Warhol showed me the wonders of self promotion and I intend to take full advantage of this.

So I get Bill to take my picture full tilt crazy Bill King style, and splash bold type across the cover—BOB STARR! Yes, with an exclamation mark, how's that for balls.

What fun seeing my colleagues' reaction to this magazine at the newsstand in the lobby of the DDB building.

Being Bob is helping me deal with Don being back in Texas. Bob ignores Robert's pain. I'm such a Gemini.

THE COMEBACK

I'M AT THE STUDIO after work having fun with Antonio, Juan and Paul and also Bernard Lennon. Bernard looks like he could be Don's brother, just beefier. Antonio did some amazing portraits of Bernard awhile ago. Bernard is very bright and entertaining, he lives with a famous gallery owner, Xavier Fourcade who represents Willem de Kooning, Joan Mitchel, Raoul Hague, Malcolm Morley, John Chamberlain and Michael Heizer to name a few.

We're about to go out to dinner and out of the blue, Antonio mentions he's looking to hire a studio manager. Without skipping a beat I tell him he's in Texas and his name is Don Hall. I give Antonio Don's phone number and surprisingly he grabs his phone and calls him. They have a brief conversation and right then and there Antonio offers Don the job! This couldn't be more perfect.

How many endings, how many new beginnings does life offer? You just don't know, but for sure Don coming home and becoming Antonio's studio manager is a major new beginning.

The gang at Antonio's has become our family. Don is loved and respected and of course he's the best studio manager Antonio has ever had.

Antonio's studio is the epicenter of the most amazingly beautiful people and Don is in the middle of it all. And it turns out Don is related to one of Antonio's discoveries, Jerry Hall. She's from Mesquite Texas, not far from Jefferson. Bill King sets up a shoot of the kissing cousins, Don Hall and Jerry Hall, y'all!

And it gets better, much better. Clairol enthusiastically approves my new campaign and I introduce Don to Rich Look, he's a music producer and head of his own production company. Rich will produce the original music for each spot in the campaign, written and performed by Don Hall. And a whole new world opens for Don.

And this is a very exclusive world, in all of New York there are a just a handful of really successful jingle singers. I didn't realize how competitive it is and what it takes to make it in this field. Singers must be competent to sight sing, that's showing up at a recording session,

The Heartbreak of Static Cling

quickly look at the score and lyrics for the first time and nail it immediately and perfectly. And Don can do just that. He's a musician, has perfect pitch and can't be compared vocally.

But the last thing the competitive few successful singers who are booked constantly want to see is another singer as good as or better than themselves.

Don was actually sabotaged at his first booking. The group intentionally went off key blaming Don. Well, that didn't last, the producer had Don sing solo and that was that.

Now Don has his music and Antonio's studio and a great group of friends. And I have the power to hire Don, Antonio, Bill King and whoever is best to collaborate with for my campaigns.

Finally things are falling into place, including a grand piano Don just inherited from Don's childhood music teacher. Amazingly we manage to fit it into our living room but he'll have to use it sparingly. Eventually we'll find a better place for it.

Half day Friday's begin for the summer at DDB. I dash home and we pack up our bags and grab a cab to Penn Station to catch the train to Sayville. We rented a house for the summer with Antonio, Juan and Paul on Fire Island.

We get to Sayville, run off the train and grab a seat on a crowded taxi/van filled with weekenders rushing to catch the ferry to fantasyland.

That ferry ride to the Pines itself is an escape

from everything. When we get to the dock at the Pines lined with yachts and we're greeted by throngs of boys in Speedo's toasting us with their blue cocktails cheering us welcome from the terrace of The Pavilions bar and disco. Toto, we're not in New York anymore, actually it's hard to tell if we're even in America. This Paradise Island is populated with bronzed beauties and millionaire party goers on the decks of their yachts gyrating to Donna Summer... Where the fuck are we?

There are no cars here, just narrow boardwalks crisscrossing the lush dunes. We walk a path lined with architectural fantasies, no two alike and we arrive at our house, a Mid-Century meets mid-seventies Modern fantasy with a fabulous pool. And the gang's all here including Supermodel guests.

It's late afternoon and we get ourselves together to go to the T Dance at the dock. Our entourage sure gets noticed, we're Antonio's people and it's so much fun, like being on a runway causing a commotion.

I remember Coney Island, the beach so crowded you can't help stepping on people as you try to find a patch of sand big enough for your towel. What an incredible contrast, and crazy how I got here from there. If I'd only known, I might not have been such a miserable kid feeling trapped in my body and the poverty of decaying Coney Island.

Before we know it the weekend's over and it takes some adjusting when we get back to the sweltering City. But work enables this lifestyle and I love my job. I'm

The Heartbreak of Static Cling

more than grateful.

And summertime in Pines paradise ends too quickly with a Labor Day celebration and thunderstorm. Fire Island will soon go into hibernation. But a whole new fall and winter season is ahead, we're liberated and at the height of our game, celebrating our freedom prosperity and glamour. We're all convinced this will continue forever and may even get more fabulous.

And smack in the face the news hits—Mark Frechette is dead.

Somehow a one hundred fifty pound barbell fell on his neck as he was working out in the prison's gym. It's reported to be an accident, a very odd accident indeed.

Recently another cult member attempted armed robbery, this time at a convenience store in Roxbury. He was caught, convicted and locked up at the same prison. This scenario seems suspiciously purposeful, but never investigated.

And I thought Mark's story came to an end for me when he was arrested and now this.

I refuse to dwell on it and just keep moving full speed ahead with the life Don and I are building together.

MAD AVE MESHUGASS

IT'S A WHOLE NEW DECADE—the eighties! And DDB moves into new digs, the agency occupies most of a sleek skyscraper on 50th & Mad Ave. My new large office is on the 44th floor overlooking the avenue of my dreams and nightmares.

One minute I'm meeting with the President of Polaroid, next I'm in Cincinnati at the monolithic granite corporate office of Proctor and Gamble, it looks like it belongs in the Kremlin. Carved in stone above the massive entrance is "PROCTOR AND GAMBLE THE BEST SOAP COMPANY IN THE WORLD." I'm almost awestruck.

The Heartbreak of Static Cling

Proctor and Gamble is the mega company founded on air. Air that was accidently pumped into their soap in the 1800s. That created, "Ivory, The Soap That Floats!" And it launched the company that makes practically every brand of soap, toothpaste, toilet paper, paper towels, detergent, deodorant, shampoo and on and on, all with different brand names competing with each other for market share even though all of them are produced by P&G.

I'm introduced to Patricia Palmer, P&G's fabric softener Product Manager. She's sitting at her desk with a thermos that has a paper label taped to it and written in thick Sharpie, "PAT" That's a warning, it's for her use only. I suspect it contains something stronger than coffee.

Pat pops out of her chair. She gives me a firm handshake and accompanies me to the focus group. We take our seats in a dark room facing a one way mirror watching ten women seated at a conference table in the adjacent room dramatically describing their horrendous encounters with static cling to a moderator. I'm immediately hooked and dumbfounded.

One of the focus group women confesses, "I get it every time I pass my maker."

What? This needs to be probed! We send a note to the moderator to have this woman expand her comment. "What exactly did you mean by getting it when you pass your maker?"

The woman replies; "When I go to my coffee

maker, my toaster oven, my mix master... static cling, it's horrifying!"

I try to maintain my composure, but Pat is wide eyed and ecstatic believing we've hit pay dirt and discovered the illusive USP, that is the Unique Selling Point that will rocket her brands market share. She takes a celebratory gulp directly from her thermos and elbows me asking what I think about that. I whisper in her ear, "Bounce and meet your maker with confidence!" Pat's orgasmic.

The focus group ladies continue to pour their hearts out describing in detail their most tormenting tragic personal experiences with static cling.

It's heartbreaking in so many ways.

Flash forward to the Air France Concorde to supersonically get me to Paris and retrieve a redhead model for my Clairol TV spot. Tara Shannon was just about to return to New York but I told her to stay there and wait for me. Clairol made me nuts rejecting every model/actress I presented to them, and this is my revenge. I have a pressing shoot date, the studio is booked and I need to be in Paris fast to drag her back in time! I couldn't think of a better way to justify my round trip on Concord and of course my two night stay at the Plaza Athenee.

Next I'm on a yacht sailing off the Bahamas with my writer and great friend Deanna Cohen and our producer celebrating the rap of our TV shoot. Bob Marley is blasting from a boom box. We're at full sale on this glorious day and with a bottle of Absolute in hand, I fall backwards overboard—I catch the terrified expression on Deanna's face through my legs as I plunge into the barracuda infested water.

When I finally manage to surface there's no boat, nothing but ocean is in sight! I decide to pick a direction and swim slowly, Marley's song is in my head, "Don't Worry." Barracudas won't get me—professional courtesy.

Suddenly out of nowhere, the bow of the boat appears in front of my face. They pull me up and the captain asks me to take the wheel and head for port.

When you fall overboard trust your instincts, choose a direction and go for it. Keep your confidence and you will be able to sail to your destination.

This lesson has come in handy many times.

Snap to the penthouse office of Chanel. I'm meeting with Kitty, the President of Chanel to present my campaign to introduce a new men's fragrance.

Kitty sits at her large round white marble desk in front of a giant wall of windows with panoramic views of Central Park. Carol, her homely assistant sits round shouldered meekly beside her. I'm with my producer and an account guy, we're seated opposite them.

Kitty is Coco Chanel incarnate in her later years. Shiny black lacquered hair, ultra white white skin, and gloss lips in a red only Chanel could create. I've toured the Chanel lipstick factory, it's in New Jersey.

She sits there glaring at me and I glare back and Kitty turns to her humble assistant Carol whispering something in her ear and the poor girl pops out of her seat and scurries out of the office.

Madam Chanel/Kitty turns her gaze again to me and announces, "She thinks she's Chanel, we allow her to believe she's Chanel, she's not Chanel." Struggling to keep a straight face I begin my pitch and present print ads and TV spots. Kitty sits there in completely expressionless silence.

Suddenly Alain, the young heir apparent of Chanel arrives late for the meeting and explains his private jet was delayed in Paris.

I go through the whole song and dance again. And after a very pregnant pause, Alain finally reacts with his thick French accent, "It's too Bwew, It's too Bwash!"

What did he just say? Too Bwew, too Bwash?? Too Bwew, Too Bwash! Why that Fwench Fwied Fwog! I'd like to swap his face Bwack and Bwew! I take a breath and simply reply, "Well, we will weconsider and pwease, excuse me, I must visit the westwoom." I run out of Kitty's office, find the bathroom lock the door and waugh my head off! "Too Bwew, too Bash!"

I return composed to the meeting exuding a most professional demeanor, not allowing myself to make eye contact with anybody and I say calmly, "We'll be back next Wednesday."

My producer and account guy are masters at

revealing no emotions. That's until we leave the building and come close to falling down on the sidewalk doubled over hysterically laughing like crazy people and trying to catch our "bweth!"

Oh, how I love my job.

THE INVITE

IRVING PLACE is going Co-op and an insider's price is offered if we decide to buy our apartment. At half the current market value this is a great deal. And the deal is done. Even with the brick wall view, this location makes it a solid investment. Now we can fix the dreadful kitchen and build some equity.

Bernard's coming over for dinner tonight to celebrate our decision to buy this place and my most recent promotion.

Don's in the mood and he's cooking up a fried

chicken dinner with collard greens, grits, fried ochre and black eyed peas and I'm drooling, his home made cornbread just came out of the oven.

Bernard arrives, and not only do they look like brothers, now they are. He tells us Xavier is having a party two weeks from now for Michael Heizer who's known for his monumental earthworks. And we're invited.

The party will be at Xavier's Bellport home. This should be fun there's sure to be interesting art world people there. We're both looking forward to it, but where's Bellport?

And now that I'm "Senior Vice President Creative Director" that mouthful comes with more travel to shoot new TV spots. I have to leave for LA in the morning.

There's some downtime and a chance to explore California and Don comes to LA to join me for a short adventure.

We take a car trip up the coast north of San Francisco to Guerneville. This small town in the redwoods is known to be the West Coast's Fire Island. Fifes is the gay resort of choice, it's on the banks of the Russian River with small cabins, a central pool, a clubhouse restaurant and bar.

Some guys choose to pitch tents and sleep near the River and some prefer the small cabins and so do we. The guests are mostly from San Francisco and LA. It's fun to see the difference. The LA guys are all tanned and oiled wearing little Speedo's sunbathing their overworked bodies by the pool. The mustached San Fran guys are in cut off jeans and plaid shirts racing canoes down the Russian River, the contrast is hilarious.

We wish we could stay longer but I have to rush back to business in LA and Don also has bookings and needs to get back to work.

We get home just in time for Xavier's bash in Bellport and we're on our way, fortunately Bernard drew us a map.

WHAT'S BELLPORT?

WE HAVE an old Ford named Betsy, our mantra when we put the key in the ignition is, "Betsy, behave" and she does -sometimes. We drive an hour and a half to Bellport and discover a storybook world right out of the "Jim and Judy" readers of my childhood. The main street is called Main Street and a lane called Bellport Lane leads to a dock with sailboats, vintage speedboats and a small Popeye ferryboat that crosses the Great South Bay to Bellport Village's very own private secluded section of Fire Island.

What's Bellport? 116

White picket fences front pristine stately homes painted white with dark green shutters, mostly all built in the 1800's landscaped exquisitely with huge trees. And it's just minutes across the bay by ferry to "Ho Hum Beach" of all things. There are no houses on this private piece of Fire Island, just a boardwalk from the bay to the ocean and it's spectacular.

Bellport Village is a best kept secret. Who knew? Well it turns out not only does Xavier Fourcade know, so does Anna Wintour, Bruce Weber, Cy Newhouse, and some very interesting people who prefer to remain incognito.

Otis lane is covered by a canopy of magnificent trees and large homes are set back deep and mostly hidden. And at the farthest point of Otis lane by the bay is the property of Xavier Fourcade. A long driveway leads to a massive vintage colonial, again white with Bellport green shutters. The house sits on two lush acres of rolling lawn that flows to the bay displaying a thirty foot, Willem de kooning sculpture. Further down the rolling lawn near the bay is a fabulous pool. So, this is Bellport Village, the un-Hamptons!

Xavier's house is classic traditional plush and comfortable. Overstuffed down filled furniture invite you to enjoy the view of the great lawn and bay and major artworks strategically placed. Xavier is a terrific host, warm with a sparkling wit countering his high gloss French accent. I can see why Bernard is attracted to him. Xavier is young enough in spirit to erase the big difference in their age and I also see why Xavier is in love with Bernard.

The party for Heizer is grand, filled with art world elite and fabulous people at home in this extraordinary setting.

Don and I are taken by Bellport Village. Our summer months in the Pines are great, but Bellport is something very different, it's year round plus that private Fire Island Ho Hum Beach is fabulous.

I have an important question for Xavier, "Who's the local realtor?"

I call Old Purchase Properties and get Mark Petheram on the phone and we make a date for the following weekend.

South of South Country Road is the most desirable and pricy location in the Village. North is more affordable, but the old adage, "Location, location, location," is everything. The hunt is on for the least expensive available property as close to the Bay as possible.

A few weekend tours later Mark drives us down Bellport Lane almost to the dock and makes a left on a hidden narrow lane named Hulse Street, (after ship captain, Hulse).

And there it is, the Captain Hulse house, now owned by Puss Landman. "Puss?"

"She's one of Bellport's old guard. All the ladies have nicknames, like Squinchy, Nabby, Lollie, Clink, Binkey and PUSS." And Puss just put her house on the market.

The house was built in 1836. Puss has lived there for sixty years, raised two sons. Her husband died ten years ago and she's ready to move.

Unlike the pristinely restored antique houses in the Village, this one needs work, a lot of work. The white paint is badly peeling and the Bellport green shutters are falling apart, hanging on by a thread.

We step inside and I've never seen so many eagles! There's eagle wallpaper everywhere, in the living room, den, powder room, dining room and even in the beyond repair kitchen. Upstairs are four bedrooms with astonishingly another variation of the eagle wallpaper. Oh how I hate wallpaper and I can tell by the peeling pieces of it there are many layers underneath. But there are four bedrooms and three baths and a large deck overlooking the backyard badly in need of help with outbuildings everywhere. There's a well house covered with vines pulling it down, an ancient tool shed, a two story guest house with a questionable tenant included and a separate garage for your horse and buggy.

And there's a prize, a fragrant majestic fifty foot tall flowering Japanese Linden tree, with a rope swing attached to a lower bow.

Don is smitten and I'm searching for my Valium. Don assures me all can be fixed... eventually. I can visualize how great this house can be, like the other magnificent restored original Bellport Village homes but eventually would take eventually years and eventually a fortune to eventually have this place stand up straight, eventually. Where's my Valium?!

15 Hulse Street is the only property situated in the best location of Bellport Village available for sale at a price that is affordable. And that's for a reason, It needs everything to bring it back from the brink, but it is an opportunity and Don is up for the challenge and I can get refills on my prescription. So, deep breath, cross fingers and here we go!

The first thing we do before attempting any renovations is move Don's piano into the house. Promise fulfilled. Don is thrilled and so am I.

So what's a dozen layers of wallpaper everywhere? It's a major pain in the ass, that's what. Don and I tackle the dreadful task for many, many weekends and a lot of Valium... And I've had it!

Errol and his band of young local handymen come to the rescue. They're far from the A list of renovators but they get the job done at a reasonable rate. The job takes two weeks, it would have taken me and Don a year. Now finally the walls are free of the bald eagle bonanza. We can celebrate the signing of the Declaration of Independence in some other way, what a relief.

We settle in, sparsely furnished but essentials are in place. I'm lingering in bed this morning and Don is at his piano downstairs. I'm transported by his music breathing and rolling like a tide sweeping me away. I'm so much in love with him.

And we're in love with Bellport. Pam and Ritchie run The Bellport Kitchen on Main Street, It's a funky charming little restaurant and they're terrific people, no pretenses, both native Long Islanders who know how to make you comfortable serving good food with a smile. Don the foodie, is instantly loved by the both of them, especially when he shares some culinary secrets.

Watching Don prepare a meal, plant a garden or create a musical composition is an object lesson for me. As a kid in Brooklyn, maybe you get a potted plant put it on the fire escape and sometimes add water, similar to the way my mom cooked. She would get frozen vegetables packed in a plastic bag and boil it in a pot, but bless her she was a career woman not the typical stay-at-home fifties housewife.

Food shopping with Don is a revelation, he knows what's fresh natural and organic and knows exactly what to do with it. And his food preparation is like a meditative act of love and respect for the ingredients. Then the magic happens, Don conducts the orchestra of pots pans stovetop grill and oven with such finesse and mastery I stay back amazed hoping to learn something about this world. Same thing when we go to a Nursery and he selects plants and shrubs, Don just knows. And I think we'll take some plants home, dig a hole and voila! Oh no, Don takes days preparing the soil and he does this with much care and joy.

It's the same way with people, Don's openness honesty and genuine interest in people not only attracts but also undoes any pretentions and posturing, instead close bonds are formed. Where I have tainted skeptical judgments, Don has an innate goodness and he believes others possess this as well. Don brings out the best out of you by example. He makes me realize how much more powerful it is to be like him.

    We're building a home together. We're building each other together, here in Bellport.

    Late afternoon and Don's almost finished constructing a low stone retaining wall encircling our Linden tree's wide trunk. Next step he'll backfill it with Don's gourmet dirt and plant dozens of Hostas, a beautiful big leaf plant that will thrive in the shade of the Linden. Too exhausted and hungry, we leave the dirt for tomorrow and decide to go the Bellport Kitchen for an early dinner.

    The place is almost empty but we find seated at the far end of the patio two familiar faces, astonishingly it's Eric Boman and Peter Schlesinger. Not since 1969, London have I seen Peter. I've heard Eric who's a greatly accomplished photographer was seeing Peter and now I realize they've been together for years.

    They met at a dinner party Paloma Picasso and Fred Hughes gave at Mr. Chow in Knightsbridge for the premier of Luchino Visconti's Death in Venice. That happened two years after I left London. They moved to NYC in 1978 and now we're reunited in Bellport. So many years have passed and now incredibly we're neighbors. We join them for dinner and they have an immediate attraction to Don. It's easy to recognize Eric and Peter will be together the rest of their lives. A perfect coupling just as it is with me and Don.

We play catch up with small talk and big talk. I can't wait to see their house, the description is Greek revival, and knowing their standards I can image how great it is. Turns out they've had the house for a few years and still working on it, I guess that never ends.

Eventually our conversation turns dark, there's something happening and no one knows what it is but gay men are dying. The news reports are vague. They say it's a rare cancer and terror is spreading throughout the gay community. This horror is labeled Gay Cancer. And immediately they crawl from under their rocks, the self-righteous evangelical monsters emerge declaring this is God's way of condemning homosexuals to damnation.

There is very little information and no government reaction to this situation whatsoever. A few deaths in San Francisco, a few in New York... Nobody we know is afflicted... as of yet.

Of course there's a lot of speculation and rumors but no understanding of where this came from or how it's transmitted or how it can be prevented treated or cured.

We collectively take a deep breath realizing all this pride and freedom and prosperity is about to take a severe turn. It's bewildering, all we can do is try to live a healthy life and wait and see.

Fortunately, Peter changes the subject with some

The Heartbreak of Static Cling

great news, Malcolm Morley bought an old church in Brookhaven and he's making it his home and studio. Brookhaven is next door to Bellport, and who could have imagined Bellport would be the magnet bringing all of us together? It will be so great to see Malcolm again.

We get back home and I fill Don in on my past with Peter in London and what I know about Eric's stellar career. We're both looking forward to cultivating this friendship. We'll be together with them again tomorrow night for dinner at their house.

Next day we're at the nursery looking for hostas to plant around the Linden tree. Our neighbor, Horace Gifford is there searching the shrubs. Horace is an architect; he's the architect who built some of the most spectacular modern houses in the Pines in the sixties and seventies. By contrast his house on Bellport Lane is one of the historic 1800's homes he brilliantly restored.

Don's disappointed in the few hostas available and Horace offers cuttings of his abundant hostas of several varieties, problem solved. This triggers me to ask Horace for some ideas about what should be done to our house and he offers to come by and take a look.

We get back home and I'm in the backyard tackling the sanding of kitchen cabinet doors. Don walks over to Horace's and returns with his Radio Flyer wagon carting a load of hostas and Horace is right beside him with his wagon also filled to the brim, what a great guy.

We invite him in to take a look at the house and I can see Horace weighing the possibilities as he travels the layout. "This is a great house, I'll get back to you with some thoughts."

That's all I needed to hear. What a daydream, I can't imagine affording Horace's services, but I'm more than excited to see what he suggests. First things first, we need to get the exterior painted and get new gutters before winter hits. Errol and his gang gave us an affordable estimate and they're about to begin.

Don decides to leave the planting of the Hostas for tomorrow. He has some plans and drives off to the market in town.

When he returns I'm still sanding those darn cabinet doors in the backyard, and something wonderful is happening in the kitchen, the aroma is overwhelming. Don's baking incredible peach pies to bring to Eric and Peter's dinner tonight. That's the Jefferson Texas about Don.

Eric and Peter's house is just outside the western limits of Bellport. It's a grand old beautifully secluded big house privately situated on several acres of lush landscape.

Eric greets us at the front porch, he lights up at the sight of Don's pies. We walk through the house to the kitchen and the place is amazing, very tall ceilings and very large rooms with all original details preserved. Eric's Scandinavian heritage is evident, the furnishings are a mix of Gustavian and American antiques in original non restored condition making an even more chic statement.

We gather around Peter in the kitchen cooking

up a storm. And big surprise, there's Malcolm Morley and his wife, Lida!

It seems like a lifetime since London. Malcolm is without the angst I remembered, he's glowing and happy. Lida is attractive, very smart and so in love with him.

We're about to have a marvelous dinner, Peter is a great cook and so is Eric. I'm looking at Don, Peter, Eric, Malcolm and Lida and I can hardly believe we're all together here and now.

It's catch up time and conversation is filled with memories and exciting new possibilities. Malcolm's description of his church/studio is spectacular. His devilish infectious smile is back. Malcolm is instantly taken by Don and thrilled we've found each other. What a great get together, topped off with the best peach pie.

After dinner Peter shows us his pottery studio equipped with a giant kiln. His work is beyond pottery, it's sculpture and very impressive. I'll never forget our time in Kew Gardens. And now it's so great to see Peter and Eric so perfect for each other. Big hugs and the night ends. Bellport has become so much more than I could have imagined.

Errol and his gang arrive early morning to begin the exterior painting. The commotion gets us out of bed and we quickly make something for breakfast on the beach to escape. We grab our things and walk down to the dock to catch the ferry. We find a seat down in the cabin behind two women cracking each other up. I recognize the voice of the dark haired gal. I've noticed her around town fascinated by her New York crazy sexy wit and style. I got her name from the cashier at the food market.

This time I just can't help myself, I tap her on the shoulder and she turns and smiles. "Are you Helen Glasser?"

"Yes."

"Helen, I need to tell you something, can you meet me up on deck?" She gets up and I follow her topside.

"Helen Glasser, I'm Robert Starr and we're going to be best friends for life." She cracks up.

"And that guy I'm sitting with is Don Hall who you're going to fall in love with."

"We'll see about this." She takes a look below and spots Don. "I think you're right... I gotta get back to Suzie, let's take a walk on the beach."

"Who's Suzie?"

"She's married to Eddie Hayes." Helen goes back to her seat and turns to Don. "Don, I'm Helen and this is Suzie... See you guys on the beach."

Don flashes his smile.

I turn to Don and whisper, "She's terrific, and why do I know the name, Ed Hayes?"

Don replies, "He's a big lawyer, *The Bonfire of the Vanities* is based on him."

"Oh, okay."

The ferry docks, Suzy and Helen take off and

disappear down the boardwalk to the beach. Don and I settle on the sand with our sandwiches. It's a spectacular late summer day. "There's something about Helen, we've got to become friends. She's really a number."

And she appears right behind us. "Hi boys."

"Helen!"

"Wanna take a walk?"

"Sure, Don, you coming?"

"Hi Helen, you go, I want to finish my sandwich I'll catch up with you."

We walk to the shoreline and somehow I feel I've known her forever. "Now look here Helen, you might not know it but what I said is true, you me and Don will be friends for life, get it?"

Helen stops dead in her tracks and busts out her outrageous laugh. "You're something else, you really are."

"So are you, you sexy thing! You married?"

"That's the problem."

"What's the problem?"

"My husband Sam doesn't like gay people."

"Oh, really? You're inviting me and Don tonight for drinks at your house and we'll see about that."

"Okay, but I'm warning you. Come over around six, I'm right on Bellport Lane."

"I know, I've been stalking you, and I'm not in the least concerned about Sam."

Don whips up another pie, this time pecan, and we take it with us on a short stroll down the lane to

Helen and Sam's house and it's impressive.

Helen answers the door holding a big glass of red wine; she's had a few bracing herself for our introduction to Sam. "Hi guys, what's this."

"It's pecan."

"Wow, Don, did you?"

"Yes hope you like it."

"Like it? I love it, come in."

We follow her into the house that's actually breathtaking, every detail restored and reconfigured into the most comfortable reimagining of its hundred year old bones with a modern twist. Helen tells us Horace Gifford did this for the former owner. Of course, who else could transform a house like this.

We sit at the island of the enormous white kitchen turned out with all sorts of salamis and cheeses and Helen opens another bottle of red wine.

"Got white, Helen? That's the only thing I drink."

"You got it." Helen pulls out a bottle of Sancerre.

"Where's Sam?"

"Taking a shower, he'll be down in a minute." Helen's wearing a low cut tight top accentuating her big tits and tight jeans. She's a sexy thang, and so much fun. But I can see she's nervous.

Tall Sam appears, he's good-looking—in a WASP way—with a square jaw and thick glasses. I guess he's a few years younger than Helen.

"Sam, we've been looking forward to meeting you."

"Hi, guys."

Helen gulps her glass dry and immediately refills it to the brim.

"Sam, Helen tells us you don't like gay people." Helen almost spits her wine across the room and cracks up. "I have to tell you Sam, I don't like gay people—gay people who don't like straight people. You see Sam, I like you before I don't like you, but if you want me to not like you, just let me know and I'll erase you from my universe." Sam seems stunned. "You should know Sam, Don and I like Helen and she likes us, and we're going to be best friends for life." Helen is now doubled over cracking up so hard her mouth can't find her wine glass. "So what ya say about that, Sam?"

Sam's deadpan becomes a sheepish grin.

"I love you guys." Helen is bent over the sink splashing water on her face.

And so, a great friendship is cemented.

Helen has two kids from her former marriage to Howard Stein, the rock promoter and owner of a club called Xenon. Her son Michael is in his early twenties, he's working at his dad's club. And Taylor, her daughter, is just a few years older than Michael and she's a big problem for Helen. Taylor is a spoiled brat and gossip columns exploit her antics.

Sam's a real estate developer. He's rehabilitated an entire neighborhood in Harlem, called Sugar Hill... He also owns the famous Puck building downtown, very impressive. He's nasty and funny and not at all the stick up the ass homophobe I expected. Lucky for him.

Helen has a small shop called The Leg Market on upper Madison Avenue offering the Silk Stocking district ladies their hose. The shop is not far from their apartment on Park Avenue.

Don and his pecan pie are a big hit and we're drunk, happy, and in love with each other, especially Helen and Don. Helen is Italian and a great cook and the topic of food sutures the two of them. My advertising adventures garner more respect from Sam and a lot of laughs.

The Bellport gossip was especially delicious. Just across the street are the Connelly's, Ilene, Jerry and their young movie star daughter, Jennifer. Helen suspects Jennifer is attracted to Sam.

On the other side of Bellport Lane are Deanna and her husband, Dr. Jonathan Anis and their young son. Deanna has a rep as an activist and this is something interesting to both me and Don especially now as the news just reported "Gay Cancer" has a new name, GRID, Gay Related Immune Deficiency which further condemns the Gay community.

But tonight is a very special event, four people bonding and having a ball, so no further talk of the expanding plague.

Sam takes us on a tour of the house and my heart stops at the sight of that gorgeous pool classically placed and surrounded by a great lawn and lush gardens. Their house is amazing but more wonderful is our new friendship.

Helen tells us about a dive north of Bellport Village called The Circle D, and she insists we go there tonight. We're drunk and why not? So we pile into Sam's white Jaguar and go north and in ten minutes we're in the middle of nowhere except for the Circle D's neon sign lighting the way.

David Lynch, John Waters and Fellini combined couldn't do any better creating this place. Country Western goes berserk! The clientele, average age seventy are dressed for a grade D western and they're all doing the two step to a really bad Elvis impersonator giving it his best on the small stage. I'm ecstatic and so is Don.

We take a seat at a small table busting a gut watching the Wild West goes Arthur Murray on the dance floor. Helen refuses Don's invite to two step with him, she can hardly stand up. I spot my favorite character on the dance floor, she's somewhere in her seventies with Aqua Netted hair piled to the sky and she's got at least two inches of thick makeup actuating her age. She's wearing an antebellum meets saloon gal get up with a corset, a big skirt held wide by lots of under layers and pink cowgirl boots. And she has a severe limp. This causes her two step to become a one and a half. She's my gal!

I get up and tap the shoulder of the craggy old cowboy she's dancing with and cut in. Helen falls on the floor in hysterics; it takes both Don and Sam to get her back in her seat.

Me and my gal circle the dance floor and now I'm in sync with her limp making it seem like an intentional dip. And now all the two steppers are imitating this new dance move. Helen's head is exploding.

We've found our place! And we can't wait to invite unsuspecting people we know in Bellport to our exclusive club.

We crawl back into Sam's car; fortunately it's a short drive home. On the way I mention Don and I have never been to Harlem. Sam offers to drive us next weekend to Bellport and on the way we'll stop off for a drink at his favorite bar.

STORM GATHERING

IT'S ANOTHER DAY in the City, the sky is clear blue now but everyone knows winter is approaching and we take quicker steps as the air has that tinge of coldness under the last vestiges of summer warmth. And with the change of season comes an evil multiplying, Gay Related Immune Deficiency is now officially AIDS. Almost imperceptivity the color in our world is slowly fading, turning to heavy grays with deep black edges. More are sick and dying and nothing is being done about it. Anger is palpable and so is fear.

We can't ignore this, it's coming closer by the day

and the sense of helplessness is killing in itself. Priorities shift, everything we hoped for worked for cared about suddenly takes a back step replaced with activism against this ongoing slaughter.

Don becomes a relentless investigator determined to uncover information about all medical developments and research worldwide happening to date. And I'm right with him digging for clues. If our damn government is avoiding this we can't.

We're in the center of a gigantic circle, at the outer edges this plague appeared and now it spirals closer picking up speed toward us and there's no stopping it.

Funding for research, care and education is almost nonexistent. We have to do something about this.

We contact our neighbors in Bellport, Deanna and her husband Dr. Jonathan, they just might help cook up a plan of action. Bellport Village has become better known, not the secret it has been. It's populated by some very wealthy and influential people. Can we somehow enlist Bellport in the fight?

Don has an idea, an auction/benefit for AIDS care, research and education. And the four of us are ignited by this possibility. We decide to incorporate and become a legitimate non-profit organization and we need a name. Jonathan suggests, STAT, I like it, being a doctor his suggestion makes sense, but I feel we need to have a name that is more inclusive and clearly defines our mission.

The stigma of AIDS is festering, a lot of ignorance is being spread and people continue to believe AIDS is a gay disease and it's not their problem. No wonder, it was positioned that way from the start.

Who are we and who do we want the people of Bellport to be? I toss words around in my head and come upon, People Taking Action Against AIDS. That's who we are and that's what we want Bellport Village to be. And the initials couldn't be more perfect Middle America, PTAAA. It's like a combination of the PTA (Parent Teacher's Association) and AAA (the Automobile Club of America).

Deanna, Jonathan and Don are excited and on board, we have a name and now we can apply for an official 501(c)3 Non-Profit Organization status.

But first, Don is compelled to lay down rules before we go any further. 1- PTAAA will be all volunteer and non-profit. We will never pay anyone a salary, including ourselves. All proceeds will go to fund AIDS care, research and education. 2- The four of us will submit possible candidates for specific drug trials, specific care services and specific educational programs to fund, and we'll have a vote. No funds will be donated to any organization for an unspecified program.

These bylaws are fundamental for us to actually make some kind of a difference, and we all agree.

Deanna offers to host meetings at her house and begin recruiting volunteers. Where and when our first auction benefit can take place is open to suggestion. Our first choice would be to get the Village to allow us to take over the dock, a beautiful venue and it's iconic Bellport. It would be held on a summer Sunday and be called, SUNDAY BY THE BAY.

We have our work cut out for us.

DEEP IN THE HEART OF HARLEM

IT'S FRIDAY EVENING and we're at Sam and Helen's place on Park Ave, having drinks with Helen waiting for Sam to get his car. A half hour passes and the doorman rings and tells us Sam is parked in front.

We get into the white Jaguar and Sam says it's a good night to see Harlem before we go on to Bellport. Don and I are excited, Harlem has been just a myth and now we'll see it with Sam the insider and Helen, this should be fun!

We pull up in front of "La Familia" an old storefront bar in the middle of decay and flattened empty lots. There's a jazz combo playing on a small stage visible in the window next to the front door. The bar runs the length of the place and behind the barstools are small tables set up against the wall and way in the back there's a large booth. As soon as our four white faces walk in the crowd becomes dead quiet until the bartender recognizes Sam and the music and conversations return to normal.

We sit at the bar and order drinks, a gal from the kitchen appears carrying a tray of chicken wings and they're delicious. We're settling in listening to great jazz and getting comfortable in Harlem.

We're really enjoying this place when we notice a good-looking young black guy enter the bar. He moves quickly through the crowd to a group of men sitting in the back booth.

Ten minutes later we see one of the men escort the young guy toward the door. They get into the front vestibule and the man shoots the kid dead. The band stops playing, conversations stop and everyone in the bar freezes. I notice Sam is not in his seat. "Where's Sam? Where's Sam!"

Helen elbows me hard to shut me up, she whispers he's in the bathroom. Suddenly a black Caddy pulls up and the shooter opens the trunk and dumps the body into it and speeds away.

The jazz band plays again and everyone in the place is like nothing happened. Sam returns to his seat and we order another round of drinks and more chicken wings. We play it cool trying not to give anyone any idea how freaked we are, or worse how we might split and get cops. So, nice and easy we smile and make happy talk with the bartender and each other for awhile.

Finally Sam signals it's time we slowly leave our barstools and walk out the door and get into the white Jaguar, then drive away in no hurry.

So this is Harlem.

On our way to Bellport I wonder if this really happened, then I see blood on my sneakers.

Helen suggests we go there again next weekend.

THE BELLPORT BLITZ BEGINS

WE' RE ON A MISSION to light a fire and enroll all of Bellport to the cause. We miss no one—first our immediate neighbors, Ilene, Gerry and Jennifer Connelly. Ilene is great looking, in her forties with signature lush long deep brown hair an elegant slim stature and a very warm demeanor. Husband Gerry is tall and Irish handsome. He's a very gentle man who made his fortune in the garment industry. And their most extraordinary brilliant and gorgeous young movie star daughter is Jennifer Connelly. She's a Sagittarius like Don and the two of them bonded immediately. It's fabulous to see the two of these beauties connect. The

The Heartbreak of Static Cling

Connelly's are now on board.

Next, we meet with Ed Hayes and his wife Suzy. Ed is a character out of a film Noir. He's great looking, dressed to kill and I'm sure he has his underwear custom made as well. He's a no nonsense attorney. If you have a problem, big or small, it will become no problem with Ed Hayes on the case. Suzy's a striking blonde former model with strong connections to the fashion world. Both are now with us and excited about our plans.

Denis Miller and Jim Johnston have a house down the lane. Denise has a high end furniture showroom in the City. Jim is a noted artist. They've become great friends and now cohorts with us committed to the success of our auction.

Malcolm Morley donates artwork for our auction catalogue cover, and promises more.

We hit every small business on South Country Road: The Bellport Deli, The Old Inlet Inn, The Bellport Kitchen, The bookstore, Old Purchase Properties, the small supermarket, the ice cream shop and everyone is on board.

Deanna has amassed thirty volunteers so far, all of them reaching out every day getting ads sold for our catalogue and commitments for donations for the auction and recruiting even more volunteers.

Antonio and Juan are spreading the word throughout the fashion world. We're getting haute couture donated by top designers and commitments from top models to populate our auction runway.

The Bellport Blitz Begins

Everyone at my ad agency is now aware of Bellport and what we are doing. The word is spreading fast and I'm determined to garner contributions for our auction from major clients.

Don's relentlessness pays off and he achieves direct contact with Dr. Matilde Krim and Dr. Anthony Fauci. Now we have a way to really find out about every drug trial and clinical study happening in America and around the world. Dr. Krim, medical researcher and founding chairman of AMFAR, American Foundation for AIDS Research, will attend Sunday by The Bay.

But there's a hitch, although the Village is all in it looks like taking over the dock is a no go. This is understandable—it would mean blocking resident access to their boats and the ferry on a weekend. Don and I plan to approach Xavier Forcade—his enormous lawn right on the bay would easily handle five hundred or so guests, several large tents and a stage for entertainment. Xavier is a very private man, we'll see.

All this is exhausting but Don and I never felt so alive.

With so many volunteers and enthusiastic feedback, all of us are even more empowered. This is our way of acting up, fighting back, and fighting AIDS. We'll also continue to march, scream in the streets, and demonstrate against deaf, dumb, and blind Reagan, who astoundingly despicably hasn't to this date said the word, AIDS.

Don has come up with a genius idea; a portion of

the proceeds from our Sunday by the Bay auction will be used to create a scholarship program for High School Seniors across the country. It will be an essay competition and these essays are to be titled, 'AIDS, Why Should I Care?' This is a great way to educate teens and their families who believe Johnny and Mary are straight, drug-free, all-American kids and so AIDS has nothing at all to do with them. A lot of eyes will be opened.

DOWN TO BUSINESS

DON IS SPENDING more time in Bellport working on the event and our house. I have to get back to work and I've got a shoot for Clairol coming up in London soon.

The success of my campaigns for Clairol has become a velvet trap. I'm getting to be known as the guy to go to for every account that has to do with fashion, cosmetics and hair products and I'm not enjoying the pigeonhole. I won't tolerate the smell of a hidden assumption that a gay Creative Director needn't pitch business categories outside of fashion. I confront the top execs and let them know I'm not all about hair and makeup! Stunned, they promise more diverse creative opportunities will definitely come my way. We'll see.

I realize my dissatisfaction is not just my assigned accounts. I feel DDB and every major ad agency has an obligation to use their power of mass communication to move the bar against AIDS and to date they've done nothing.

DDB is my home, it's still the best agency in the world and my years here have been the greatest. Here at this agency Don and I will be able to light a fire, we just need to finalize a concept we've been formulating, an idea that would be impossible for them to pass up. We're really close to a great plan, when I get back from London we'll nail it and I'll set up a presentation with the powers that be at DDB.

London is a short two day shoot, there's no time to find Samantha and have some fun with her again. I'm staying at Blake's, a very chic boutique hotel popular with the ad and film industry.

I'm on my third Martini at the intimate clubby bar at Blake's. Mark Mayhew, a producer who used to work at DDB is sitting at the bar spots me and walks over to my table. "Bob! Hi, what are you doing in London?" I fill him in and he continues, "I'm here with Bob Lenz, he knows your work and wants to hire you."

"Who's Bob Lenz?"

"He's the Creative Director of Backer and Spielvogel."

That piece of news wakes me up. That agency is

hot at the moment, known for very creative work with major accounts. "Okay Mark, introduce me."

Mark pulls up a barstool for me next to Bob Lenz. "Mark tells me you're Bob Lenz. I'm Bob Starr, you want me, you pay me, you got me."

Lenz cracks up and tells me he wants me to meet Bill Backer when I get back to the States.

"Okay, Bob Lenz, call me." I get up, walk back to my table and trip turning it over with a crash. How's that for a first impression?

I go directly to Bellport from the airport. The house is finally all freshly painted and looks terrific, it's so good to be home. Tomorrow my folks are coming and we're preparing a small party for them. Helen, Sam, Ilene, Gerry and Jennifer, Malcolm and Lida, and my sister Carolyn will be also be here.

Carolyn is six years older than me. So when I was ten, she's a rebellious teenager, as rebellious as a girl was allowed to get in the stifling fifties. We were never that close, she got married at nineteen, a disastrous marriage ending in divorce affecting her greatly. I'm glad she's coming to visit.

Don catches me up with some great news, Deanna and Jonathan sold their house on Bellport Lane. And what's great about that? Well, they bought Gray Dunes, the very big estate on Otis Lane close to Xavier Forcade's home and it has more than an acre of lawn directly on the Bay. Sunday by The Bay now has a location, how perfect.

The Heartbreak of Static Cling

Don unrolls blueprints of our house Horace dropped off. Wow, if we only had the bucks this house would really become everything we could have ever wanted. There's got to be a way, maybe it could be done in stages and we set up a meeting with Horace.

It's Saturday and Ted, Zelda and Carolyn are here in Bellport The look on their faces when they arrive will always be remembered. They're astounded by Bellport and in awe of 15 Hulse Street. Ted and Zelda are filled with pride and joy for me and Don. Carolyn carries a tinge of jealousy but she's also happy for us.

My folk's reunion with Malcolm is all hugs and kisses for him and his wife, Lida. Ted and Zelda meet the Bellport crowd and they're thrilled. And they love Don almost as much as I do.

We promise to come to Miami Beach and visit as soon as they settle into their new condo. Yep, my parents are making the mandatory Jewish retiree migration from Brooklyn to Florida. They've worked hard all their lives for this.

It's a lazy Sunday and we're taking a break, no talk of the benefit, no company, no nothing but me and Don doing a little gardening, the newly planted Hostas look amazing around the Linden Tree.

Something catches my eye, there's a small stream of smoke coming from the top floor window of the guest cottage. At first it looks like Joey, our inherited twenty year old tenant is just smoking a joint. But the smoke darkens and thickens. I run to the door and call his name, no answer, the door is unlocked and I run upstairs. The window sill is set on fire by a candle. Joey is stoned in a stupor on the floor and I quickly soak a bath towel and extinguish the near disaster.

I pull Joey to his feet and shake him by his shoulders. "Joey, you almost burned the house down! This is not working, get your stuff together and move out, I'll give you an hour, understand?!" He nods yes. "One hour Joey, forget this month's rent just leave."

I keep an eye on the cottage and finally see Joey carrying a suitcase to his wreck of a car and drive off. What a relief.

It takes awhile to settle down from the drama and Don and I don't want to talk or think about anything.

Especially our upcoming appointment on Wednesday with a doctor Matilde Krim referred us to. We'll be among the first to get the blood test.

We lock up the house and drive back to the city.

FATHERS AND SONS

IT'S TUESDAY and my dad's last day of work at Saks Fifth Avenue. He's now finally retired and I'm giving him a surprise sendoff. I've hired a vintage Rolls Royce and chauffer and stocked it with champagne and caviar and plan to abduct him as he leaves Saks for the last time.

And there he is, I spy him leaving Saks from the backseat of the Rolls and examine his forlorn expression, a life's work finished. He's about to make his way to the subway home and I instruct the chauffer to leave the car and show my dad to his vintage Rolls Royce. I wish I would have had this filmed. He was astounded. The chauffer opens the door for him and he finds me with a bottle of champagne in hand, I pop the cork and we have a ride through Central Park.

I'm grateful to be able to give him this gift at this time in our lives. We talk about the good times, his love of cars, his Kaiser Manhattan, our breakfasts at the coffee shop on 47th Street before going off to my office and him to his job at Saks. And now here we're in a chauffeured Rolls looking forward to his hard earned reward, retirement in Miami Beach.

And we circle Central Park again for the fun of it and then to my apartment on Irving place. I give him a hug and his chauffer drives him home to Brooklyn.

That evening Don and I are watching some dumb movie in bed. The phone rings, It's Don's sister Ronnie and she seems upset, I hand the phone to Don and his expression darkens, he mutters a few words and hangs up. "My father died, I'm going to Texas tomorrow, come with me."

Lights out and we hold each other tight.

Early morning I make calls to my agency, book our flight and postpone our doctor's appointment.

We get to Jefferson, Texas and I get myself a small room at a bed and breakfast. Don's staying at his mom's house. We agree it's best for him to be alone with his family initially.

Don and I have had long talks about our fathers. There are many similarities, heartbreaking disappointment, denial and a distance too far to cross. The hurt is deep, long lasting undermining self confidence and ruining a carefree childhood. It lingers even when years pass and there's some resolve and healing. But down deep there's love and that's undeniable. Don realized long ago it's up to him to forgive and overcome the obstacles his father built. His strength is a beacon for me.

Don's Texas is all gentile charm hospitality and grace deeply rooted in Jefferson. It's North East Texas but looks like the Deep South. Ms. Virginia DeWare stands at her portico in period Southern Bell attire welcoming tourists to view her antebellum Jefferson home.

Don told me of his mother Norma graciously guiding guests through her antique shop and his father Floyd serving up the best food and hosting loyal patrons at his Club Café.

Jefferson has a brochure made years ago, on the cover is a well dressed young gentleman assisting a lovely debutante exiting her horse drawn carriage in front of Ms DeWare's home, that gentleman is Don.

Don calls and tells me to come to the services at the Church at One PM and we'll go back to his mom's house afterward. He sounds like the time alone with his mom was healing. she's always been his great supporter. He said she's looking forward to meeting me and so are his brother and sister, John and Ronnie.

Don's the youngest, John's in the middle and Ronnie the oldest, six years older that Don, same difference in age as me and Carolyn. I always wondered if things would be different if I had a brother close to my age. It didn't seem to help Don that much. John's a good guy, straight and everything Floyd would want in a son. I guess Don and John had a good relationship, but he never expanded on that. And Ronnie, like my sister married young and had her own life early on.

The landmarked, Union Missionary Baptist Church, circa 1847 is filled with faithful friends, neighbors and family. I take a seat in the back row and notice how respectfully dressed up the congregation is, Floyd's Club Café was the popular meeting place for so many.

I spot Don and his family in the front row. Prayers and eulogies are a wonderful tribute and very moving. I'm thinking about how this deeply rooted Southern Baptist religion must have challenged Don growing up.

We meet outside in the front of the Church. I want to hug Don, but I don't, I want to hug his mother, sister and brother but I don't. This is not my Jewish family in Brooklyn. But I show them love with my demeanor and they're very warm in return.

We get into separate cars and drive to Norma's.

This is Don's boyhood home, it's modest and charming. Norma's friends prepared food and more neighbors continuously arrive with offerings.

I finally get a good look at Don's family. Norma is a weathered Texas beauty with perfect features and tight ringlets of silver hair. John and Ronnie both more resemble Floyd, good looking but not the good fortune

The Heartbreak of Static Cling

such as Don's. I examine Norma's mannerisms, her walk and the way she holds her head. Don has so many inherited traits from her. I eye an old photo of Norma on the mantle that confirms her great beauty early on. And I feel her radiant warmth directed at me, I guess she realizes how much in love I am with her son. Ronnie and John are cordial, John more friendly.

More neighbors arrive and I corral Don and ask him to join me outside. We slip out the side door for a cigarette "Don, you okay?"

"Yeah, I'm just concerned about my mom."

"Is she ill?"

"No, just alone now even though she has a whole bunch of friends around her, you know what I mean."

"And she has you and John and Ronnie, do you want to stay here with her for a few weeks?"

"I don't know right now... She sure likes you."

"I love her... I love her for giving you so much; her beauty, her strength, and her love." We embrace and Don hangs his head over my shoulder.

We decide Don needs to stay with Norma for the night and I get a ride back to the bed and breakfast.

Tomorrow morning is the burial; Don tells me I don't have to be there. I'll leave this to his immediate family and see Don afterward.

Daybreak I decide to take a long walk. Life, love and death are too much on my mind, I've got to shake it.

I walk under tall Mesquite trees dripping with Spanish moss and watch smiling strollers and feel the simple peace and calm breeze with no dark cloud undertones. Jefferson makes Bellport seem chaotic and Manhattan insane.

I wonder on and find an old Cajun café with a view of the Caddo River and the bayou beyond. Sweet Tea is served in a mason jar, crawfish, swamp fries, and the weight of my concerns lift.

We could live here, what more do we need? I wonder what Don would think. It's a daydream but I have to ask him.

Would I live in Coney Island again? Hell no. But this isn't Coney, It's his home, or is it now? We could be happy here without the soul crushing hedonistic money hungry ladder climbing and impending doom.

I try to erase thoughts of our upcoming blood tests but it's impossible. Who the fuck knows what's in store for us? Let it go Robert, let it go for now.

I get back to the bed and breakfast and call my office. Winnie, my secretary tells me a Mr. Lenz called and wants me to call him. Shit! I don't want to talk to him now, but I have to. I call and tell him I need to put off going any further for now, I have several campaigns in production and I need a month to finish them. He seems okay with this, good I need more time. It's also good to show Lenz I'm in no hurry. Do I really want to leave DDB? Not really, but what If I get a giant offer, what would I do? That could mean a lot of things like we could finish the house, and travel the world in style. Would it be worth paying the price of more pigeonholing? They want a Creative Director to primarily handle another damn hair product account. I'll ask for the stratosphere and not settle for anything less. We'll see.

Don calls, he's planning to make an early dinner for his mom and comfort her. We plan to get together after she's tucked in.

Don arrives at the Bed and Breakfast around 9:30. We need a drink and go to a quiet place on the Caddo he knows well. We have no conversation until we settle into a secluded table with a view and a bottle of white wine.

"Have you thought about staying here for awhile?"

"I don't think so, she's okay, Ronnie plans to stay with her for a couple of weeks."

"I had a crazy idea this afternoon... I love Jefferson... what do you think about you and me living here? We could get a great house here and..." Don looks shocked and he takes my hand and busts up laughing. "What's so funny?"

"You wouldn't last here a week Robert, neither would I, this *was* my home. My home is with you in New York and we have a lot to do, very important things to do. I love your fantasy but everything we're dealing with won't go away, we can make a difference and we have to."

"I love you Don, more than anybody in the whole world, it was just a fantasy, you're right, there's no escape to roses and lollypops. Let's go home."

GET ONBOARD

WE' RE READY, set and armed with a presentation that will empower the advertising industry to take action.

Don's brilliant essay scholarship program, 'AIDS, Why Should I Care?' is the inspiration for this concept.

I set up an appointment for us to make this proposal to Jack Mariucci, head Creative Director, and top DDB execs.

The conference room is well attended. Don's presentation begins with a short background describing People Taking Action against AIDS, our benefit, Sunday by The Bay, and our educational scholarship competition.

The Heartbreak of Static Cling

I take over and lay out our proposal:

1- Recruit powerful ad agencies and secure top TV commercial directors to commit to produce and direct the wining concepts of a competition between top creative's at DDB, Y&R. J. Walter Thompson, and BBD&O and as many agencies we can get involved.

2- Creative concepts will submit in the form of storyboards for 30 second spots. The strategy is to create TV spots which will move people to realize AIDS affects everyone and it's urgent we all become actively involved the fight against AIDS.

3- An appointed panel of Creative Directors from the various agencies will judge these storyboards. Winners will be assigned top directors such as, Tony Scott, Ridley Scot, Bob Giraldi, David Fincher, Michael Ulick; all who agree to direct incurring no fees.

4- Contributing ad agencies will have their media buyers secure donated prime air time for winning spots on major national networks.

5- The fully produced winning spots will premier at an awards presentation fully donated by the venue and covered by the media.

They sit there silently dumbfounded. A minute passes and then Jack springs from his seat. "Terrific... We're doing this!"

And "ADS AGAINST AIDS" is born.

Don was so right when he said we have a lot to do and we can do it. And we just did.

PUT TO THE TEST

IT'S BEEN two days since we've been tested and we're in a cab going to Central Park West to the doctor who won't give us the results over the phone. Small talk won't do, no talk can distract our minds racing as our cab crawls uptown through thick traffic. What if? What if? I can't stop what if?

Joni Mitchell, "A Case of You," plays. I wish I could sing, can't even remember the full lyrics. But Don knows it and softly sings that song as the cab rolls to a stop.

We're here in the small waiting room and before we have a chance to sit a nurse escorts us into the doctor's office. He seems happy to see us. Don adapts an upbeat mood, I try to follow his lead and smile shaking the doctor's hand. He warmly asks us to take a seat then sits himself behind his desk and opens folders.

And he begins, "Don, Robert, how long have you been living together." What the fuck does that have anything to do about this?

Don answers, "About twelve years."

The doc replies, "Wonderful." He shuffles papers and continues, "Robert, your results are negative."

I hold my breath. "But, Don... your test results show you're positive." Both of us freeze expressionless. I'm struggling to take shallow breaths, Don is stoic.

"The good news Don, your T-Cells are strong, nearly 700."

I blurt out, "What does that mean?"

Don shuts me up. The doctor continues, "It means you don't technically have AIDS, Don, we caught this early. There are a few things we need to do now."

I force myself to breathe, Don is completely composed. "I want you on Bactrim, It's an antibiotic that can prevent Pneumocystis Pneumonia, and I want to monitor you twice a month. Also Don, AZT is a drug showing promising results, I'm sure it will be approved soon. But right now, just the Bactrim and monitoring."

Don takes a few minutes and then begins, "Doctor. There's some evidence Pantamadine in an aerosolized formulation could be much more effective against Pneumonia and much better tolerated."

The doctor is taken aback. "We're looking for funding for our next phase of research."

"How much is needed?"

"Quite a bit Don, we'll get there."

"We'll be able to contribute by the end of June."

"Dr. Krim told me of your organization, PTAAA and the Benefit you're planning, we're very proud of you. Don, we're learning more every day and you will be among the first to benefit from our research. Your immune system is good now and the plan is to keep it that way."

I can't keep my mouth shut any longer, "Doctor, you said Don technically doesn't have AIDS?"

"Don has no opportunistic infections and his T-Cell counts are good. Technically both those factors are used to diagnose AIDS, especially if T-Cells drop below 200. Don, do you have any questions."

"No."

"If you have anything you'd like to discuss with me, call any time. Okay then, I'll see you in two weeks." He writes a prescription and hands it to Don.

I call a cab from the reception room and we wait for it outside, needing oxygen.

"Don we're going to beat this, we know too much, he's a great doctor and connected to Krim and Fauci."

Don manages a slight smile.

"You wanna go to Texarkana tonight for dinner? I'll invite Juan and Paul."

"Okay, good."

The Heartbreak of Static Cling

We get in the cab, I hug Don and whisper, "There is no way this is gonna get us."

I can't show the horror penetrating my soul. My strength is his strength and his strength is mine. It's not easy to keep calm when you need to yell and scream at the top of your lungs and curse the universe. But I'm doing exactly that with a smile.

"Robert, when we get home I need to work on some lyrics."

"What are you working on?"

"Lullabies, songs from the father to the child, it's a way to help fathers bond with their children sharing messages of hope, acceptance, joy and unconditional love."

"Wow, Don there's nothing like that. All the lullabies I've ever heard are from the mother to child. This is really great, how many songs so far?"

"Six, maybe more."

"Okay Don, get them ready to record, I'm producing your album."

"Really?"

"Really, it's a spectacular concept and very needed, how about calling it Daddy's Lullabies?"

"Perfect."

"I'll leave you alone to work on it.

I watch him at his piano composing a new lullaby, certain he feels this will be his legacy. I need to go for a long walk and have a very serious talk with myself.

My head is a jumble of disconnected thoughts, my

heart is racing breaking and in my throat. Everything about everything has just changed and there's no way to make sense of it. I'm silently screaming, *goddamn motherfucker son of a bitch* why him, not me?! Can't I just rewind today and switch things around? Take me, not Don, not Don! I'm the bad one, I'm the fuckhead guilty one who encouraged anonymous sex for "harmless" kicks, goddamn it, goddamn me, God give me AIDS. Not Don!

I collapse hysterically sobbing on a bench in Washington Square. Eventually catching my breath my dreadful thoughts take a turn. Okay, Robert, your overwhelming guilt and your horror is not important. Don is important, the most important person in this world, the deepest love you will ever have, fight like hell for him with every ounce of your being, take care of him, never stop and make life wonderful for him somehow. There's no time to spare Robert, live life with Don now to the max with a vengeance.

We need help. It's too much pressure being strong for each other when we need help being strong for ourselves as well. We have to find someone, a therapist who'll see us together and also separately.

This is gonna hurt, but it's not gonna kill. I must believe this.

I walk back home and we go out for dinner.

NEW NORMAL

SO MANY THINGS are in the works, and that's a very good thing. Horace is on board and Hulse Street is being reborn, his plans are fabulous, we decided to tackle the first floor and leave the rest for later. This will make a major difference. Don and I couldn't be more excited to get this done.

Don's lullabies are incredible and almost ready to begin recording. This labor of love is healing in many ways.

Ads Against AIDS is in full swing, major ad agencies, directors and production companies have coordinated and calls for storyboard entries have been sent to hundreds of creative teams. We should have the wining TV spots ready to premier in about six months.

Sunday by the Bay promises to be more than imagined. Donations are pouring in including major artworks from Morley, Keith Haring, Robert Mapplethorpe and more to come. Spectacular designer fashion creations arrive daily. So many ads have been sold that our catalogue is on its way to become the size of Vogue. Tents and food services have all been donated. Our army of volunteers has grown and a miracle is about to happen this summer.

Most importantly, Don's health is holding steady and his persistent extensive drug trial investigations reveal research developments and new treatment possibilities empowering him. He's gained access to worldwide leading doctors including Dr. Joseph Sonnabend, a pioneering AIDS researcher and co-founder of AMFAR with Dr. Matilde Krim.

A new year is on the horizon and it will be a celebration in spite of it all. Antonio, Juan, Paul, Bernard, Xavier and Don and I are invited to the star studded glitterati New Year's Eve party at Mr. Chow. This promises to be much more glamour than necessary, good!

Don and I have new tuxedos and I hire a Rolls Royce Limo with Chauffer for the night, now that's a good fuck you to AIDS.

Antonio introduced Michael Chow to his wife, Tina. She's a spectacular beauty, exotic and fragile.

The Heartbreak of Static Cling

Michael installed Tina as the face of Mr. Chow's working at the restaurant while also rearing their two children, China and Max.

Tina and I are great friends she's invited me to Mr. Chow to lunch with her several times. Our recent get together was a bit heart wrenching. She pleaded for me to help her escape Mr. Chow's; would it be possible to find her a position at my ad agency? I'd hire her instantly to be my assistant, if I only could. We'd have so much fun devastating potential clients with her beauty and brains. Maybe I can find a way.

It's a clear cold night gliding in our Rolls watching people on the move, or trying to be. Finding a cab in NYC New Year's Eve is next to impossible. We spot two couples desperately trying to grab a cab.

I lower the window. "Need a lift."

They freeze in disbelief as we pull over and I open the door. "Happy New Year, get in."

"Holy shit, you're the greatest!" The fun begins, they offer a vial of Coke and we speed uptown to drop them off at their party on East 65th street. "Hey you guys, we'll never forget this!"

And here we are making our entrance at Mr. Chow's, New York at its best and best of all we're here with our phenomenal family of the brightest stars celebrating a new year, celebrating each other and celebrating being alive.

I watch Antonio, Juan, Bernard, Xavier, Paul and Don, each so beautiful, each possessing uniquely brilliant genius lighting up this world and my life. And we're instantly surrounded by so many more astoundingly talented glamorous and famous, I'm so lucky.

I notice Bill King isn't here, hope he's okay. I pray they're all okay. I smack myself out of these thoughts with more Coke and champagne.

Our big round table is a feast for eyes. Exquisite food continues to be delivered along with endless champagne, drinks and visits from even more spectacularly sexy gorgeous ones attracted to the our orbit.

The thrill of it all is reflected on Don's beautiful face, our eyes meet, no words necessary.

And then Antonio insists, "Do the Bette Davis joke." Not again, practically every time we're out together, "Do the Bette Davis joke!" And now everybody is demanding the damned old Betty Davis joke and I can't get out it, so here I go again.

"Bette Davis and Tallulah Bankhead are filming at Warner Brothers starring in separate pictures. Both hate the films they're struggling to make. At lunch break they run into each other in the commissary, Bankhead approaches Davis, 'Bette Darling, Bette Darling, I can't stand this one minute longer, I'm going to strangle that Pig director.' Bette pounces, 'Tah Lu Lah! I detest my so called co- star; can someone please explain the attraction of Aqua Velva?' 'Aqua Vulva darling!' 'Sorry, I just washed my hair. We're getting the fuck out of this dump! Let's go for a car trip to the desert!' And so, Bette and

The Heartbreak of Static Cling

Tallulah escape in Bette's convertible. Bette lights her tenth cigarette, floors it and they speed away. They're thrilled to escape Hollywood and as the sun sets they find themselves plowing through a deserted sandy highway somewhere in the desert and, *POP! PHISSSSH!* Tallulah yells, 'What was *that*, darling?' Bette pulls over to the side of the road, lights her fifteenth cigarette exhales and announces, "*Flat tire!*" Tallulah bolts out of the car and starts jacking it up. On each upward bump from Tallulah's jack, Bette puffs joyously. Tallulah continues jacking up the car when a sneaky slithering snake makes its way up her leg, up her skirt and attacks! 'Bette, darling, Bette darling, I've just been bitten by a *rattlesnake! Do something!*" Bette pops out of the car and informs Tallulah, 'I'll go find a doc-tah!' and Bette marches down the lonely highway chain smoking until she discovers a little house displaying a doctor's shingle hanging off the front porch. Bette bangs on the door until finally the doctor appears, Bette dramatically lights another cigarette, 'Doc-tah, doc-tah, my friend was just bitten by a *rattle—*' she inhaled and continued, '*—snake*! What are you going to do about this?!' The doctor tells her he's in the middle of birthing a baby, he can't come with her but she must immediately rush back to her friend and suck out the poison three times. Bette stamps out her cigarette and marches back to Tallulah who is now writhing on the ground grabbing her crotch. 'Bette darling, Bette darling, my pussy is in flames! What did the doctor say?' Bette ignites yet another cigarette. 'The doc-tah said,' she exhaled, 'you're going to die!'"

This performance has become humiliating but they're all in stitches, especially Antonio! Is it Bette or is it my Tallulah Bankhead writhing on the floor grabbing my "pussy in flames?"

It's near midnight and the wattage of the evening ramps up. We're dancing on tables, tongue-kissing everybody and 1985 is no more.

I embrace Don and excuse myself. My tradition on New Year's Eve is wherever I may be I go alone outside and look up at the sky and pray. To whom or to what I don't know, I'll never know, but that's not the point, it's the act of praying that's important. And now there's only one thing to pray for.

BALL BUSTER

I'M IN BED replaying our first meeting with Rosemary. Thank God we found her, it wasn't easy. I stopped counting how many shrinks we've interviewed. Some after two minutes we knew there would be no way we could tolerate being stared at blankly scribbling notes, never saying a word. Others were so unattractive it was impossible to stay another minute in their office.

We get a recommendation from Joseph Sonnabend and book an appointment with Rosemary. She's in her late sixties, and she smokes, hallelujah! Rosemary has an understated style and warmth and she exudes a keen knowledge of our circumstance. She talks straight talk, straight to the heart of the matter and we can talk to her, she hears us and understands and we hear her. We need her help, help she is more than capable of providing. She will see us together and separately once a week for much needed hour and a half sessions. We found our Rosemary.

We're in bed and a persistent discomfort increases and I turn to Don, "I got a ball ache."

"What?"

"My left ball, it's like a dull ache and it's getting worse."

"Tomorrow you're seeing Dr. Brown, go to sleep."

Dr. Brown has been my doctor for a couple of years. He's a general practitioner, gay and handsome. He arranged an appointment for me to see him this afternoon.

Of course I arrive on time, I'm always on time. Brown's all business after he hears more of my complaint. I drop my pants he feels my balls and tells me I need to see the Urologist he recommends... As I pull up my pants up he's on the phone.

"Robert, he'll see you now, here's his address."

"Now?"

"Yes he's expecting you." The urgency is disconcerting, what the fuck?

I get a cab to the fancy address on Park Avenue. The office is clubby and opulent. And I'm immediately directed to an examination room.

The Heartbreak of Static Cling

Same routine, I drop my pants, and matter of factly the doctor explains, "Robert, you have Testicular Cancer, it's your left testicle. You need to be admitted to the hospital now; I'll arrange it with New York Hospital."

"What? *What?!*"

"Robert, you have Testicular Cancer and you need an operation as soon as possible."

"A biopsy?"

"No, your left testicle must be removed."

The room spins, I come close to falling to the floor but the doctor catches me and puts me in a chair.

"There's no biopsy possible for this, it can be replaced if you so choose." He retrieves from one of his cabinets an orange egg shaped silicone object, it's a prosthetic testicle and I'm about to pass out. He hands me a paper cup of water.

I manage to say, "I need to make a call."

He hands me a phone, I give him the number an ask him to dial.

"Don, Brown sent me to this urologist, he just told me I have to go to the hospital now. I have Testicular Cancer."

"What's the address I'll be right there, I want a second opinion get another doctor's name from him, I'll be right there."

Before I know it Don is here talking to the doctor. "Come on I got the address." Don pulls me up out of my chair. He has a cab waiting.

We get to an even fancier doctor's office on Fifth

Avenue. Same examination, same diagnosis. Don is holding me by the waist helping me stand up straight. This doctor calls the original urologist a few minutes pass and, "It's confirmed, they're waiting for you at New York Hospital."

With everything going on with Don, he's sitting close to me in the cab telling me everything is going to be all right. I take his strength into me. "Don't worry Don, what's a little cancer, plus I'm demanding the largest size implant.

I've never been to New York Hospital. It's a tall gothic tower on the East River's edge. We're greeted by Dr. Lu, the Chinese surgeon who will castrate me. "So nice to meet you Doctor Lu."

"Mr. Starr, we will operate tomorrow morning, I need to do another examination and then you can take a shower and rest, I'll give you a little sedative."

"Gee, thanks, how about Morphine right this minute?!" The doctor remains expressionless.

Don stays with me until I settle in and tells me he'll be back a little later.

After another short examination Dr. Lu explains the operation. "You'll have a slight scar on your lower right side like an appendix scar." He continues with a presentation of various sized silicone balls. I point to one a horse would be proud of. Another Chinese deadpan glance and he chooses one more fit for a human. Then he fills a small syringe and tells me it's Valium and a nurse takes me to my room and I'm instructed to take a

The Heartbreak of Static Cling

shower now and another in the morning. I guess you have to be Mr. Clean to get your ball cut off.

The Valium kicks in, making me slightly less suicidal. And after my first shower I get into bed and make a promise to myself to be as strong as Don and drift off.

Through my fog hours later Don and Bernard come into focus. What a surprise visit, I'm looking at both of them dealing with their own horrific HIV battles cheering me on. I know Don brought Bernard with him for his own support as well as mine.

I put on a happy face like I'm here to get a haircut. We have some laughs and a saint of a nurse appears and shoots me up with another Valium shot and I'm off to dreamland.

At daybreak I'm awakened by a chubby nurse ordering me to shower again and put on the glamorous gown she delivered. Where the fuck am I? Oh, time for castration. My body is vibrating under the force of the shower and my deep breaths almost drown me.

I dry off and struggle to tie my festive gown correctly and here are the orderlies with a gurney for my amusement ride. They transport me down endless hallways, I count the fluorescent lights passing over my head quickly and I'm shoved into an elevator ascending to the lovely surgery floor.

My heart is pounding as they lift my body up and onto the operating table. I do my best to avoid focusing on the décor of stainless steel monstrous contraptions surrounding me.

Miss Anna Sthesia, my happy anesthesiologist appears at my side, she jabs a vein in a second and smiles. "Now just relax, this is strong and it'll be all over before you know it."

"Gee, thanks, Anna." Lights out.

And just like that, I'm in a heavenly comfortable bed and as my fuzzy vision sharpens, I guess I'm dead. I'm in an enormous well decorated suite with a fireplace and tall windows overlooking the East river way below. So heaven is a penthouse? Don comes into focus, "Don, Where am I?"

"This is the private suite used by the Shah of Iran and other dignitaries and now, you!"

"What?" Just leave it to Don to make this happen.

Dr. Lu appears. "Robert everything went very well, there's no evidence the cancer spread. You'll feel some pain at the incision on your side which will subside in a week or so. In two weeks you'll need to begin a regimen of radiation treatments as a precaution in case errant cancer cells are present. I need you to tell me if you would like to eventually have children."

"Children?"

"We can freeze and store your sperm now because radiation will render your sperm impotent."

"No, I don't want children."

"Are you sure?"

"Absolutely."

With that Dr. Lu disappears. Interesting how

immediate that decision was.

"Don, how did you do this?"

"I have my ways." Don cracks up. "Do you like your accommodations?"

"Can we get a two year lease?"

I subtlety slip my hand to my crotch to check out the goods. "Damn it! Don, I told that doctor my left was always bigger than the right, get him back here now!"

Don lifts my gown. "Calm down Robert it's perfect, you're just upset about the whole thing."

I'm such an idiot, how dare I throw a shit fit, I'm alive. "I'm sorry Don, I'm okay. I can't imagine how you did this for me, this place is amazing, I love you so much."

"Get some rest, order room service, they have a very special menu up here. I'll be back later."

Do I want to have children? I never did. I wouldn't burden a child with my genes and I never felt I would be able to raise a child the way a child ought to be raised. It takes more than love, you need to be an example of how to love yourself and I've always struggled with that. Don would be a much better father. He told me he would love to have a child. He would be a great dad. Maybe that's what's in our future, if there is a future.

The ordeal is half over, at least it was quick. I'm home walking with a crutch. Radiation is coming up soon and I'm really looking forward to it, just as much as having all my teeth pulled, oh well getting nuked could be fun.

It's called of all things, The Stitch Clinic. And I'm here at Stitch in a nuclear bunker below ground, how James Bond.

I'm on a hard bed of steel and lasers are pinpointing exact locations on my belly for my tattoos. Tattoos! Yep, these little dots will guide the death rays to zap me exactly where needed. The fun continues when a nuclear engineer places a protective shield around my genitals to isolate surrounding areas from the radiation to come. Once the placement of this contraption is complete and I'm pinpointed by lasers, the guy disappears into his protective bunker within the bunker.

And with an unworldly dark sounding buzz, every hair on my body stands to attention in sync with the vibrating undertone of the bombardment. Robots reposition the apparatus to lock onto the other tattoo locations and repeat the radioactive blast. I've always wanted to be in a sci-fi movie and here I am, it's a small price to pay to put this fucking cancer behind me.

LAYING DOWN TRACKS

THE ARRANGEMENTS are finished and the recording studio is booked. And now we're beginning to lay down tracks for the first cut of Don's album, "Daddy's Lullabies."

MY LITTLE HERO
Words and Music by Don Hall

Look at that expression on your face
You're my little gift to the human race
You grow a little everyday
to fill a special place in my heart.
You don't have to be a doctor or a lawyer.
You don't have to be a poet or a king.

You don't have to be more daring
than Tom Sawyer,
or outdo anybody when you sing.
You just have to be you because
being you is the best thing you can be.
If you're good at being you,
you'll be happy your life through
and you'll always be a hero to me.
You don't have to be the brightest
or the smartest,
or know all the answers from the start.
Maybe sometimes being unsure is the hardest
it's the only way you learn to trust your heart.
So each and every day, whatever comes you way,
keep your eyes wide open and you'll see,
let the light shine through,
you'll find what's right for you
and you'll always be a hero to me.
You're my little hero I'm so proud of you
You're my little hero,
may all your dreams come true...
You're my little hero, you're my shining star
You'll always be a hero to me
just by being who you are
You'll always be my little hero
just by being who you are
You'll always be a hero to me
just by being who you are.
My little hero

Had I received messages like that from my dad, how much better my childhood would have been.

Recording sessions are scheduled evenings. Don and I live for these sessions.

Our engineer's recording studio on West 57th Street is in the Steinway Building. It's small but fully equipped. Don's charts call for a wide variety of instruments for each song. And with Don's good relationships made with the best studio musicians in the business we're booking them as needed. All but the piano, that's Don's domain.

When he finalizes his tracks, his voice reaches your soul.

WORKING IT

I'M BACK at my job only taking one day a week off to enjoy my nuclear attacks, just two weeks more and I'll be fully toasted.

Rosemary is really helping, our time with her is absolutely necessary. Another blessing, Don's health is holding steady. He's so energized by our upcoming Bellport event and his recording sessions it's almost impossible to believe he's HIV positive.

But every day we learn our closest friends also carry the virus. We're all dealing with it, living with it constantly and leaning on one another for support.

181 The Heartbreak of Static Cling

I've put Bob Lenz and Bill Baker on hold. They think I'm playing hard to get and they're right. I really don't care right now, there's too much going on. I can't think of changing agencies now but I don't want to kill the possibility, I'll call soon and meet with Backer to find out exactly what they have in mind. It can't hurt, it's just exploration.

The more we do the quicker time passes. I'm fully booked with a production schedule that will take me to LA again. Hopefully Don will be able to join me. We should be back in time to on get everything in place for our Sunday by The Bay, there's a lot to do.

Horace Gifford is a genius, on paper his plans where terrific but the results are astounding. We're overwhelmed by the transformation. Every detail is done to perfection. The effect is a house created and maintained impeccably this way, there are no missteps. It's all authentic, correct and gorgeous. Hulse Street will live for another hundred years.

Living to the max is working and it's giving us great joy, hope and a life we love living. I'm determined keep this going.

California here we go again. I have three weeks to shoot two Clairol spots. I'm at the Beverly Hills Hotel in my favorite bungalow #8 and Don is here with me.

Mary Kay Stolz is a great friend we met in New

York through Antonio. She's now living in a terrific house with a fabulous view of Silver Lake. Mary Kay is a most stylish person and a great deal of fun. Currently she's a creative director at FIDM, the best school for fashion on the West Coast.

Don and Mary Kay have play dates while I'm shooting. I join them and more of our newly acquired California friends at cocktail parties we host at our fabulous digs at the hotel.

Our California gang, Mary Kay, David Wolfson, designer, Maryanne Brauback, film producer, and surprise, Ilene and Gerry Connelly are here renting a house while Jennifer is shooting another movie. So we have ourselves a West Coast Party! Damn right we're celebrating life.

One location of the TV spot is a gas station somewhere off a freeway in Pomona. Michael Ulick is directing, he's a great director and a good friend. And of course I have my two most cherished accomplices on set, Patty Wilson, the greatest stylist there is. Nothing can stop her. I've *actually* seen Patty drive on the sidewalks of New York to get to a shoot on time, and the wardrobe choices she brings with her are all fabulous and in amazing quantities for selection. We've worked together on photo shoots with Bill King and now all the TV spots for Clairol with Ulick. And here's Max

Pinnell, the incredible bald Australian hair dresser who is one of the few people on earth who can double me over in uncontrollable hysterical laughter when I least expect it.

The action of the spot is very simple; a gal with gorgeous hair pulls her VW convertible up to a gas pump and fills the tank, her long blonde hair shines in the sun, cut to a guy filling up his pickup truck distracted by the sight of her. It makes sense with the voice over copy but that's not the point right now.

We're in the middle of shooting the scene and I get an elbow in my ribs, Patty whispers, "Did you get a load of that??" She points to a woman watching us; she's holding the hand of a young cherubic little boy. Is she looking to be discovered? Her lacquered black hair is teased to an inch of its life and her camera ready Technicolor dramatic makeup is sparkling with glitter. She's wearing a pink tube top accentuating her enormous tits and tight black tights emphasize her bare midriff and her major ass all balanced on six inch reds spiked heels. There she is, Ramona from Pomona who probably drove by this gas station and realized we're filming here, so quickly she gets home dresses to be seen, grabs her kid for a prop and shows up with a toothy smile. Everybody auditions constantly in California.

It's impossible not to stare, but I have a job to do,

I must pay attention to our brilliant blonde actress struggling to get the gas nozzle into her gas tank and toss her hair at the same time.

Max turns me around to face him. He has something very important to tell me. "Robert, did you see what just happened?" "No, what?" "Patty went over to Ramona and child and offered the little innocent one a bag of Cheetos." "And?" "And, Ramona says to the darling child," What do you say to the nice lady?" "And the adorable child's eyes open wide at Patty, and suddenly he turns into a demented Hyena from Hell and *hisses* at her!

That did it; I can't breathe laughing so hard. Max runs me into the trailer where Patti is recuperating from the attack of Ramona from Pomona's deranged demented toddler. We take another line or two or three of coke to calm ourselves.

Just another Clairol shoot.

Our cocktail and coke parties are a big hit at the Beverly Hills Hotel. Room service actually provides refills for our little glass vials. The major actress, star of our shoot spills coke all over the bedspread. Max chases her out of the bungalow and runs after her through the hotel yelling, "You're just a dumb fucking model!"

They love me here, I'm a regular.

I have another week of this entertainment to go.

The Heartbreak of Static Cling

Don has to get back to Bellport tomorrow, things are heating up with our event and Don has a doctor appointment. He packs up and before he leaves he makes me promise to behave myself.

Of course, I do.

THE MAIN EVENT

IT'S SATURDAY EVENING and the enormous white tents are up, everything looks spectacular, every last detail is double checked by volunteers. Tomorrow will be Sunday by The Bay! Don and I can hardly believe it.

We arrive early and the day is spectacular, blue skies and a delicious cool breeze from the bay. And to our amazement, a long line of excited bidders have already formed at our entrance gate. We get a message from our parking volunteers we better start letting people in.

The Heartbreak of Static Cling

Our event is officially open and they keep coming. It looks like everybody from Bellport and Manhattan are appearing in droves.

Don and I are in awe standing among hundreds of families, friends, neighbors, notables, celebrities and seasoned auction goers all excited and energized by the opportunities presented. But more than that, everyone is celebrating being here to participate in the fight against AIDS.

When an idea is realized beyond all expectations the high is overwhelming. More than anything, the most magnificent visual for me is the look on Don's face, so full of happiness and love for everyone who helped make this possible.

The silent auction tables are crowded with bidders eagerly writing their offers.

There's food, drinks and music on the rolling greens leading to blue waters of the Great South Bay, this a very elegant event. Fantastic silent auction items range from vacations to estate jewelry and collectables in so many categories bidders keep coming back to compete and up their bids. We allow more time for the silent auction to continue giving everyone enough time to get their bids in. And when the silent auction closes the main live auction event in the biggest tent begins.

There's a large stage and a runway between the two banks of a hundred chairs. Within minutes after we announce the live auction open all seats are taken, the huge tent is packed, standing room only. Next year we'll

The Main Event 188

have to get an even bigger tent.

We start with a brief thank you to all and introduce our auctioneer to great applause. He announces, "We begin with fashion." The runway is now lit with spotlights and music pounds the hearts of the crowd. Supermodels strut in Armani, Gucci, Prada, Chanel, Karl Lagerfeld, Thierry Mugler and more. Are we in Paris? The biding goes wild and wilder higher and higher.

After blockbuster bids and big applause our auctioneer announces, "Now to works of art. We begin with artwork by Robert Mapplethorpe."

I thought the fashion bidding was crazy, now it's a feeding frenzy! Each of four Mapplethorpe photographs are fought for feverishly, every winning bid brings applause and gasps. "And now works of Keith Haring." Again there's a wild bidding war. Each time the auctioneers hammer falls applause grows louder. Amazing works of major artists continue to ramp up more energy from the crowd. Don and I sit there astounded. Next, the auctioneer offers a spectacular array of furnishings and jewelry. And when the final item brings the last winning bid, everyone goes berserk!

It's a standing ovation for Dr. Mathilde Krim as she appears onstage and underscores the importance of these wonderful contributions to fund vital research care and education for the fight against AIDS. She graciously thanks the founders of PTAAA and all the volunteers for Sunday by The Bay.

The party continues into the night. Don and I find Deanna and Jonathan beaming and we make a date tomorrow to review the event and tally up the proceeds. We did it and it is a miracle.

Our first Sunday by The Bay netted nearly four hundred thousand dollars.

Now we can help fund the vital research and drug trials Don has identified. Now we can fund good food and comfort for those in need battling AIDS. Now we can continue and expand our essay scholarship program and educate more teenagers in more High Schools across the country.

The New York Times article headline: The Little Village That Could.

Sunday by The Bay is officially on the map.

This is how Don is dealing with it.

GIVE US A BREAK

WE'VE DONE EVERYTHING we could for now, even though Sunday by the Bay is a successful thrilling achievement Don's diagnosis continues to be an issue even with every distraction thrown in its way. A bigger diversion is needed. We need to go away, far away for enough time to really be away from everything if that's at all possible.

Italy for a month or more, I can do it and so can Don, we need to do it and do it now.

But there's a hitch, I get another damn jury duty

notice I've ignored many times but now I'm being seriously hounded. Confident I just have to appear and tell them I've got a date with aliens from planet X and I'll be excused but I hold my breath because this time I have to show up at the courthouse downtown.

They check my summons handed to them and with no further questions, I'm taken into a large jury room and hear the judges first words, "Good morning ladies and gentlemen of the jury." Oh shit, this can't be happening. The melodramatic judge continues, "This is a very serious case involving multiple first degree murder charges. This trial will necessitate a sequestered jury and it will continue for approximately three to four weeks." You've got to be kidding. No, he's not kidding and I'm trapped. Italy has just become a crushed dream.

The judge shuffles a few dozen papers before him and announces, "I will now read a list of names, please listen carefully. If you have any knowledge of a person I'm about to name immediately raise your hand. Again listen very carefully."

The judge scans the papers before him and begins, "Jimmy Fist, Tony Hammer, Sam Snuffer, Shorty Fingers, Vito Bonacruncha." The judge pauses and scans the room examining the horrified jurors. "Nothing rings a bell?" He continues, "Jack Shmucker, Dave Decapatini, Harvey Hatchitari, Ed Hayes."

My arm shoots up and I'm waving my hand like a lunatic. "Your Honor!"

"Yes I see you, do you recognize one of

these names?"

"Yes Your Honor, Eddie Hayes."

"Do you know this person?"

"Yes Your Honor."

"How do you know this person?"

"He's my neighbor, he's my friend, and he's my lawyer." The judge lowers his glasses to the tip of his nose and glares at me. "Bailiff, escort this gentleman out of this courtroom. Sir, you're dismissed."

I can't wait to tell Ed how he saved me from juror hell... On second thought, should I even mention it?

I tell my agency I need to take my vacation early and there's no two ways about it. Somehow they understand. Again, I decide not to call Bob Lenz, I just can't deal with ad agency business right now.

And it's full steam ahead, we need to get out of Dodge.

Alitalia to Florence, our rented Audi is waiting and we drive to Tuscany we're booked to stay at a monastery—Don's idea. As I imagined the monastery is ancient and beautiful and basically uncomfortable. Don loves it. And if he loves it so do I.

We explore with no maps and let the majestic Cyprus lined roads take us. We get out of the car and hike through lush vineyards on gentle hills revealing breathtaking countryside landscapes and villas. Don has amazing energy. I'm huffing and puffing in the heat of the day and he's smiling and climbing the hills vigorously. This trip is already lifting the weight of the world. And Don especially is in culinary heaven, nothing can compare to real Tuscan Italian food to feed his soul. I've never felt such joy watching him savor every flavor.

It's our second night at the monastery sleeping on narrow separate hard beds in our sparsely furnished small chamber. I'm more than eager to begin our journey south. Florence and Rome are brief but wonderful stopovers on our way to Sorrento to get aboard the ferry to magical Capri.

Waterman ink blue that's the color of the Mediterranean and Capri rises from the sea before us, it's heart stopping.

We're greeted at the dock by a driver in uniform who takes our bags and stores them in the trunk of a Mercedes with The Grand Hotel Quisisana insignia on its door and we begin our assent to the top of Capri to this magnificent Hotel. We're speechless.

We enter the glamour of another era and greeted by a concierge who guides us followed by two luggage carriers to our suite and it's enormous. The bellboy raises the metallic shutters of giant windows revealing spectacular views. Regaining my breath I turn to the concierge and say, "What, no terrace? I specified our need for a terrace when we booked." Don looks at me like I'm nuts. And immediately the concierge escorts us to a top floor more spectacular larger suite with an elegantly huge terrace affording even more mind blowing views of the cliffs of Capri descending to the Mediterranean and Capri's signature archways rising from the sea. "That's better, thank you."

This is what I wanted for Don and so much more. We wash up change clothes and go down to the outdoor bar at the front of the hotel for martinis and people watching.

Don takes a sip of his frosted giant martini with an elegant twist and he's now able to speak. "Robert, wow!"

We make a toast with our crystal martinis, "Here's to life."

This outdoor bar is a magnet for faithful residents of the hotel and Capri's elite. I notice an exotic comfortably ensconced dowager lounging at a nearby table loudly dictating her exacting instructions for the cocktail creation she demands. The waiter replies, "Of course Zelda, we never forget."

That's all I had to hear, I turn to her, "Zelda!" She smiles at me. "Zelda, that's my mother's name, how fabulous!"

She's amused. Don's embarrassed by my approach. "And what are your names?"

"I'm Robert Starr and this is Don Lamar Hall!"

"Are you new to Capri?"

"Yes, it's gorgeous!" Suddenly another creation approaches Zelda's table.

"Zelda darling, it's been much too long," They air kiss passionately and I wonder how this woman is capable of maintaining an erect posture due to the weight of her giant Emeralds, Rubies, Safire's and enormous Diamonds around her neck, wrists, ears and fingers, enough to choke several horses.

Zelda directs her companion's attention to us and, "Robert Starr, Don Lamar, this is my dearest friend, Madam Bulgari."

Well, Madam Bulgari lights up at the sight of us. "Hello you handsome gentlemen!"

Mesmerized I reply, "I think you should consider ordering something a bit lighter on the rocks!" Don turns red, Bulgari and Zelda crack up.

We down another majestic martini and decide to walk and find a restaurant Don researched not far from the hotel, it's supposedly spectacular. And it is, no description of its location or cuisine can do it justice. The restaurant is a magical structure hanging onto the ledge of a cliff overlooking everything Capri has to offer. Where's the ketchup?

Satiated and floating on velvet air we return to our suite. I order two more amazing martinis for nightcaps on our extravagant terrace. I light candles and room service delivers in seconds. The moon creates sequins rolling on the ocean. Candlelight and that moon conspire to adore Don's spectacular face. I can feel my heart pounding and breaking, I keep that well hidden.

This is the honeymoon denied by the vile bigots who vow never to allow our marriage. Fuck them. We're here alive and in love.

Don eventually drifts off under glorious Italian sheets. I look at him peaceful and comforted and slip out of bed, walk out to the terrace and quietly close the terrace doors behind me, I light a cigarette look up to the stars and my endless painful tears could fill another ocean.

Somehow eventually I manage to compose myself. I can't let on how terrified I am. I never can let him know.

Our wakeup call is early, today we're taking a long hike up to visit Tiberius, actually his ancient palace, Jovis (Villa Jupiter), completed in 27 AD. Tiberius sodomized two boys during a sacrificial ceremony on the island and when they complained he had their legs broken. He also diplomatically sexually assaulted women. From sexually depraved to simply sadistic, during banquets, Tiberius would fill his drinking companions with vast quantities of wine before tying ligatures around their genitals, preventing them from urinating.

And so, Capri continues to be the playground of the rich, powerful and debauched.

A Capri breakfast on our terrace and we're off. We're just minutes into our climb and suddenly we have company, he's absolutely adorable and so in love with both of us. We've been adopted by a dog who we immediately name, Gino Lollobrigida.

Gino leads us all the way up to the ruins of the perverted emperors' palace. Even the view is hedonistic. Gino knows this place well and proudly shows us where his ancestors peed.

I'm astounded at Don's energy, I'm struggling to

drag myself up this mountain and he's running and jumping with Gino!

I'm so happy to finally satisfy business associates who often wished me to go take a hike. Maybe one day they'll reciprocate and leap off a cliff. Oh well, I promised myself to forget the wonderful world of advertising on this getaway.

Gino shows us his favorite trail down the mountain and as soon as we get back to our hotel we order room service for our pooch. We can't take Gino with us to explore the grottos by boat, but he understands and snuggles on big down pillows luxuriously waiting for our return.

Both grottos are astonishing. We couldn't leave Capri without becoming tourists. Back at The Grand Hotel Gino greets us at the door leaping up into Don's arms. I wonder if Mr. Gino Lollobrigida has a passport.

Our last night in Capri is sad but we have more exciting Italian adventures planned. We walk Gino with us to a crowded outdoor restaurant hoping he recognizes someone. It's not going to be easy to say goodbye, but we know Capri is his home. Everyone at the restaurant is in love with Gino especially a very stylish lady named Juliette who Gino has been continuously flirting with. Juliette announces she's more than thrilled to give Gino a home at her villa here in Capri, Gino is no dummy. But Gino must have his last night with us at the Grand Hotel Quisisana. Juliette will pick Gino up in the morning.

With a heavy heart it's goodbye Gino, goodbye

Capri, we love you both, and you too, Juliette for adopting our pooch.

Aboard the ferry speeding away Capri grows smaller in the distance floating like the sparkling jewel it really is.

Mario Andretti has nothing on Don behind the wheel of our Audi careening up the narrow hairpin twisting terrifying Amalfi coast roads with no guard rails and crumbling edges with signs marking locations where cars careened off the cliffs. My handprints are permanently imbedded into the armrest as Don continues to accelerate. Oh what a heart pounding joy speeding to Ravello!

Thankfully we decide to make a pit stop in Positano. Don wants to see Le Siranuse, Positano's most renowned hotel. Spectacular wine and antipasto and afterward we're taken on a tour of available suites. I venture into one of the master bathrooms and crack up; the bathtub's spout is a giant gold penis! How Italian. Don is doubled over.

We'd love to stay but Ravello calls.

Don's racecar skills continue up the Amalfi coast until we come to a sign pointing left indicating the road to Ravello. Well, I thought I was going to have a heart attack on the Amalfi racetrack but that was kid stuff compared to the hairpin turn blasting off up a nearly vertical twisting dark narrow road ascending close to the edge of the atmosphere. Finally I'm able to exhale when we arrive at The Caruso, Ravello's beyond belief hotel.

The Heartbreak of Static Cling

We quickly check in and find a terrace located way above the world for cocktails and dinner just as the sun finally sets.

And as soon the evening darkness settles in, astonishing fireworks explode before and below us. This is the place the Kennedys honeymooned. We're actually in heaven orchestrated by the Gods.

All this will forever be with us.

Our trip is coming to an end and we're driving back down the coast and stop off again in Capri to see how Gino is doing. Well here's a dog who knows how to live, he's not only pampered and adored in Juliet's luxurious villa, Gino now has a boyfriend, a poodle no less! Love abounds doggy-style in Capri.

AND NOW FOR A COMMERCIAL BREAK

ADS AGAINST AIDS are almost ready for its premiere. Storyboards were submitted by creative teams from five of the biggest ad agencies. Four winning concepts were shot and are in final stages of editing. The winning ads are powerful concepts incredibly produced and promise to be very effective.

That's well and very good, but as far as I'm concerned this project is already a big success; Major ad agencies and creative talents were awakened and ignited by the challenge and finally used their talents and

The Heartbreak of Static Cling

abilities to move people's perceptions about AIDS and they now realize how important it is to get involved with this ongoing battle.

December fourth is the date, the Waldorf's grand ballroom is booked and invitations to the press have been sent.

Don's been working on getting notices of our second PTAAA scholarship competition out to a bigger number of high schools across the country. Sunday by the Bay's second year already looks like it will be even more successful. Volunteers are working continually empowered by the amazing energy created and the amount of funds raised at our first event.

But numbers are not so much our friend now. Don's T-Cell counts are falling, hovering around the dreaded 200 count. And horribly there are still no breakthroughs. Sure there's hope but not nearly on this horizon... AZT has caused more harm than good and Don has abandoned it as advised. How beyond frustrating knowing practically every current drug trial happening all over the world is still adding up to nothing, and still maddening little governmental help continues this disaster. And death is all around us constantly.

But we can celebrate a victory. Don directed PTAAA to fund phase four trials of aerosolized Pantamadine, and now it's been approved by the FDA. This will help save many with AIDS from the horrible death of Pneumocystis Pneumonia.

It's not easy to concentrate on any ad account with what we're dealing with. But I force myself into that world for escape.

Daddy's Lullabies is doing wonders for Don. The album is beautiful and we live for ongoing recording sessions. We keep busy moving on giving each other strength.

Light the lights, the premier at the Waldorf arrives and the ballroom is filled to capacity. Curtains part lights dim and the winning TV spots so well crafted and powerfully conceived grab the audience by the throat.

Major applause, I'm on stage with my fellow creative directors, we are the four who followed through with Ads against AIDS and made certain these winning spots will definitely air prime time on national networks.

Jack Mariucci takes the podium and thanks all for their work and contributions making this important project happen. Creative directors representing different agencies take their turn at the podium. It's all beginning to sound a bit self- congratulatory and aggrandizing; they know the press is eating it up.

It's my turn to put in my two cents. I spot him in the audience and gesture for him to come up on stage. "I want you all to meet Don Hall, he's the founder of PTAAA, that's, People Taking Action Against AIDS. Don is the one who brought this challenge to our industry. Don Hall is the inspiration and spark that created Ads Against AIDS."

The Heartbreak of Static Cling

A well deserved standing ovation rewards Don as he humbly utters, "Thank you."

More applause and waves to everyone and Don and I find Sam and Helen in the crowd and we go out to dinner, (not in Harlem). And finally take a deep breath.

ANOTHER DAY ON THE JOB

AT BILL KING'S studio for yet another fashion shoot and Jerry is up to her old tricks, she's a no show, my clients are getting antsy and the account execs panties are in a knot.

I thought I taught Jerry a lesson the last time she pulled this stunt and went missing. It was a Celanese SuperSuede shoot and of course I booked Supermodel Jerry Hall. I had Bill lacquer the backdrop high gloss comic book yellow to contrast the shocking blue Super Woman Super Model Jerry Hall's SuperSuede dress, and

The Heartbreak of Static Cling

no Jerry!

I was not about to let her get away with this again and I become a film noir detective hunting that dame down. My contact at her model agency spilled the beans with a hot lead.

I tell the crew I'm on the case, cool your heels, I'll be right back and dash out of the studio and bolt out in front of a bus to nab a cab to floor it to the diamond district in the West 40's.

The street's cordoned off, turned into a movie set for Marathon Man, starring Dustin Hoffman.

I spot the star's trailer and dash through body guards and barriers and pound on Dustin's door. He opens it and there she is cuddled next to him. I grab her, "You come with me right now Jerry!"

Dustin turns white. "Where are you taking her?"

"She's on my set today Dustin, not yours!"

I shove her into my waiting cab and give her a good talking to.

And here we are years later waiting for her again... wait a minute... Miracle! Super glamour girl finally arrives dazzling and just a fifteen hundred dollar an hour late.

I guess she's learned a lesson—well, almost.

This business is getting on my nerves. Sure it's fun and pays the bills but it's become repetitive and more bills are mounting up, living life to the limit costs a fortune. My patience is wearing thin but I'm pushing pause. Moving to another agency doesn't feel right now.

But when it does it will happen for sure and quick.

I get home from the shoot and find Don upset. "Robert, I got a call from Juan."

"Antonio is in the hospital."

"What?"

"It's not good he's in LA, UCLA Hospital."

"Damn it, are Juan and Paul there?"

"They're on their way."

"So are we."

Don tells me Antonio has been pretty sick, he went to Puerto Rico to see relatives or doctors, who knows what? But he got a lot sicker and maybe because UCLA Medical Center is one of the best in the world, he's there.

Juan and Paul are booked to stay at the Shangri La Hotel in Santa Monica, I immediately make reservations.

I've been upbeat strong and full of hope and joy to the point of passing out. But now this is very different, facing this is impossible. I can imagine how much harder it is for Don.

So I shoot myself up with delusional obscure optimism and backbone and present the most positive outlook and tell Don I'm so glad Antonio's at UCLA where I'm certain they'll get him back on his feet soon.

Don is also acting. We're doing this for each other and for ourselves. We know as pressure builds we will explode and we'll have to do that with Rosemary's help.

We arrive at the hotel late afternoon. Juan and

The Heartbreak of Static Cling

Paul are already at the hospital. We drive to UCLA finding our way through the enormous medical center to see Antonio.

Expressionless Tina Chow gently massages Antonio's feet. Juan and Paul hover at his side. Antonio is slightly conscious, just enough to manage a small smile of recognition. Juan and Paul are trying their best to be happy to see us. There's absolutely nothing possible to say.

He's lying there peacefully hooked up to an IV and monitors, no grotesque apparatus apparent. This is not a quarantined ICU, it's a quiet room with just us and Antonio until Jerry Hall appears in all her glamour but in obvious shock and not knowing what to do. She gets on the phone and whispers "I don't know, I don't know, I... Okay, but... hold on." She covers the mouthpiece and pulls me over to her. "Mick wants me to wear a mask, talk to him."

She hands me the phone. "No Mick, you can't get it that way, no she doesn't need it... That's not necessary... absolutely not necessary." I hand the phone back to Jerry. She finally hangs up and walks over to Antonio and kisses his cheek.

We're just standing there silently; Tina continues her loving massage and without words we take turns leaving the room for a minute but Don doesn't leave Antonio, he's holding his beautiful hand. That hand that created miracles that will live on forever.

I'm alone in the hallway silently yelling silently

hysterical, silently taking deep breaths and fighting to find strength to return to the room. There's nothing that can be done but we're here now with him and he knows that.

Jerry sheds her sleeveless fur coat and pulls up a chair next to Antonio and smoothes his forehead with her cheek.

We're there for hours but we don't know that. There is no time now, there is no reality but this moment.

Jerry slowly gets up and whispers asking if we can give her a lift to her friend's house when we decide to leave, I nod yes.

More minutes more hours more time with Antonio until we manage to say "We'll be back tomorrow, Antonio." We hug Juan, Paul and Tina and leave with Jerry.

We manage to find our way outside of that hospital and force ourselves to deeply inhale the night's crisp California Jasmine air, a small comfort.

Jerry gets in the back seat with I don't know what to call it; it's a big rectangular box some kind of a case, a makeup case I guess. She tells Don the way to find her friend's house in Beverly Hills, it's 1:30AM.

It takes Don just about a half hour to find Jerry's friends street and suddenly Jerry's Texas twang has something important to say. "Mick won't marry me."

"What?"

"Mick won't marry me!"

The Heartbreak of Static Cling

I tell her, "Look Jerry, if you want Mick to marry you, Mick will marry you."

"Mick won't marry me." I turn and see her in the back seat fingering her pussy. "I do this and tell him, smell! And he still won't marry me!" Jerry's craziness is just what we needed.

Eventually Jerry recognizes the house. "This is it, park!" Don pulls over and we get out of the car. Jerry sets her makeup case on the ground in front of tall hedges and stands on it, now she's almost seven feet tall yelling, "Angelica! Angelica, Angelica!" Lights go on the gate opens and a woman in a white bathrobe appears.

"Hey Jerry! Hey you guys, come in." This woman in fluffy slippers and her bathrobe is Angelica Huston.

She brings us into her warm comfortable unpretentious home, exactly how she reveals herself. Jerry introduces us and she instantly makes us feel like we're old friends. We settle into fat sofas In front of a fireplace and she brings large glasses filled to the brim with Brandy.

I watch Jerry abandon her Supermodel glamour and become a vulnerable person whose hurting bad.

Sitting here with Don, Jerry and Angelica Huston is some kind of a miracle. Angelica is magically healing, caring and loving sharing her wonderful history with Antonio. What an amazing woman. We spend hours till dawn healing. I go to the kitchen for wine and get a glimpse of snapshots taped to the refrigerator door of Jack Nicholson and Angelica, a dreamlike visual on this very surreal night.

We're so thankful for Jerry's thousand watt glamour and comedy bringing us to Angelicas warmth compassion and wisdom.

Afternoon arrives quickly and we're here again with Antonio, today it's just us and Juan and Paul. There's been no change but we want to believe he seems better. You need to see what you need to see. But what I see in Don and Juan's eyes is unbearable. They are seeing everything too clearly.

Our session with Rosemary is day after tomorrow and it's urgent. We stay at Antonio's bedside most of the day. Tina returns and again no conversation is possible.

Somehow we manage to control ourselves to say I love you Antonio. And leave him to go home.

Antonio Lopez
February 11, 1943—March 17, 1987

LEVERAGE

I GO ON like everything is normal and life is okay, maybe if I do this long enough I just might fool myself.

It's strange stepping foot into this office building again after so many years. Backer now occupies DDB's former floors. Getting out of the elevator I see the place is renovated but I'm able to spot where my tiny first office was as Lester Feldman's young assistant art director. The receptionist announces me and I'm greeted by a secretary who escorts me to Bill Backer's office.

Here he is, the man who created, "I'd like to buy

the world a Coke" And I wonder if he's got any.

The short Southern gent greets me with a smile and explains his proposal including responsibilities I would shoulder. Of course, the main account I'm desperately needed to save is Helene Curtis; Suave Shampoo and all products from this client. Same pigeonhole as Clairol. But Backer offers a carrot, a promise of creating campaigns for their other clients, interesting assignments however vague.

My responsibilities would also include supervising six creative teams of art directors and copywriters, and a senior copywriter, with my approval will be hired to work with me.

Okay, let's cut to the chase: What's the offer? It better be big enough to leverage DDB. Well bang a gong, get it on... Two and a half times my current salary plus a mega entrance bonus!

Stone faced I tell Backer I'll get back to him, I shake his hand and leave.

I hit the streets imagining what I would be able to do if I decide to go for it. There might even be some magic drug for Don I could afford?

Maybe this is my revenge for being pegged as the "fashion creative director" I'll make them pay and pay big.

But DDB is my home, is it time now to leave the nest? One thing for sure, their reaction to this offer will be very telling.

I get back home and report the events to Don. He

has a wisdom about him that matters. And after a lot of talk we decide to just let it ride and wait for DDB's reaction.

After Antonio's death everything changed. Time changed, fear changed and there's even more urgency to live now.

The weekend is here in Bellport. We're so grateful for this place. April is more than half over and PTAAA is in full force preparing for another Sunday by The Bay in July. I try to keep Don out of continual meetings with volunteers and make sure he has time to rest and have some time for ourselves, but this work is top priority for him, this is his purpose and energy.

I'm in front of the house doing some gardening, suddenly I see Bernard's car speeding down the lane. Xavier is in the passenger seat, Bernard turns his head and looks at me with a strange expression and continues driving away quickly.

Monday evening is our Rosemary session and I can't wait. This Backer thing is hounding me and there's much more of course.

Next day at work I make an appointment with Jack, and I'm rehearsing how exactly how I'm going to approach this, but I know I'm much better winging it so that's what I decide to do.

Jack sees me the end of the day and I just let it out. He knows how I feel about DDB. He knows my frustrations here and also he knows my loyalty. This might put me at a disadvantage but whatever; I need to know what DDB will do. Jack can't help being impressed by Backer's offer. I'm valued here working successfully with clients most creative teams run from. Jack promises to bring this up to the powers that be. I tell him to take his time.

A few days later and still no news from Jack, what kind of game is this? He damn well knew I was talking backwards when I said take your time and if their reaction is nothing, then Bye Bye DDB. I'll give it no more than a week.

I fill Don in on the latest DDB drama and he hits me with news.

Xavier Forcade dies of AIDS, April 28th, 1987.

ZIGGY AND BOOTS

BOOTS is gray, he wears white boots and he's brilliant and affectionate. This cat just shows up at our door and won't let us go. I'm not one to allocate miracle attributes to pets but this one is remarkable. Boots is completely independent and doesn't need us but he won't leave our side when we're here in Bellport. I had a cat door cut in the upstairs deck room. He instantly worked out which tree to climb to get up and over the railing onto the deck and into the house with a comfortable bed and food and water always available. He comes and goes as he pleases and we love him for that.

The final counter offer from DDB was infuriating and I've accepted the position at Backer. I'll begin in three weeks giving me time to prepare for the transition from DDB.

Ziggy is sage green metallic and a convertible. It's our shiny new VW we decided on after I almost blew my entire entry bonus from Backer on a new Mercedes SL, it was creampuff color with saddle leather interior and I could taste it. But Don pulled me out of the showroom and talked some sense into my head. We don't even drive to Bellport anymore, we take a limo so the car is just for jaunts along Long Island and Ziggy is perfect. I park it in our driveway and stare at it for hours. How crazy, but cars were the only thing that brought me and my dad together. He had a weird car, a 1954 Kaiser Manhattan which he repainted at least five times. It was originally baby blue with a navy top, a real head turner. That thing looked like it escaped from a Coney Island ride. As a kid I simonized its big toothed smiling grill with my dad.

We love Ziggy and Boots. And we're taking full advantage of everything Bellport, the beach, the best friends and neighbors and our finally finished home. What seemed last year insurmountable to create Sunday by the Bay is now a joy almost on automatic and heading for even greater success.

I'm not giving a thought to my new position at Backer, however it turns out to be will be just fine, and that change had to come. Both of us are moving forward putting away what hurts as much as we can.

And here I am my first day at Backer. My new secretary introduces herself and shows me to my new enormous corner office that was once was Bill Taubin's, a legendary DDB creative director in the olden days. I'm taken by the honor of occupying this space now. It's comforting to have some connection to DDB.

Backer and Lenz show up asking how I like my new digs and if anything is needed. I tell them I'm fine, I'll just rearrange the furnishings. They seem very pleased I'm here and leave me to settle in. I close the door and move the giant brilliantly designed desk to face the view of the city I promised myself to conquer a long time ago and sit there in disbelief. The rest of the day is filled with introductions, all seem pleasant enough and my secretary delivers a key to the executive gym on the floor above. Okay, I'm officially a Mad Man!

Half past five I leave the building on a cloud so wound up I decide to walk home. My obscene salary is causing a maniacal grin on my face, people notice and that's unusual in New York. I try to control myself before a cop pulls me in.

Whatever happens, however long it lasts this move is worth it. And it's all because I overturned a table drunk in London to the delight of Bob Lenz. I couldn't make that up.

Somehow I feel somewhere in my guts this balloon is too big not to bust, but right now I just don't give a damn.

I get home hug Don and we go out for an especially great dinner.

LIKE A ROLLING STONE

AT ANTONIO'S STUDIO Don is helping Juan and Paul archive Antonio's life's work, a monumental task. They tell me they have to leave to get some materials and I should wait here to let Jerry in, they'll be back soon.

I'm alone in the studio with Antonio's spectacular work, flat files filled with more and more, a lifetime of genius here for the world to treasure. I'll never forget watching Antonio at work creating magical worlds.

Suddenly there's a knock on the door and, "Hi, it's Jerry!" I open the door and Jerry appears in all her glamour arm in arm towering over Mick Jagger at her side.

"Jerry, Mick! Come in." I'm reduced to a babbling teenager in a star struck frenzy desperately trying to be cool, yeah sure. I tell them the guys had to go out to get supplies; they'll be back soon... "Would you like some wine?" I need some right this second. Riffling through cabinets I find nothing, No drop of anything!

Mick says, "No problem." He pulls out a joint, lights it and passes it to me. From Mick Jagger's lips to mine! The Jewish expression for this is *'plotz,'* and I did as discretely as possible.

I pass the joint to Jerry and say with a potent pot swagger, "Hey Mick, I spoke to you from the hospital when you had some concern about Jerry wearing a mask."

"Oh, right, mate."

Mate! Somehow I keep breathing. "Thanks for setting that straight. Jerry told me you were a close friend of Antonio's."

"Very close, look at this incredible work... Brilliant." He takes another drag and passes it to me again. I want to lick it.

Jerry is amused at my battle to be coherent. She cracks up at my expression as I give Mick a head to toe once over, and so does Mick. There he is wearing normal jeans a T-Shirt, a lived in wool blazer and a warm smile, just a normal playful ordinary guy, *Mick Jagger*! Have you ever seen this "ordinary guy" on stage?!

Finally Juan, Paul and Don return and I'm so relieved. Juan just says, "Hi Jerry, hi Mick," like they're next door neighbors like Fred and Ethel Mertz who just dropped by.

Don, bless him, he picked up a couple bottles of Chardonnay. I pull him over and show him the last of the joint I pocketed and will keep forever. I've turned into a very troubled teenager with a crush.

After a Chardonnay or two or three, I'm able to reminisce with Jerry about our time with Angelica. Mick overhears the events of that night and appreciates what a gift it was. What a nice regular ordinary truly great guy he really is.

I pull Jerry close to my Jacque Fath Green Water perfumed neck and whisper, "Mick will marry you, and if he won't, here smell!"

BACK TO BACKER

IT'S BEEN several months and it's not easy getting used to the culture here so different than that of DDB. This isn't an exclusive creative family, Backer is just all business, and that's okay, I'm here to definitely give them the business but unfortunately I have to be a teacher as well. My creative team's former mentors ignored explorations necessary to create unexpected invention. Their recent presentations were predictably expected and what I consider invisible advertising.

      Years ago Lester Feldman taught a class once a week at SVA and asked me to fill in when he was unavailable. Eventually I took over his class and renamed it, "What's the Big Idea." It was about how to think logically and ask insightful probing questions that could solidify a strong strategic platform enabling the creation of unexpected concepts to be executed and evolve. The class was fun at times, but some students were just asleep at their desks.

Here there is no nap time and it's taking a lot of patience. If nothing else they'll get a swift kick in the ass and thank me for it, eventually.

Taking advantage of the executive gym I hired a personal trainer to help me unwind and get me in shape. Well this didn't go over big with a fat ugly account guy who was offended by my workout thinking it was maybe, too gay? So asshole complained and I had to let go of my trainer. This is a very forward thinking ad agency isn't it?

Nonetheless I'm getting paid the big bucks and I won't let any bullshit bother me.

I reviewed several portfolios of "Senior Copywriters" to consider hiring and take some weight off my shoulders. But from what I've seen these contestants would be more of a burden.

Finally after rejecting everybody, Lenz brings me a portfolio that's not so horrible, actually there is some competence visible. So I set up an interview with Miss Senior Copywriter, young Wendy Wannabe. Petit aggressive and so desperate to become one of the good old boys, she in the middle of our interview pulls out a cigar and lights it.

As Addison DeWitt so eloquently said to Eve

Harrington, "You're too short for that gesture." I really wanted to use that line but held my tongue waiting for a more appropriate moment.

I just clearly suggested, "Put that out please." She almost argued but smartly stopped herself with a grin and killed the cigar.

Could I possibly work with her? Maybe her ambition would be a motivation to accomplish something with our baby creative teams and free me to actually do some gratifying work.

Beyond the over self confident façade, there is some transparent vulnerability, her saving grace.

After debating myself to exhaustion I've decided she might work out and I hired her. The cigar thing however obnoxious was amusing.

Instant buddies, she's doing everything in her power to make that happen, she's no dummy. I'm playing it for all its worth and actually her better side reveals itself surprisingly when least expected. But I am well aware she would cut my throat for my office.

I give her the lowdown on the slow progress of our creative teams and also a crash course of "What's the Big Idea." She gets it and calls it brilliant, yep, she's no dummy. "Now dear Wendy, apply this to our teams and bring them back with good work."

Miracle, this is happening. She is less intimidating than me. Some of our women art directors are paired with women copywriters. And Wendy's cigar knows how to empower women. Good.

Life at Baker is slightly more tolerable now. I'm appreciative and invite Ms. Wendy to lunch where she probes me trying her best to find cracks she can exploit and I do the same, it's fun. Whoever said advertising is competitive?

It's all a much needed diversion. Don is doing well, but there's constant underlying fear and continual bad news about those closest to us. Celebrities are dying, distant friends are dying and friends are testing positive daily. And still no substantial effective treatment is available anywhere.

Bad news travels fast, Bill King is sick. I call his studio and his assistant confirms this but tells me Bill continues to be at his studio mostly every day. It's been a long time since I've seen him.

I get to 100 Fifth Avenue and Bill is there, well almost there. He's stick thin walking slowly but brightens when he sees me. I hug him, or is it his skeleton I'm embracing? He wants to show me something and takes me to his storage room a floor below his studio. It's filled to the ceiling with exquisite English antique furniture. I knew he loved this stuff, but not to this extent. He's proud of his collection and I tell him how great it is.

He's exhausted and I can't bring myself to say much. We get back in the elevator up to his studio, I pinch his bony ass and kiss him, I say goodbye and he gets out of the elevator, the doors close and I know I will never see him again.

Bill King dies November 19th, 1987. He is 48.

TAKE THREE

OUR PTAAA Sunday by The Bay does it again even better and nets more than our past two events and again all the proceeds will fund much needed AIDS care, research and education.

But with great success, intrigue finds its way to those who believe they could personally profit by infiltrating our board.

A fundamental rift between the founding members has arisen and Don and I have no choice but to withdraw PTAAA from any further involvement with Sunday by The Bay. This split is hurtful, very unfortunate but necessary.

We created a miracle, a successful miracle, an all volunteer selfless miracle putting Bellport on the map and making a big difference in many lives. And we will continue PTAAA as a fundraising nonprofit organization firmly adhering to our founding principles.

There's a more immediate event coming up, Don's fortieth birthday. His health is holding steady now and nothing else matters.

On my fortieth birthday Don threw a party I'll never forget. Our Bellport house was filled to capacity with guests and Don cooked his astounding Southern fried chicken and soul food for everyone, how this is possible I'll never know.

Texarkana is our favorite restaurant. Abe De la Houssay and his wife Helene are great friends and fabulous restaurateurs. As the name of their restaurant suggests it's part Texas, part Cajun and up to Don's standards and that says everything about the food. I booked the restaurant and invited everybody. Great pictures of Don, the boy in Texas are displayed on the walls and straw cowboy hats are provided to all.

Don arranged to perform a set with a gal he met through his voice coach. They're terrific together accompanied by a group of the best studio musicians backing them up.

What a great celebration.

Don is now forty, he's okay and I don't care about anything in this world but that.

Happy Birthday, Don.

MERGER MANIA

IT'S HAPPENING everywhere, Doyle Dane Bernbach will become DDB Needham Omnicom Worldwide, give me a break. And Backer Speilvogel becomes Backer Speilvogel Bates. Now if that's not a Backerbreaker I don't know what is.

Merge ad agencies that are creatively oil and water, mix them all up, hold your nose and drink that down. The only ones who like this kind of cocktail are the CEO's and their stockholders. They're drunk on merger mania and cashing in big time.

And many heads are rolling... Including mine.

Yep, I knew it in my gut this wouldn't last. I just didn't know how long it would take to happen. There's an epidemic of head on collisions rocking Madison Avenue and it's spreading fast.

My salary needs to be cut to show even more profit, Miss Cigar will stay for now, just give it a month or two, darling.

Where I go from here, who the fuck knows? I'll wait for the dust to settle before thinking about another move.

But too soon I get a call from Peggy Persky who's proudly perky, say that ten times! She's a friend of a friend, a copywriter at an agency I've always admired for their consistently mundane awful work.

Peggy is also amusing; marketing herself as The Midwestern Woman therefore she perfectly understands the needs of all American Women. She knows what women like to wash their clothes with, what they brush their teeth with and what douche they desire, you name it, Peggy's from the Midwest and she knows. Evidently she's also been living in Manhattan for most of her life. Her adoring mundane Advertising agency bought this crap hook line and sinker installing her with the Proctor & Gamble account, how appropriate.

Peggy is also a cunning feminist, surrounding herself with women who agree men are to be used because women are so much smarter.

Of course she likes me a lot, it's the position I've

held and my envious creative reputation. Maybe she can get some by association. Her antenna detected the news of me being let out in the cold by Backer and she pounced offering me an interview with the brilliant head of her agency. No thanks.

Or, on second thought, who gives a shit? I need a job now. Oh yeah, it could be horrific but what's the alternative now that so many great agencies have merged to oblivion?

I'm in it for the money, now more necessary to fight for Don's life. My only priority is keeping him healthy, whatever it takes. Creative ambition no longer drives me. I tell Peggy I'll think about it and get back to her.

Later that night Don and I are walking to a restaurant with Juan and Paul. Juan and Don are in a conversation several feet ahead of me and Paul. I whisper to Paul, "If that fucking mark on Don's ankle is KS I'm going to kill myself."

SUSPENDED DISBELIEF

I NEED to convince myself completely. I have to make myself confident beyond any doubt, I have to do this or I'll collapse the scaffolding Dcn needs now. That angry little son of a bitch spot on his ankle is KS and that Kaposi Sarcoma will be rendered insignificant and will not spread. Nothing in this world will convince me otherwise.

Now this fucking KS labels Don with AIDS. Labels can and will be removed. I have no choice but to kill fear immediately.

I've believe in many things: In whiter than white, brighter than bright, I believe in scrubbing bubbles, I

231   The Heartbreak of Static Cling

believe it's you only better and just do it and only your hairdresser knows for sure, I believe things go better with coke and Mister Clean, motherfucker I'm a madman with a vengeance and I also believe we'll absolutely survive this.

Do what we need to be done and do and more to get whatever it is wherever in this world it may exist, we'll get it and Don will be okay. I need this belief to be normal, think clearly and continue to reinforce this belief with every ounce of my strength.

Okay, radiation—stop this now, calm this now, do what you can and give us the time to find something better because we will. I refuse to let this crush us. We will overpower this, there cannot be any doubt.

I'm taking that damned job. Don is taking that radiation. And we're grabbing it all by the balls and squeezing hard.

Working with Peggy is like radiation, no problem I know what that's like, I've endured it when they removed my left ball but that turned out to be no one's advantage, it was replaced with solid brass. Bring it on Perky Peggy just throw whatever garbage you have at me, I'll handle it. Just don't get me mad, you don't want to see me mad. I'm using you and this job to keep my sanity.

Don's radiation isn't going well. It's making the hideous spots angrier, now his ankle is swollen. Doctors decide to back off and consider Chemo. Okay Don, no problem you'll see, a little chemo and that'll get it.

I have to go to Cincinnati to Proctor & Gamble

with Perky to witness another focus group investigating static cling, of all things. My static won't let go, for me fabric softener is no savior, neither is this job. And now the fucking static has deafened my right ear, my emotions are on overload but I refuse to let it show.

Don's thick black curls are graying and thinning. I catch him crying in the bathroom mirror.

"It'll grow back, you'll see."

The chemo is working and just one more dose and done. His ankle swelling is down and the marks are faded somewhat. We have a reprieve. He's feeling better and we're taking full advantage of this.

Jennifer Connelly is starring in another movie that begins shooting soon in LA. Ilene and Gerry rented a house there and invited us.

We're going and that's that, and from there we're going to Cabo San Lucas for a week and forget about everything.

If the ad agency doesn't like this they can shove it. Nothing will get in the way of our plans.

Wait a little longer he'll heal some more and we're off to LA LA Land.

The house is on Stradella Road, Beverly Hills, it's some tacky glamour fantasy. The pool is surrounded by Roman Columns and statuary, the craziness of this place is amusing. Ilene, Gerry and Jen get the joke of it and we laugh our heads off. Being with them is exactly what we need. Don is having fun and you can't put a price on that.

There's a great scene Jen is about to shoot and

we're invited to come see the set and watch the filming.

The Rocketeer is set in the thirties. This scene takes place in a spectacular deco nightclub only Hollywood could build. Jen appears wearing a white satin gown incredibly stunning. The camera follows her walking through the nightclub. Billy Campbell is co staring. He's secretly lurking in the club and finds the villain, Timothy Dalton escorting Jen. The orchestra onstage features a giant clamshell that opens revealing a deco diva chanteuse with a velvet voice singing, "When they begin the beguine." This Hollywood Glamour transports us to 1938.

Of course we ruined the shot by getting too close to the action but all is forgiven. How great it is watching Jennifer, what a beauty. Billy Campbell isn't too shabby himself. He's a great guy, extremely handsome in a boyish unassuming way and a lot of fun.

That Cole Porter song haunted me all the way down to Cabo. We booked ourselves into Hotel Cabo San Lucas, the oldest hotel there. It's a big old Spanish hacienda like place with magical gardens, alluring seaside pool and the best mariachi band, more like a mariachi orchestra. I request that song and their interpretation is magic with the best Margaritas.

This heaven is so necessary now. The romantic days and nights are healing and the best escape, a much needed pause of the horror show.

But there's no stopping it.

Tina Chow dies of AIDS January 24th, 1992.

Horace Gifford dies of AIDS April 6th, 1992.

Ted and Zelda B. Starr

Carolyn, Mom & Me

Toddler me
Into leather early on!

Abraham Lincoln High

Mr. Leon Friend

Grads: Carol to Pratt, Me to SVA

School of Visual Arts (SVA)

Andrea at Max's

The Chelsea Hotel

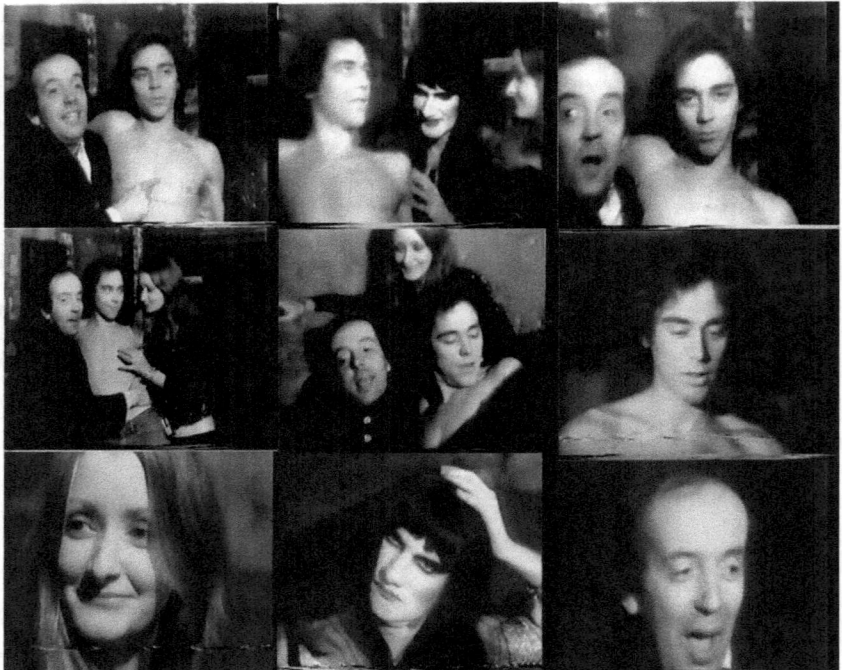
Anton Perish presents: Frankenstino, with Taylor Mead, Jayne County, Katrina Toland, filmed at The Chelsea

Anton Interview with Andrea "Whips" Warhol

Malcolm Morley brought me to London

The Royal Botanical Kew Gardens photoshoot by Peter Schlesinger

BILL KING invites that guy we met briefly by chance that day, to have dinner with us in Chinatown.

And that was that.

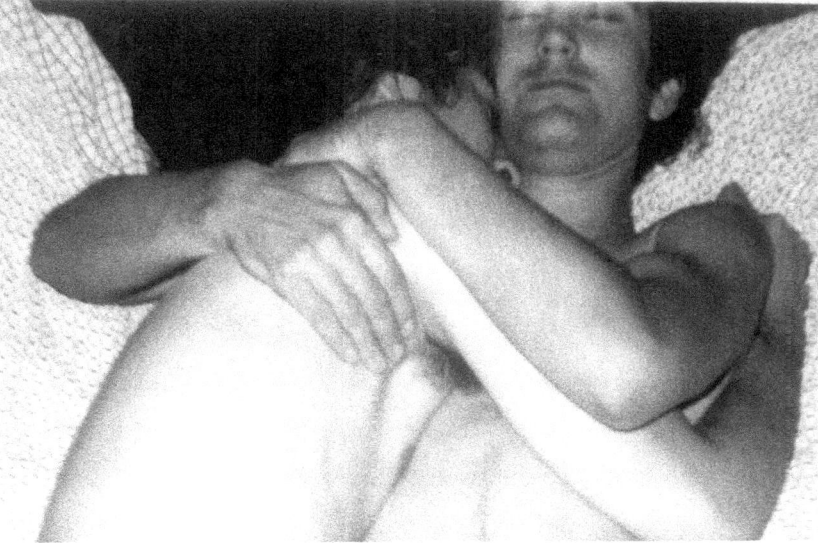

Jerry Hall and Don Hall. Photo: Bill King

Cover Photo: Bill King

PURE GARBAGE
Holly Woodlawn, Don Hall, Elda Stiletto, Jamaica Kincaid, Fast Eddie, and band

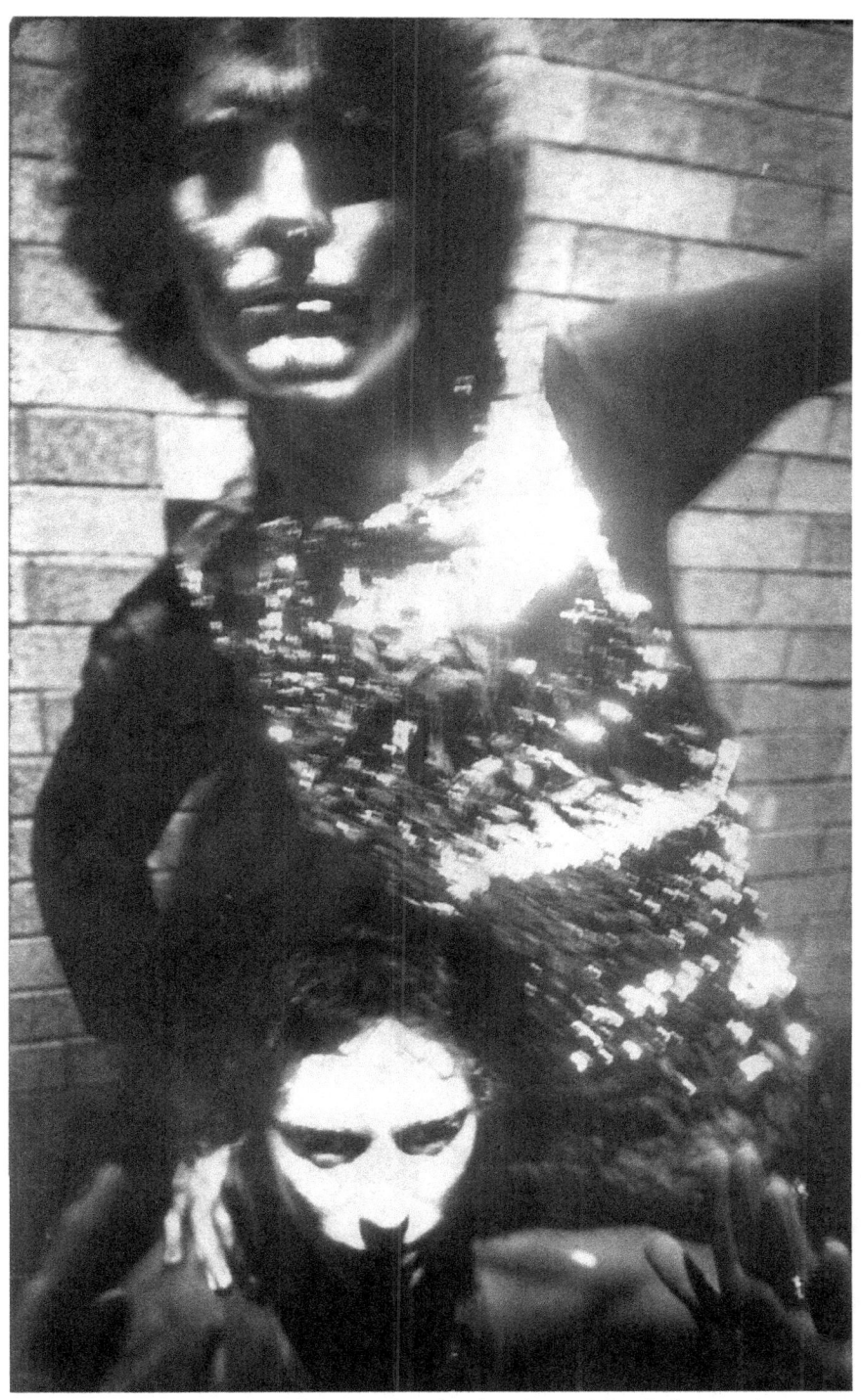

Don Hall and Robert Starr performing in a Marta Minujin happening at the Museum of Modern Art (MOMA)

Fire Island Pines

New Year's Eve at Mr. Chow's

top row: Paul Caranicas, Jessica Lange, Don Hall, Christian, Ed Hayes

bottom row: Corey Grant Tippin, Jerry Hall, Antonio, Me, Nancy Lucas

Mick Jagger & Jerry Hall

photos + artwork
Courtesy of the Estate of Antonio Lopez & Juan Ramos

Tina Chow

Don with Bernard Lennon

Juan Ramos and Don

SUNDAY BY THE BAY

JULY 9, 1989
BELLPORT VILLAGE
LONG ISLAND
12:00 NOON

Don in his garden

Jennifer Connelly and Don

Ilene Connelly

Eric Boman and Peter Schlesinger

Tony Frere and Joey Arias

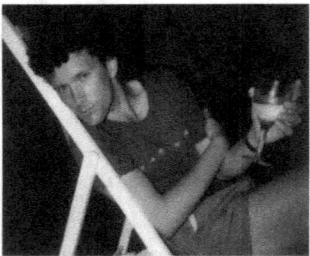

Zelda at the Gay Parade

Zelda and Holly

Todd and Holly

Zelda and Helen Glasser

Mary Kay and Zelda

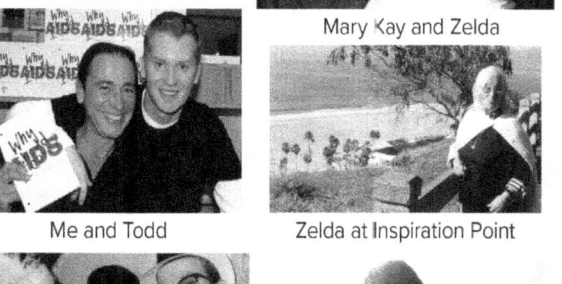

Jennifer Connelly

Me and Todd

Zelda at Inspiration Point

Holly, Me, Connie and Brent

photo: Frank Stiefel

THEY CALL IT AN AD AGENCY

I GET BACK to work and Peggy's enraged. Turns out two of her masterpiece TV campaigns targeted at her beloved Midwestern American Woman bombed magnificently in focus groups. And it's absolutely my fault because I had nothing to do with it, perfect logic Perky.

She's had it with me and I've had it with her. She has no power to fire me but she manipulated my reassignment to partner with another copywriter whom she sold to management as a perfect match.

The Heartbreak of Static Cling

Hello Hilda Hack, a more appropriate name couldn't possibly be imagined. I thought these dinosaurs were extinct, but this environment nurtures this species.

This agency is somewhere between Christmas and being buried alive. I've trudged through enough garbage here to build a landfill to Mars. My tolerance meter explodes and I'm out of here for good.

I need to take care of Don. He's now on more meds; one of them is an infusion supposedly to prevent blindness. These infusions are given at the doctor's office. But now it's recommended he get a port installed in his arm so he can hook himself up at home. Now we have an arsenal of drugs and a rolling steel rack with a monitor and infusion bags hanging on hooks and he soldiers on.

Don convinces me to call Jack and ask him to get me back to DDB. Not an easy decision but I know he's right, I've got to work just as much as Don has to finish recording Daddy's Lullabies. We have to continue living.

I don't need to explain much to Jack, he knows all about that agency. He also knows about Don and asks how he's doing, I sugar coat it and tell him I really need to be back at DDB.

It worked and I'm back and I don't care about the cut in salary. It's just saving me being here, even though there's a distinct aroma of the recent merger lingering in the air. The work is still challenging, standards remain high and I'm home again.

Don calls me at work and tells me to meet him at the hospital. Bernard had a seizure and he's about to have a brain operation. I grab my things and rush to

Lenox Hill.

Don's already there waiting with Gary, Bernard's new boyfriend. Suddenly metal doors swing open and nurses are wheeling Bernard out of the operating room and bringing him into the ICU.

I catch a glimpse of Bernard, his eyes are wildly open but he's not there.

As soon as we get home the phone rings. Gary tells us Bernard died. The horror of it all is too close.

Daddy's Lullabies are finally completed and it's a miracle. He's managed to do whatever he needed to maintain his strength. It's been four years since his KS diagnosis.

Rosemary is helping us enormously, but my last session with her was a horrible shock. She tells me Don is settled and accepts his fate. His main concern is what this is doing to me.

How can I deal with that? She makes suggestions, I can't hear her and I don't want to hear her... I can't accept his "fate" I won't accept his fate. I'll show him how strong I am, he doesn't have to worry about me. He just has to show me how strong he is and reject what he thinks is his fate and continue fighting for his life. I will never stop fighting for his life. Never.

I can't hear Rosemary any more. I'm trying to erase what she said and run out of her office.

GRIEF TAKES THE F TRAIN

TWO STRONG nurses, one male one female are holding me up to be able to walk with them, they're taking take me to Coney Island because Don asked them to do this.

    The F train pulls into the station and they sit me between them keeping me from sinking to the floor of that subway car. I can't talk to them, I can't talk at all. Why did Don demand this? What did they understand so well they complied? Why is he sending me home to Coney Island today? Is he sick of me being with him constantly, sleeping on the floor next to his hospital bed, does he need to be alone to be at peace so he can finally go home? Will I ever see him alive again?

The F Train speeds to memories of decaying amusement parks and my miserable childhood. The past months come back at me unbearably. There's no humor here no relief and no time anymore, it's impossible.

Somehow Don had a reprise a short while ago and his doctor stopped the IV treatments temporarily. Free of that apparatus he was able to record, mix and finalize his vocals for his album of lullabies. And he never stopped his relentless research. He found promising news of a vaccine trial in Switzerland. Doctor Roka's results were published and so compelling Don was determined to meet this doctor and wanted me to come with him to Switzerland. But I couldn't afford it and my newly reestablished job would be jeopardized. I'll torture myself for this forever.

Don seems strong enough to travel and I can't stop him. I get him plane tickets and book a good hotel near Roka's office.

He calls me from Switzerland and shares his concerns about Roka after meeting him. I strongly demand he come home immediately. Next day he calls again telling me after more investigation and more research he's decided to take Roka's vaccine, he tells me it can't hurt. I believe he's too thorough and too smart to be duped. I repeat to myself, "It can't hurt."

Don's home for a few weeks and he's showing

renewed energy. Could Roka's vaccine be working? Could this be the miracle found?

No not at all. Dr. Roka's vaccine is worthless. I had no idea Roka told Don to stop taking Bactrim in order to get the full benefit of the vaccine. When Don finally mentions this to me I go nuts wanting to go to Switzerland and strangle that quack motherfucker.

Don crashes in pain and I'm sitting beside him in an ambulance racing uptown with sirens screaming blowing all red lights speeding to the emergency room at St. Luke's Roosevelt Hospital.

Brain scans, negative, clear. Many IV mega antibiotics including Bactrim are infused he's on oxygen and stable finally comfortably breathing again.

Next day we have surprise visitors, Jack with his assistant Ruth appear at Don's bedside. A very nice gesture and much appreciated.

Two weeks of intensive care and we're finally back home, It's nearly midnight, Don gets out of bed and walks to the window, opening it he leans outside and erupts in howling anguish brokenhearted angry loud and furious yelling at God shattering the universe with soul crushing gut wrenching grievance until he's exhausted and purged. My face is in a pillow weeping when he slips back into bed. The phone rings, it's a neighbor, I tell him, "We're just going through a hard time, sorry you were disturbed, thanks for your concern."

Weeks pass and Don amazingly is on level

ground. I'm at work not getting any assignments lately, I'm just sitting in my office wondering and suddenly a knock on my door, it's Ruth, Jack's assistant. She struggles to express empathy, "The merger is causing a major shuffling and unfortunately people will have to be let go, I'm sorry Robert."

Infuriated I blurt out, "Do you know what it takes and what it costs to care for your loved one who's dying?

Stunned for a minute, she manages, "Do you want to talk to Jack?"

"He sends *you* in here to do his dirty work? I never want to talk to him again."

Ruth backs out of my office and closes the door. How much loss can be tolerated?

That evening with Rosemary she tells me they did me a favor. "A favor?!"

"Now you can spend more time with Don."

I try to let that sink in. I try to believe her and understand.

And we do have more time and decide to go to Bellport, Don is back again on his IV routine, we pack up all his medical gear into the trunk of a Limo and head out, Don sleeps most of the way there.

I open our front door and call for Boots, he usually comes in a flash but I hear something strange and run upstairs. Boots is lying in bed on the pillow crying out. I go to him, he's obviously in pain, teeth are missing and he smells horrible. I carry him downstairs, we get him into his carrying case and we drive him to the vet.

The Heartbreak of Static Cling

Next day the vet calls to tell us Boots has FIV. That's what they call AIDS in cats, Feline Immune Deficiency! Now I want to buy a gun.

Trying to defend our house from rancid intruding Possums, Boots lost the fight. The vet says Boots responded to antibiotics and he's in no pain. And then he asks if we want to see Boots one more time, he must be put down, there is nothing that can be done. Even Boots succumbs to AIDS. Fate twists its knife.

Just a week later at Irving Place, Don wakes me up late at night. He's in terrible pain and distress not breathing well. And again we're in an ambulance. There's a lot of confusion, his doctors are unreachable and he's stuck in a terrible ward, His back hurts I can't find more pillows. I go nuts on all of them and have him moved into a private room on the top floor of the hospital where he gets the attention he desperately needs and he's finally comforted.

The next morning Don makes a strange request, actually a demand to the nursing staff that I am taken away to Coney Island. They don't explain anything to me, they just grab my arms and tell me we need to go and leave Don for a while.

The subway screeches past tenement windows just a few feet away from the tracks snapping me out of my terror and back to this surreal journey to Coney Island accompanied by nurses.

Finally we're at the end of the line, Stillwell Avenue, Coney Island. The nurses hold me up and walk me slowly down the station's stairs and onto Surf Avenue where a hidden ride still exists, Coney's oldest carousel. I stop there and watch the carved stallions glide to the mechanical orchestra and my eyes fix on the brass ring I caught a long time ago. What was that supposed to mean?

A familiar metallic smell mixes with salt air, it's the perfume of the electric rides sparking near the ocean and it gets stronger when we approach the Cyclone. I was twelve when classmates picked me up by my arms and legs and threw me into that beast of a roller coaster. My fear turned into an addiction, riding again and again.

Numb and heartsick I climb into the front car I knew a lifetime ago. The nurses are hoping this joy ride will jolt me back to my senses. I'm wishing it would eject me to my death.

One nurse sits beside me and the other stronger nurse is seated behind me, ready to grab me in case I decide to jump.

The vintage wooden Cyclone creaks and crawls up and up higher and higher. All of Coney Island is now below me. The dormant Parachute Jump still stands by the sea like Coney's Eifel Tower. The Wonder Wheel continues to turn cars that seem to swing off their hinges over the wide boardwalk. It's all still here but I'm not. You would think this a great place for a kid to grow up. It wasn't. They thought it might make me feel better, it doesn't.

We reach the highest peak and the Cyclone crawls

The Heartbreak of Static Cling

to a completely exhausted stop. It seems nothing at all is in front of us. And then we're suddenly plummeted vertically off this cliff at speeds robbing every breath blasting us into hair pin turns slamming us side to side rearranging our intestines until it's finally done with us.

I'm unchanged. The nurses keep a close eye on me. I stay in my seat to ride again, maybe this time it'll work. Maybe this time I will jump? But no such luck.

We're heading back to the subway and I stop at a tragic souvenir stand and buy a pinwheel and a Steeplechase grinning face t-shirt for Don, terrified of what may be ahead.

I'm back at the hospital and find Don is sitting up reading the New York Times, both chest tubes seem to be doing their job. But there' something about his expression, like he's disappointed he wasn't able to die before I returned. This kills me but I can't show it. I just unpack the souvenirs.

The nurses leave us and I show him the stuff I bought, he doesn't like the pinwheel, I immediately throw it away and show him the t-shirt, he likes that.

And then he says, "Robert, find yourself another boyfriend."

No "boyfriend" will ever become the one and only love of my life. My heart shreds and all I can manage to say is, "I love you Don more than anybody in this world and I always will."

Very deeply inside of me I know he knows this, he just doesn't want me to be alone. But if Don goes, no matter who or how many friends I may or not have, I will always be alone without him. I also know Don will always be with me keeping me alive.

It's evening, Don's asleep and I need a drink bad. I quietly leave his room and head for that bar I found close to the hospital. The Martini's are big and cheap.

I sit on the barstool avoiding my reflection in the mirrored wall of bottles. This old New York bar is almost empty, just a few local drunks sitting alone. I finish my drink and head back to Don.

He's still asleep and he looks peaceful. I slip off my sneakers and lie down on the floor in front of his bed and finally get some sleep.

Suddenly Don's voice wakes me up, "Robert something's wrong! Something's wrong!"

I run to his side, he's gasping for breath. I bolt to the nurses' station. "He can't breathe, get help now!"

The nurse does her thing and in a minute doctors run into Don's room, I follow but can't see what they're doing; a doctor turns and tells me I have to leave his room, "He needs to be intubated." I force my way close to Don, "Do you know what they want to do to you?" He nods yes gasping. "You're okay with this?" He again nods yes. More doctors appear and I'm thrown out of the room. I go to the nurses' station and collapse in a chair next to her. "Would you let them to do this to your husband?" She doesn't answer.

More doctors run to Don's room with a gurney and they roll him out quickly to the ICU. I follow them,

The Heartbreak of Static Cling

I'm barred entrance. Finally they emerge and tell me he's on a respirator and under sedation not in distress. I peek inside the room and nearly pass out.

I'm in a waiting room on the phone. First I call Don's sister and tell her she and John needs to come now. Then I call my mother, I'm a terrified child and I need my mother, hearing her voice helps.

Hours pass and a doctor approaches me. "He's comfortable and awake, you can see him."

I rush to the new room they moved him to, he's calm and the machine is doing the work.

Unable to talk now with that ventilator down his throat breathing for him, he's able to write notes on a pad. He writes, "Let me rest now, you get some rest, I'm okay." I kiss his hand and leave trying to keep my balance.

More phone calls to everyone we know, all are on the way to see Don. After sitting in that waiting room for an hour, I decide to drag myself to the bar in the middle of the afternoon.

I run back to his room and visitors are seeing him one by one. More appear outside his room, waiting. I can't say anything to any of them and they're so heartbroken they can't say anything either.

I'm about to go in to see him and a doctor stops me, "He needs to rest, no more visitors. Come back tomorrow morning, you can't sleep in this room."

Somehow I get to Irving Place. I haven't showered in a month. I dry off and throw myself in bed trying and avoid looking at the window where Don yelled at God. Finally I slip into a coma like sleep.

I'm back at his side early morning, he seems composed. I see his sister and brother in the distance and I leave to let them visit. Now I'm in the waiting room with Ilene Connelly, my mother and my sister Carolyn. Don's brother and sister are white as sheets.

Don's doctor appears in the waiting room and urgently tells me to follow him. He takes me into a room displaying X-rays of Don's lungs. He uses a pointer and tells me these spots are blebs. What the fuck are blebs? He explains they're like blisters and this is very bad. "Prepare yourself he's not going to make it, you should think about removing him from life support." The air is sucked out of me.

I return to the waiting room sit quietly for ten minutes before I can explain what the doctor just showed me. And when I tell them there's no response from anyone. They want me to make the decision I could never make.

Suddenly Don's doctor runs frantically into the waiting room. "Robert, he's doing it himself, come with me!" I run after him, Ronnie and John are running behind us. Don is in severe distress fighting for breath, the ventilators are of no use anymore and the doctor removes the apparatus. Don struggles violently gasping fighting for his life and I see the monitors going crazy, his doctor shuts them off.

I'm standing there paralyzed. Ronnie and John

The Heartbreak of Static Cling

are behind me. I can't stand Don's suffering and I tell the doctor to up the Morphine. And then dreadfully, finally, Don becomes still. I look up at a clock on the wall and I can't read it, time doesn't work anymore. Time no longer exists.

It's September 2nd, 1993. Don lived 43 years and nine months.

I go to him and look at his beautiful face and his open eyes that no longer see. Don, where are you? My body begins to convulse I can't feel my legs I'm uncontrollable shaking. The doctor yells my name like a slap in my face. I'm completely frozen and destroyed.

They leave me alone with him. I pull back the sheets covering his body. My agony and furious anger at this world is crippling, I die with him.

Our life together is gone forever. I drag what's left of me out of this room.

Don's memorial service at Riverside the next day is filled to capacity. His body is in a plain pine coffin covered with spectacular flowers a friend delivered. I get up to the podium and try to talk. I don't know what I'm saying and finally shut up. Jennifer Connelly walks up to me and I take a seat. She recites a poem. I don't understand a word but I'm sure it's beautiful. She takes her seat and one of Don's lullabies, entitled "Dreaming", fills the air. "Forever may you dream."

The casket opens, I kneel down to him and kiss his lips for the last time and walk away. One by one the mournful pass by Don to say goodbye and they walk past me in deep sorrow. I'm in deep numb oblivion.

Someone somehow gets me back to Irving Place. A lot of people are here. I pour myself a stiff drink, bring it to my bedroom and shut the door until all of them are gone.

WHERE AM I?

THIS HOUSE we made our home is no longer, it never will be again. This place of dreams realized is now hollow empty rooms as empty as Bellport itself.

It's pouring rain again perfectly as I play a CD of Jessye Norman's Richard Strauss operas, Don's favorite. I blast it loud and look outside at his garden still alive and thriving because of him.

I want to kill myself but I can't. Don would be very angry, I can't have him mad at me. I'm suffocating here.

New York is a ghost town drained of color with streets filled with walking dead. And Bellport is even more painful. I put Bellport up for lease and list Irving Place for sublet. Both are taken within a week.

I need to get the hell out of here now.

Don wanted to go to a holistic healing place in Mexico called Rancho La Puerta. I'll go there for him. But I'll have to wait a couple of weeks for an available room. I need at least a month there, maybe more until I see the light or drop dead.

I can't wait weeks to leave New York. I call Ilene Connelly knowing she's in Santa Monica with Jennifer again. Thankfully, she tells me to stay with them until I can get down to Mexico.

The plane reaches altitude and I wonder if I'm nearer to Don. New York below is a rotting corpse. The only relief is seeing my life there disappear. The flight attendant brings more vodka. Who am I and where am I going?

Who the fuck cares and who the fuck knows?

Ilene and Gerry are warring, divorce is imminent and Jen is in the middle of this but they're kindly trying to shield me. I'm very grateful I can't endure any more drama. I escape to the beach for long walks trying to breathe.

Gerry leaves and Ilene is going to San Francisco for awhile so it'll just be me and Jennifer. I tell her about Rancho La Puerta, it's the kind of place she would love, she's so much like Don.

Time has come for me to get on a plane to San

Diego where I'll be met by the bus to Mexico. We drive over the border and through the desert. Don loved the desert, I never understood why.

Tacate is not far into Mexico and it's a short drive to the base of Mt. Kuchuma and Rancho La Puerta. I'm greeted by BJ—strange how may BJ's are in my life—and she hands me a booklet listing all the programs and classes offered and asks me to select ones of interest.

I tell her I can't make any sense of anything, just tell me what to do. She understands and shows me to my room.

This old casita is instantly comforting, I unpack my bags and BJ appears at my door again, handing me a schedule and tring to explain, but I stop her. "Just tell me what to do." She points the way to the dining room for dinner. I ask for it to be delivered to my room and she leaves.

I collapse in bed feeling like I just walked from New York to Mexico and pass out.

A few knocks on my door and I'm almost awake as sunlight cracks through the window shutters breakfast is being delivered and my untouched dinner is taken away.

Like a controlled zombie I follow BJ's every instruction. Whatever exercise, hike, meditation, lecture, yoga, sweat lodge, body work and physical therapy she signs me up for I force myself to obey. I'll do this for however long it takes knowing how much it would mean to Don.

Gradually weeks of this insane routine begins to

wake me up, forcing me to get to the other side of the nightmare.

I spot Jennifer, a big surprise. She tells me she also needed to get away. Jen's an avid athlete, challenging hikes and all the rest are perfect for her, actually easy. She's climbed Mount Everest twice so far. We're on different schedules but we connect at dinner. She asks me to stay with her in Santa Monica when I leave here, a glimmer of happiness. I had no idea what I would do if I ever leave this place.

Just at the end of Jen's second day, Jen tells me her father wants to come here to talk to her. I suggest she tell him to vent his problems over the phone, but she won't.

The next day I find out Gerry did come to see her and Jen went back with him to L.A. I'm not surprised, just disappointed.

I'm coherent now enough to put a sentence together and partially understand what's spoken to me. Many days of meditative organic messages and activities were just mumbo jumbo garbled incoherent noises, now it's beginning to make some kind of sense, I hope.

My stay here is coming to an end, I can feel it, I can feel there could be a different life ahead for me. I love the staff here for being so respectful and understanding. It's time to give them something in return, a thank you celebration at my casita.

It's astounding I can imagine celebrating anything.

I coerce a staff member to drive me to town to get

the best tequila, and I sequester a blender from the kitchen. I've had gallons of holistic healing cocktails and now I just want to drink the hard stuff and show my appreciation.

But when the much appreciated gathering ends, a realization sets in: I may never truly heal but I can't allow it to stop me from putting one foot in front of the other.

I walk out into the desert night that's lit by a big moon. The clear sky is black velvet and diamonds, air is quiet nearly silent, and this is Don's magic desert, he sent me here.

Now I understand your love of the desert. You are right here with me now, Don, and you always will be.

LIVING WITH JEN

JENNIFER is warm and very supportive. I run lines with her of film scripts delivered almost daily, astoundingly Jen not only knows her lines but also the dialogue of every character in the script she reads just once. Being here in Santa Monica with Jen is a blessing.

Now my long walks on the beach have a new rhythm, I've learned how to power walk at the Ranch, empowering me through the grief. I have no idea about tomorrow and I just don't care.

I'm feeling strong enough to make contact with a

271 The Heartbreak of Static Cling

few old friends who moved here awhile ago. BJ Dockweiler... Well this BJ is the wife of Frank Steifel who produced many of my TV spots. Frank and BJ are living here in Santa Monica and I decide to reconnect. They're coming over tonight with a friend they want me to meet. I'm looking forward to seeing them but not really interested in meeting anyone new.

It's great seeing Frank and BJ again and they introduce me to a creature to behold. Todd is tall, stick thin with a beautiful face framed with the brightest orange red hair on the planet. Best thing about him is his humor and thick Long Island accent. He's playing it very shy, but I have an idea he's not.

After enjoying the ocean view from the terrace for a minute we go out to dinner. I'm not the Robert they know, I have little to say and they understand, they told Todd all about it. His New York absurdity lightens the mood, it's a good distraction. Todd's another New Yorker searching for a new beginning here in LA. He could become a friend.

This first social interaction is a good beginning even though it's taken a lot of strength to manage my emotions. I have to keep it all inside me I must be in control, no one would be able to tolerate my pain, nor should they. I guess if I continue putting myself out there I'll get better at it. Todd and I exchange numbers and I ask Frank and BJ to keep in touch and thank them for Todd and a great reunion. This year is ending finally, goodbye and good riddance to 1993, the worst year of my life.

Living With Jen 272

I get a call from Bellport; my tenants have decided to move and now I have to make a decision. Being a landlord thousands of miles away is not working. It's winter and my old house is vulnerable, pipes freeze and I can't deal with any of that. I'll keep the memories of Hulse Street in my heart and now it's time to really let it go. Irving Place is less a maintenance problem so I'll hang on to it and lease it out for the time being.

It's dreadful returning to Bellport to get it ready for sale. I need to get rid of a lot of things and store the best of it until I find a place of my own in California. Going through everything here is killing me. I find a team that conducts estate sales. After a week of sorting and packing I find a moving and storage company. And the estate sale liquidates all the rest, including Don's piano, the hardest thing to let go.

Friends and neighbors here in Bellport loved Don. I plan a memorial service at the local Unitarian Church and hire gospel singers from Brooklyn. Don's ashes are now in a unique wooden box created by David Ebner, Bellport's acclaimed woodworking artist. His genius creation for Don will be here tonight for the memorial service.

Lightning explodes the sky with crackling violent thunder rattling the old church and drenching Bellport with torrential rain appropriately ordered by God. The church is filled, I say a few words then ask if anyone would like to speak and a few take their turn praising and mourning Don. Hard wind turns the rain sideways hurricane style now even heavier, I'm wondering if that

Gospel group from Brooklyn will ever find Bellport. But they suddenly run into the church drenched and ready to lift us all.

They get up on a small stage and they begin and sing loud to God and even louder to Don's soul. These Gospel singers are pure Brooklyn and that says it all. This is something new for our old Bellport Unitarian Church. Everyone's on their feet jumping up high to the leaking rafters.

This is my final good bye to Bellport.

This door is closed.

BOOM TOWN

SANTA MONICA. It's January 16th 1994, it's nearly 5AM. Jen and Billy are asleep in another bedroom in this penthouse by the Pacific, I'm in bed thinking about Bellport being no more, the house sold quickly and I'm trying to convince myself I did the right thing, If I didn't let it go, it would never let go of me.

Eventually I find peace with it and fall into a deep sleep. *BANG! BOOM!* I'm slammed out of bed wide awake, was it a nightmare?! What the fuck! I get back in bed guessing a garbage truck just crashed into the building?! And then again a bigger *CRASH!* And the room jolts and the corners of the walls split and ceiling begins to crack open. It sounds like a freight train crashing and everything is exploding. I hear the kitchen blast to bits smashing dishes glasses, the refrigerator crashes to the floor, and suddenly violent much harder sharper upward thrusts erupt and I'm airborne and my bed is a trampoline! I grab onto the sheets as the bed hops across the room toward the wobbling wall of windows that explode and shatter showering glass shards at me. My bed keeps hopping and sliding toward the giant open hole in the wall and I'm about to be launched out of the 20th floor of this building!

I could not invent a more perfect ending to my life, thrown out of a penthouse clinging onto California king size bed sheets plummeting twenty stories to my death in the Pacific! I'm terrified and hysterically laughing and yelling, "Here I come Don, here I come!"

Suddenly the upward jolts stop and become just a mean rumbling, and I hear Jen screaming, "You okay? We got to get the fuck out of here!"

I find shoes in the dark and frantically stuff everything I can find into a duffle bag. Jen and Billy Campbell are at my door, "Robert, hurry up, let's go *now!*"

Feeling our way in the pitch dark hallway to the stairwell and again *BOOM* after *BOOM* aftershocks big ones. We're hanging onto the wobbling handrail running down endless flights of stairs the building keeps shaking with constant aftershocks. We hear people screaming in the stairwell below. Finally we reach what's left of the lobby looking like a bomb went off. We climb over the rubble and bolt outside. Every car alarm in LA is going off at the same time punctuated by loud transformer explosions.

Fast and very cautiously we run cross cracked open streets to Billy's Jeep and make a fast getaway avoiding a possible total collapse of the building's twin towers that would crush everything within blocks.

Billy's brother's house is in the Palisades, we're hoping it still is there. Billy maneuvers the Jeep through streets that look like a bad science fiction World War III movie. More transformers explode, car alarms never stop.

The house is standing showing little damage and Billy's brother is harboring terrified neighbors whose homes were destroyed. He pours us drinks and throws some pillows on the floor for me to pass out. This is January 17, 1994 and this is the 6.9 Northridge killer earthquake. Welcome to LA LA Land.

Aftershocks hit this house hanging on a cliff, who the hell can sleep? Every time I try to doze off another jolt hits.

Daylight and I have no idea where I am. Jen and Billy are awake. My scrambled brain decides to call Frank and BJ. I hope they're okay, maybe they'll let me stay with them, help!

Billy and Jen drive me to Frank and BJ, they can't believe what I look like; shell shocked would be an understatement. They were lucky, only their chimney crashed to the ground like every house on the block. BJ shows me to the guest bedroom and I finally collapse.

The next few days we sit mesmerized watching the devastation on the news, freeways split in half, buildings collapsed demolished and more and more dead and buried in the rubble. Big aftershocks keep coming; we run outside and watch the swimming pool waves become fit for surfing.

Gradually it all calms down and so do we. Frank and BJ are a miracle, I don't know how to repay their kindness. Week's pass and life returns to something close to normal.

I really enjoyed my first initiation to life in LA.

Frank wants me to meet a friend of his. Pacy is a partner in a small ad agency in Santa Monica. Frank arranges a dinner at a newly reopened Mexican restaurant.

Pacy is small statured with big ideas and a sharp wit. Still struggling with grief also just beginning to shed my earthquake PTSD, I'm not really into meeting Pacy, but who knows?

Obviously Frank filled Pacy in on what I've been through with Don and also my career at DDB. Pacy was familiar to that and out of the blue he offers me a job at his agency. I don't understand why or what his offer means, I try to make sense of it but can't imagine being at all interested. I just take another sip of my drink and blankly stare at him listening to his pitch.

He tells me he and his partner, Bill Zimmerman create political advertising. I reply, I'm not into politics.

He tries to explain what propositions are. I tell him I've known a lot of hustlers and hookers. He's amused but continues and I cut him off, "Pacy, I'm not interested in politics unless you're doing something for the fight against AIDS." Pacy is persistent and tells me they do a lot of good for a lot of causes and the job would be on a freelance basis. I could just try it out and see if it fits.

It finally dawns on me, idiot, jump at this chance, you need to go back to work.

WORK IT OUT

WHO WOULD have thought it would take a catastrophic earthquake to start my life again, but it did. Working with Pacy is what I needed, a new challenge moving me forward. Pacy is a joke a minute, his partner Bill is a savvy lefty political consultant and the assignments are for all the best causes like clean energy, banning frivolous lawsuits and gun control for starters. Budgets for production are on a shoestring compared to what I'm used to, but big ideas don't need big production budgets to accomplish great results.

Work It Out   280

The small office is situated in Santa Monica's idea of an office building. It's a three story Mediterranean affair with a courtyard with a fountain a few blocks from the beach, a big contrast to my office on Madison Avenue.

The barebones staff includes a secretary, Bill's assistant, me and Pacy. It's efficient and oddly less political than the agencies I've worked for even though politics is what this place is all about.

Freelance is something to get used to but it seems all of California is freelance. Actors, directors, screenwriters all are freelance workers and then they're not. There's a freedom to this, no one here has a steady gig. The old system of a nine-to-five reliable life doesn't exist anymore, I learned that lesson.

The truest security is being secure in your own talent.

I'm gradually regaining security with the help of weekly phone sessions with Rosemary... Losing Don, losing my career, my home in New York and my closest friends to AIDS undermined every ounce of me. Now it's about rebuilding.

This job however temporary confirms California is my new beginning and now it's time to find my own place here. BJ and Frank have done more than enough, bless them, it's time to move on.

Someone guess who is looking over me. Pacy tells me his friend Jack is going on an extended trip for a year and he's subletting his apartment in West Hollywood, a one bedroom, fully furnished and he's asking $500 a month.

West Hollywood, I had ideas about West Hollywood, a gay ghetto populated with boys named Scott, Trey, Skip or Chaz. "Hi, my name is Skipper and I work out." But why the fuck not, I need a place of my own.

I get to Alfred Street and find it's a 1920's two story Spanish style building; it's shabby but located close to everything and not in the middle of Boys Town. Jack is an interesting older guy, a writer and a professor and very amicable. The apartment is surprisingly well furnished and comfortable. Now I have a job for awhile and my own place in West Hollywood. Stranger things have happened.

Now settling in I make arrangements to get Ziggy, my cherished VW convertible shipped here. Surprisingly, I'm getting to love West Hollywood; it's more diverse and interesting than imagined. A big facelift is in the works, all of West Hollywood's main street, Santa Monica Boulevard is about to be rebuilt and tree lined and that will make a major difference.

A studio apartment has just become available, I tell Todd and now he's my next door neighbor. Living here is actually becoming fun, but heartache emerges when least expected.

I've been searching for an IBM Selectric, my favorite typewriter and I found one for rent. I figure it could help purge the hurt. I can't do it continually to Rosemary or to anyone, it's best to put it on paper. I want to hear the hum of it, the clicking keys, feel the electric keyboard and watch typewritten papers pile high.

Without notes I begin a science fiction AIDS thriller set in year 2084 Don is the lead character, a genius geologist in charge of monitoring the robotic mining fields in US Africa. An enormous earthquake cracks open a mountain in Zaire exposing a deeply hidden secret laboratory. And on and on, the pages fly out of my typewriter and I'm there with him discovering the unknown monstrous origin of HIV and the mutated vengeful virus it's become and now unleashed. The purging of my anger and eventual justice of it all is cathartic.

I joined a bereavement group that gathers once a week. All of them lost loved ones. Their horrible stories allow space to let loose everything I've stuffed inside me ready to blow up.

Rosemary, science fiction, working with Pacy and whatever it takes, I just force myself to do it.

Tony Frere is an old friend, a TV commercial producer from New York who moved to LA awhile ago. He heard I'm now living in LA and got my number from Frank and he calls to invite me to his house in the hills for Thanksgiving dinner promising I'll flip out to see who else will be there, I try to guess but he won't give me a clue.

Tony knows everyone from my past. He's especially close to Joey Arias, the infamous performer who amazingly becomes Billie Holiday when he sings. Tony is smart, sly and successful, and he always keeps his secrets secret. What a surprise, I can't wait.

I drive up the hill not far from my place and it's a whole different story. The hills above West Hollywood are coveted and very pricy. Tony's mid-century house is understated and comfortable, not one of the architectural extravaganzas in the neighborhood.

Tony looks great, his toothy grin gleams in contrast to his dark skin and he's still wearing his signature thick glasses. He literally pulls me into his place and there she is, Holly Woodlawn, the one and only Holly Woodlawn. I haven't seen Holly in years, I love Holly; we've known each other since 1968 way before she became Holly Woodlawn, the Andy Warhol Superstar in Andy's movie, 'Trash.'

Lou Reed immortalized Holly with his song, 'Walk on the Wild Side.' And a few years ago Holly met Jeff Copeland, a great writer who was determined to collaborate with her and created a terrific exposé capturing Holly's outrageous life story with a book titled, 'A Low Life in High Heels.' Reading it actually gave me a chance to laugh out loud. Nobody on this planet but Holly could live that life.

What a reunion, how fabulous, Holly and I are back together again. This is the best kind of collision you can have in LA.

I flash on Todd, he's been dying to meet Holly. I ask Tony if I can invite him and of course he says yes. I quickly drive down the hill, Todd's not home and I leave a note on his door with the address and return to the party. Holly is now surrounded by a crowd of intriguing guests. We'll have our time together later, as she said so many times, "We're sutured at the hip."

I walk out to the terrace for a cigarette and encounter an interesting oddity sitting on the deck brooding. He's got New York City written all over him, must have just gotten off the plane. He's all in black of course wearing a beat up motorcycle jacket. He's bald but not just bald, he's bald everywhere, no eyebrows no eyelashes, not a hair anywhere. He's got a great shaped head and a sometimes pretty sometimes thuggish face.

I approach this creature and he recoils, he's got his guard up and an overload of attitude I've encountered in many sleazy New York gay bars. But this is no obstacle, I'm one of them, I've been there done that and I'm intrigued. There's something familiar about him.

Two seconds into the conversation I recall a photograph by Robert Mapplethorpe, a portrait of a black guy and a very white guy in profile, both of them from planet Alopecia, and this thing sitting here is the white guy. He's Robert Sherman, also known by his drag name, Constance Cooper. Gradually his NYC night crawler attitude loosens and we connect. Connie and I become good friends, we both know that. He just has to get used to the sunshine.

Finally Holly and I are together reminiscing and boy have I missed her, I didn't realize how much until now. Todd arrives and practically shoves me aside when I introduce him to his idol, Holly. Todd's like a kid in a drugstore, let him enjoy the high, I'll have a lot of time with Holly we're reconnected and realize we live near each other.

I guess even with all the shit that's happened, there's something to be thankful for this Thanksgiving.

EXIT IRVING PLACE

I'M PACKING up quickly and getting this place ready for sale as soon as possible. It's time to let New York go completely. And I have to get to Miami, my mom's in the hospital recuperating from a minor operation and my father is lost without her.

Finally the moving company picks up everything adding it to Bellport's storage. I've hired a local Gramercy Park Realtor and Irving Place is sold in a flash.

My dad meets me at the Miami Airport in tears

fearing the worst, who will take care of him if she's gone? I calm him as we drive to the hospital. Zelda is mad at me, she didn't want me to go out of my way to visit her, but she gets out of this quickly and we embrace. She's doing fine and will be home soon. I convince my father she'll be okay and home soon. And I take him to his favorite spaghetti and meatballs joint in a mall. Boy do I hate Florida.

    I try advising him to get his prostate removed. His doctors gave him the choice of radiation because he's terrified of operations. He was told prostate cancer is very slow growing and this will help but it's not working and he won't listen to me. I try to comfort him and hope to change his mind but he's stubborn.

    I get a call from Todd he has some news. Holly just moved into a studio in our building upstairs from Todd and he's in heaven. Next he tells me there's an apartment with a pool available nearby on Willoughby, not far from Alfred Street, the rent is $1,200 and it could be great. Jack will be back soon and I'll have to move and I need to get my stuff out of storage.

    Zelda's finally home and on her feet, Ted is relieved and I'm on a plane back to California.

    The corner of Willoughby and Croft is surrounded by tall hedges hiding the building completely. I ring a buzzer at the gate and an older man with a Russian accent lets me in. This 1940's duplex was completely renovated by an architect a year ago. Boris bought the place from him. The apartment is large with some great original deco architecture and it's updated beautifully, but the best is just outside the kitchen door, a big patio with a fabulous private pool. I'll take it right this minute but Boris the Russian needs to haggle, I too know how to haggle and we seal the deal.

    Now I have a place with my own lease that's large enough to get most of my things out of storage, I'm home at last and that pool makes me feel like I'm in some movie, an omen of things to come.

    I promised myself to reach out to old friends and call Marianne Braubach, Don and I visited her long ago when she was single and living in Brentwood, we met her through Antonio. She's a film producer and married to yet another Robert, a computer whiz who invented a foldable soft keyboard. Marianne invites me to a fundraiser to benefit the homeless at their home in Pacific Palisades.

    I'm kind of familiar with their neighborhood close to Santa Monica, but it took me a couple of wrong turns to finally find their house. It's a great looking modern house, the door is ajar and I can see lots of people are already here. I find Marianne in her kitchen preparing appetizers. Big hugs and I let her get back to her crudités and search for her husband, Robert. He's a great guy and very friendly, he brings me to the bar for a drink and then the perfect host goes to greet new arrivals.

    I decide to take myself on a tour and wander through the house, it's impressive and I notice she has an

Antonio artwork beautifully displayed, seeing it gives me a warm sense of connection.

I also notice I'm being followed by a tall slim grey haired man. Wherever I go, from room to room he appears examining me. It's creepy and I keep moving to get out of his sight but it's impossible, he's always there studying me.

I dash into a small den and I take a seat on a sofa. He appears again and takes a seat beside me. And now with a thick Russian accent and a terrible stutter he begins, "Aaaar yoyoyou annnn actooor?"

I turn to him, "Everybody in LA is an actor."

He continues, "Yoou, woudddd be perperperfect for mmmy new mmoooovie."

"Oh, really, how great, what's your name?"

"Sergei Bodrov." He spit that out without a hitch.

"I'm Robert Starr, give me your number, I'll call you."

He reaches for his wallet and retrieves a card and hands it to me. It reads Sergei Bodrov and a phone number.

I stand up and tell him I'll call him tomorrow and walk into the main room hoping he won't tail me.

Marianne is making a speech to the gathering about the need for their contributions and on and on. There's no way I can talk to her about what just happened, I'll call her later. Sergei is standing at the back of the room and I can feel him examining me. Is this a come on? Somehow I don't think so but whatever it's uncomfortable. I can't really have a visit now with Marianne and Robert. I'll see them another time, and I slip out the door.

I get home too late to call Marianne and decide to wait till tomorrow. Could the Russian possibly be for real?

TO LIVE AND DUI IN LA

I'M SITTING by my pool and I hear someone at the gate. It's a messenger delivering a script. Turns out Sergei is real, Marianne informed me he's an Academy Award winning director for best foreign film. After that piece of news I called Sergei and here's the script. He wants me to read it and make notes. After reading a few pages, he's not going to be happy with my notes which are becoming a rewrite. But so what, he asked for it. It's supposed to be a comedy.

It's so crazy here lounging by my pool reading a

script for a movie I'm being considered for... Things happen to me, I should be used to it by now.

The timing couldn't be more perfect, my freelance with Pacy is over. I knew it would come to an end sooner or later, it served its purpose and I'm grateful. So now I'll just have to become a movie star, this is LA isn't it?

They're here, my first pool party guests, Holly, Todd and his new roommate, Brad. Todd and Holly both moved out of the "Alfred Apts." Todd moved up the street to a rental in a Spanish duplex, and Holly found a roommate on Sweetzer, an old alcoholic we've nicknamed Lurch. It's a hot day and I've supplied a lot of wine and we all take the plunge, Todd is of course totally naked, it's his new liberation. His roommate Brad is great looking in his Speedo's, Holly wearing her man's boxer shorts as a bathing suit is a sight to behold doing the backstroke.

I tell them all about the Sergei saga and decide Holly has to meet him, I'll figure out where and when.

Brad is interesting and very smart, he has a sharp mind and explodes in laughter at my obscure humor and I like him instantly. He's a Realtor and his career holds a wealth of fabulous Hollywood stories but there is an indication his personal story is more interesting.

There's nothing like being unemployed and hosting a pool party with good friends and reading a movie script the director had delivered to you for approval. This is LA fantasy land, so forget your troubles common get happy, here we go.

The Heartbreak of Static Cling

I continue with my script notes even though Holly cautions me to be kind. "The script's written by the director and his wife, so don't be too critical, okay?" She's been through this, she knows.

Sergei calls to invite me to a party next Saturday night at his house in Venice to celebrate Russian New Year and most of the cast will be there. Perfect, I'll bring the script with my notes and Holly.

On Russian New Year's Day, I call Holly, "Get dressed, you're going to be discovered, again!" Early evening I pick her up and she's dressed to kill, literally. She installed herself into a very gay gown and she's douched up to the hilt. Warhol Superstar meets the Russian director, I can't wait. I stuff her into Ziggy and get on the road to our destiny in Venice.

It's somewhere in Venice I've never been, finally I find the house near the canals.

Carolyn, Sergei's wife answers the door and Sergei hands us two glasses of Vodka. The house is filled with guests and Holly makes a grand entrance and she's well noticed and recognized. Sergei has no Idea who she is but he's filled in quickly by his guests.

I realize I very much like Sergei. He's kind, generous and also humble thanking me for my notes. He tells me he's working on a revised script and he'll get it to me in a couple of weeks.

I've looked up his accomplishments and they're impressive. I still can't believe he wants me to be in his new film. He tells me he's considering me for one of two principle parts and he says it would pay scale plus ten percent. I ask about the ten percent and he explains it's for my agent. I tell him I don't have an agent and ask if I could get the ten percent above scale and he nods yes. I hug him and we toast to that.

Holly and I mingle and chat and somehow I find myself blitzed on vodka dancing on a table in the backyard and Holly tells me it's time to leave, mission accomplished.

We get into my trusty Ziggy and slowly make our way out of the maze of streets. Suddenly a motorcycle cop out of nowhere pulls me over. He orders me to get out of the car and walk a straight line and then he asks me for my permission to take a breathalyzer test. Sure, why not?

The cop handcuffs me and orders Holly out of our car and now a cop car joins the party. Holly and I are chauffeured to the Venice police station. I ask what did I do to be pulled over, he answers, "Your tire crossed the white line." How tragic.

We're escorted into the police station and they instruct me to empty my pockets. I have about eighty bucks I want to give Holly for cab fare but they won't allow it. How the hell is she going to get home? She's completely broke and they could give a shit.

I blow Holly a kiss as they take me to a holding cell. What now? Hours pass and they pull me out of the cell and I think, great this will be over soon and I'll probably have to sign something and be released. No way, after about an hour in the holding cell they handcuff me and I'm shoved into another cop car.

The Heartbreak of Static Cling

"Where are you taking me?" They don't answer.

I try to recognize a few landmarks for a clue to where they're taking me but who knows where, everything is totally unfamiliar. Finally twenty minutes later, welcome to the Valley and the Van Nuys jail.

This dank horror of a place is my new home. I'm thrown into a small freezing cold cell with bunk beds and a steel toilet. I pull my shivering self onto the top bunk and stare at the metal ceiling etched with porno graffiti. How the hell did inmates do this and with what? It's weirdly erotic.

Why did they take me here? Oh yeah, I crossed the line so now I'm doin' time shaking hung-over quaking, locked up they're making me do The Van Nuys Jailhouse Blues!

I have no idea how long I've been here, don't know if the sun's up and don't know what the fuck is going on. Now a clank of keys and the cell door opens. A cop drags me off the bunk and handcuffs me and this time for good measure he secures the handcuffs to a chain around my waist connected to ankle shackles. I'm Hannibal Lecter being moved into a jail bus. I don't bother to ask where they're taking me, I know by now they won't give me the time of day.

I had no idea jail buses have a separate compartment, a cage for the criminally insane and it's reserved for me.

The morning sun warms me through my caged window, just another day in my life. We make several stops along the way to who knows where and at each stop new assorted drugged out gang bangers and hookers get on board for the ride. They sit side by side unchained staring at me in my cage. Suddenly one of the inmates kicks my cage and yells, "What the fuck did you do?"

I answer, "I ate my mother's baby, wasn't so bad, she was just my half-sister." And he leaves me alone.

Again I'm searching for something recognizable to figure out where the fuck we're going but nothing's familiar until we reach downtown LA and our tour ends at the infamous Twin Towers Jail. This is jail number three.

My lovely fellow travelers disembark first and then two cops approach my cage, open it and hold my elbows steady so I can hobble in my leg shackles out of the bus.

This jail is much fancier than Van Nuys. It's enormous and just as cold. I guess they keep it this way to keep prisoners compliant; it's hard to cause trouble when you're frozen stiff.

My jail bus buddies are marched into a lovely communal cell so they can be social. And of course I'm thrown into solitary. What the fuck is happening? No one will talk to me. They just give me a rotten apple a slice of bad cheese and I settle in for another festive night. I've come a long way to restart my life in LA and here it is.

Good morning, I'm now taken out of my cell chained up again and hauled to and planted into another jail bus. Now where, Disneyland?

The bus makes a turn at a sign marked "LAX." Horror hits, I realize I still have a New York drivers

The Heartbreak of Static Cling

license, are they putting me on a plane in chains and deporting me to New York?

Instead, my guided tour of jails continues. This one is called the Airport Jail, who knew this existed? In a perverse way it's a relief, I would be mortified being seen on the red eye in shackles.

My solitary confinement here is similar to the Twin Towers just a bit smaller and a degree warmer, how luxurious. The food is the same, another rotten apple and cheese. Welcome to jail number four.

Another day passes and suddenly the bars open and a diminutive troll sitting on an office chair rolls himself into my cell. He tells me he's my public defendant and when I see the judge, just say not guilty. "What? How can I plead not guilty, I failed the breathalyzer?" He repeats, "Plead not guilty." And he quickly rolls himself out of my cell and the door clangs shut. I love the surreal, this is truly David Lynch casting.

More hours pass and a guard comes to visit. He attaches my handcuffs to leg irons and drags me to an elevator. We arrive at a long narrow room with chairs facing a draped wall. Other inmates sit comfortably uncuffed, side by side. I, of course, remain fully shackled and separated from the others.

A guard announces, "Stand up when your name is called." The curtains part revealing a courtroom behind a wall of thick glass and the judge is seated. Prosecuting attorneys and my mutant public defender are seated at their desks facing the judge. Proceedings begin, a name is called, an inmate rises, questions are asked and the judge dispatches quick ugly decisions.

My name is called and I try my best to stand up but it's impossible with all the weight of the steel apparatus attached. Two guards grab my elbows and prop me up to a standing position.

My public defendant creature lifts his body out of his chair to his full height, possibly four feet, and addresses the judge. "Your Honor, Robert Starr is a first offender; he has a clean record and should be released under his own recognizance."

The prosecution consists of two Black attorneys, one male, one female and both are smugly grinning. The male prosecutor rises and addressees the judge with a smile. "Your Honor, Robert Starr is wanted for attempted murder and armed robbery in Oklahoma, he's been a fugitive on the run for six months and has been finally apprehended." I hold back any reaction as he continues, "Your Honor, Robert Starr has distinguishing tattoos on his torso." What? What? That did it! I'm about to double over hysterically laughing but I stuff it pretending to have a sudden coughing fit.

The judge orders the removal of my chains and tells me to remove my shirt and present myself to the court. That's all I needed to hear. Judge just you get ready for this!

I'm unshackled and my performance begins, a spontaneously choreographed striptease, one button at a time and I take my time. The expression on the prosecutor's face is worth it. And now for a fabulous finale, I perform a shirtless pirouette displaying my tattoo-less torso, voila!

The Judges lifts his gavel and slams it down hard silencing the courtroom. "Robert Starr is guilty of DUI; he's to pay a fine of five hundred dollars and attend driver's education courses, release him."

Finally I'm no longer Hannibal Lecter in chains and a guard walks me to a holding cell where I remain for many more hours and rewarded with another rotten apple and something that looks like cheese.

It's 2 AM and I'm released from my cell and taken to the front desk to retrieve my belongings. I ask to make a call for a cab to get me home. The miserable desk clerk attending to her nails tells me there's a pay phone a half a mile down the road at a liquor Store. "I've just been charged with a DUI and you're sending me to a liquor store to make a phone call?" No answer.

This dark street is just below the overpass of the 405 freeway and I sense trouble lurking in shadows. Finally I see a neon liquor store sign and a pay phone attached to the side wall. Still shaking from being refrigerated and chained I manage to call a cab.

Another agonizing fifteen minutes a cab pulls up in front of me.

I get into my apartment turn up the heat full blast, fill the bathtub with hot water and soak for hours contemplating the significance of mistaken identity. I lost my identity awhile ago big time, am I mistaken?

God knows what time it is or what day it is, I dry off and crawl into my warm bed.

And then it hits me, Holly! What happened to

Holly? I grab the phone, she's probably in a coma at this hour, I'll leave a message.

Surprise, she answers. "What the fuck happened to you? I called every fucking jail in LA and no one heard of you!"

Not shocked at that, I give her the short story and ask how she got home.

"I grabbed a cab, ran upstairs and stiffed him."

That's my Holly!

I pull the covers over my head determined to sleep for a year.

WHAT'S AN EX-CON TO DO?

I'M SNAPPED out of my beauty sleep by a UPS guy leaning on my doorbell. He delivers nine boxes filled with hundreds of essays submitted for Don's scholarship competition entitled, "AIDS, Why Should I Care?"

Don's legacy will continue. I'm going to publish a book of these essays, adding a subtitle: "Teens Across America Speak Out."

I crack open a carton and it's daunting, I begin reading and realize the essays fall into several categories such as: "I'm HIV Positive, I'm Fifteen" or "My Friend/

Boyfriend/Girlfriend Got It" or "Someone in My Family Got It" or "I Thought It Wasn't My Problem" and more. Overwhelmed, I call Holly for help and she's onboard. We spend days reviewing and sorting all of this. I love Holly.

Rosemary is thrilled I'm committed to this project and she offers help to get this book published. She's an amazing blessing.

I barrel ahead with this project only interrupted by my weekly DUI group sessions. They describe bartending at eighty miles per hour while entertaining hitchhikers, other distracted text addicted group members top these antics with their own hair-raising crashes and road raging on the rocks. And not one of them spent any time in jail. I'm finding this all very amusing, actually I'm looking forward to our weekly happy hour for more stories from brain dead LA drivers.

Reading essay number 857 the phone rings, it's Sergei. I fill him in on my guided tour of jails, he's horrified. Sergei realized at his party which character I should play, it's the caterer. I guess it was my go go dancing on top of the tables that synched that roll. His revised script is almost finished and he'll send it to me shortly. He tells me three scenes will be highlighted and he wants me to learn them to audition on tape.

Audition? I thought I had the part. He explains it's just a formality. Yeah okay, formality. I didn't pursue him, quite the opposite. Okay, everyday living in this town is an audition.

The Heartbreak of Static Cling

I go back to reading essays. This is going to take some time—good, what else do I have to do? Oh yeah, learn my part and audition.

A week later and here it is, the final script delivered by messenger. It's much improved and the Caterer's scenes throughout the entire film are really good, especially one hilarious encounter with cockroaches, I'm glad that scene was highlighted. The audition should be fun, if nothing else.

The caterer has an affectation: he keeps a handkerchief hidden in his shirtsleeve pulling it out occasionally to wipe his damp forehead. I dress for the part in a white shirt and black slacks and shove a hanky up the cuff of my shirt. The audition is on Wilshire near the Miracle Mile, how fitting. It would be a miracle if this is for real.

It seems legit, I've watched many auditions for my TV spots, so it's very familiar except this time I'm in front of the camera.

The casting director instructs me to present a different scene, not the cockroach fun, but a drunken scene where I fall into a chair next to an invisible friend and share my thoughts about an off camera character. Take three and the casting director wants an explosive laugh at the end of my dialogue, I have no idea what I'm supposed to be laughing about but I accommodate and we're done.

I leave the camera room and Sergei and his wife Carolyn are there. Big smiles and I pull out my hanky wipe my forehead and leave.

Back home I get back to reading essays for a few more days. I'm sitting by my pool with a glass of wine and a pile of essays and the casting director calls. He tells me I got the part and he will contact me with shoot times and such. And then he says it pays scale. And I ask, what about the ten percent above scale Sergei promised because I've no agent. He tells me he'll get back to me on that.

This is one of the most surreal conversations I've ever enjoyed. I plunge into the pool and float in complete disbelief.

Another week and another hundred essays read. The phone rings and it's the casting director and he tells me very matter of factly, they've decided to cast someone else.

What?

He repeats this and I ask if this has to do with the ten percent? He just simply says, "They decided on someone else." And he hangs up.

I immediately call Sergei and get his answering machine. I leave messages, and I never hear from him again. This is a perfect ending to a typical LA story.

This is painfully disappointing. But I've overcome more horrible disappointments, compared this one is nothing.

Actually it's an inspiration to create a new breakfast cereal, it has zero calories, zero nutrition and it's made with one hundred percent artificial ingredients.

305   The Heartbreak of Static Cling

And its brand name is LA Flakes. The graphic on the cereal box is a dotted outline of a person with a subtitle, "The celebrity spokesperson for LA Flakes didn't show up for the photo shoot."

LA Flakes: A perfect souvenir for sale at LAX.

THE ONE MAN SHOW

I OPEN THE ENVELOPE and Antonio's portrait of Paloma Picasso is on the cover of an invitation to a one man show for Antonio at the Louvre. Paris, how perfect, the Louvre even more. The opening of this spectacular exhibit and tribute is a must see.

After all that crap movie star bullshit an escape to Paris for Antonio at the Louvre is exactly what I need.

I don't want to go alone, I call Ilene Connelly and we're off to Paris, the complete opposite of LA.

It's mid-October and Paris is what Paris is, magnificent. Ilene booked us into a small hotel off the

Champs Elysees. We check in and go for a Parisian stroll and suddenly we're different people with whatever identities we desire to create. It's wonderful to be able to star in your own movie at will.

After a great dinner we discover a club on the boulevard and venture in, it's Paris to the hilt, my favorite is a topless six foot femme fatal beauty wearing a Chanel bag around her neck bouncing off her naked tits sipping her whiskey so chic so nonchalant. Yes, we're not in LA.

Next day we hit the flea markets and get back to the hotel to ready ourselves for a night of fashion glamour and Antonio's genius.

The sun is setting as we walk across The Pont des Arts, a walking bridge over the Seine to the Louvre in golden light and we're not alone. This evening it's a promenade of famous photographers, supermodels, major fashion designers, magazine editors and artists and performers all headed for Antonio's one man show, a sensational visual.

Entering the gallery I'm hit hard by the soundtrack, it's Don's voice, a recording he made inspired by Antonio's first book entitled, "Antonio Girls." I'm with him again at this astounding exhibit. Paul is mingling with the glamorous but so many now can only appear in Antonio's work on these walls.

Antonio lives on in our hearts and his work will live forever.

ART SUPPLIES MAKE A BUCK

ENDLESS ESSAYS are edited and ready for publishing. And another starring roll becomes a possibility. A new art supply supermarket and frame store has opened just blocks away and they're looking for sales help. Why not? I'm unemployed and constantly amused by my many interviews at ad agencies in LA. Most of their "Creative Directors" are young enough to be my children. When they review my portfolio their reaction is the biggest threat is sitting opposite them. How unfortunate.

The Heartbreak of Static Cling

This is LA and I'll try anything, even a job selling pencils.

They sell art supplies and an assortment of arts and crafts materials including my favorite paint by number sets and a large inventory of kitsch decorations. Also there are endless isles of shelves with thousands of premade frames, perfect for your favorite photo of your dog or your darling child's crayon drawing. Best, there's a desk manned by "Design Consultants" who can custom make the perfect frame for whatever and include as many custom mats they are able to convince you to add to your order. And if this isn't enough there's "artwork" actually printed pictures of artwork on canvas framed and waiting to take residence over sofas.

This strikes me as the most perfect pop tart environment for me to spend my days.

I'm immediately hired and given a green polo shirt with the store's logo and a name tag to help get me get into character. I'm ready for business quickly learning the cash register and thrilled at my new roll selling picture frames and pencils on Santa Monica Boulevard.

They ask if I would like to become a "Design Consultant." Sure, why not? I'll have to take a few classes in order to be "certified." This seems absolutely certifiable so I accept.

Classes are held at another location near Westwood. The instructor is maybe an out of work elementary school art teacher? And he gets down to business lecturing about primary colors.

Art Supplies Make a Buck 310

One day I'm in the Louvre, next I'm in the loo, ah sweet mystery of life!

I keep my mouth shut and let him make many mistakes about "the world of color," the chromatic scale and such; I just nod my head at his wisdom and accept my new "certification." I'm so proud.

Turns out this gig isn't so bad. The best of it is guiding the tasteless to make less horrible choices, and teaching novices how to use art supplies. The worst of it is unloading massive boxes filled with art supplies and frames at 6 AM and restocking miles of shelves. Oh well, it's a workout more interesting than the gym.

The manager tells me they're looking to hire more sales help. Light bulb, Holly! I tell the manager I have the perfect person for the job and run around the corner to Holly and Lurch's apartment. I bang on the door, no answer. It's unlocked, I let myself in Lurch isn't home but Holly's here passed out in bed surrounded by empty gallon bottles of cheap Chardonnay, her favorite "Fish Piss."

I check if she's breathing and try to shake her out of her stupor. "Holly get up you got a job! You'll be my playmate at the frame store!" Miracle, this information brings her to semi consciousness. I help her clean up and dress her in almost clean chinos and a shirt with just a few stains and walk her around the corner to the store.

She's become somewhat coherent so I answer questions for her and she's hired.

Holly arrives at her first day at work wearing the green polo with the stores logo and a name plate that

The Heartbreak of Static Cling

reads, "Harold."

This is exactly what I needed, a costar in this movie with both of us in character as salesmen. And this is exactly what Holly needs, lifting her out of her fish piss fog.

They try to teach Holly how to use the cash register. The vignette of "Harold" the cashier is hilarious.

Fortunately there's a microphone next to her if she needs assistance and Harold's' velvety voice wafts throughout the store. "Manager to the cash register, manager to the cash register."

Finally, she kind of gets the hang of it, well almost. Harold is very generous, I catch her shoving items into plastic bags and giving it away. Harold is very popular with her customers.

We are working in this chain stores' new crown jewel. The manager announces a grand opening cocktail party and we're all invited to meet the founders and top execs.

Cocktail party, that's all "Harold" needed to hear. This soiree is to take place at the store tomorrow evening; the store will be closed to customers for the event.

It's 7 PM, all the staff is here at attention in their green logo shirts and smiles greeting the top brass. And then, Holly Woodlawn makes an entrance in a festive cocktail dress adorned with her name tag; Harold. She's accompanied by Lurch. Cocktails? You bet.

The expression on the faces of the managers is priceless as Holly with Chardonnay in hand introduces herself expressing her joy of being a salesman here at West Hollywood's most glamorous new store.

Drunken Lurch in search of his tenth cocktail stumbles and crashes into a display of hundreds of tiny frames which explode all over the floor. I decide to go out for a cigarette and bust a gut.

Lurch is shown the door. I go back inside and see Holly on her knees picking up the mess, I take over and she returns to the execs and apologizes for her "husband's" state of drunkenness.

Astoundingly, they pour her another drink.

Oh Holly, what would I do without you?

"Harold" and I soldier on for months, occasionally she's a no-show, but eventually returns refreshed. Unfortunately the novelty of this show is wearing thin for the both of us.

The straw came one early morning at 6 AM. "Harold" and I are schlepping and unpacking cartons and restocking shelves when the manager instructs us to clean the bathrooms. And that did it, art supplies and frames galore but janitors no way.

And so ends our stellar performance, we bow out and run off stage.

JUST LOOKING

LOOKING FOR what for who for when for where, looking for someone I recognize in the mirror. I need a Director. And Todd brings him to my place. Monty, a spectacular Director, so he believes, and he just might be right. He's young energized determined producing and directing his masterpiece and it's a silent film! Why not, dialogue has become passé, just *act* and the world will notice!

He's here for a reason, I could feel it but never expect what he's about to tell me. He's getting a car salesman's license! And lightning strikes, why the fuck not?!

Nothing in this town is more important than the car you drive, not even your mother. Many sleep in tents on the sidewalk to make payments on their new Lamborghini. Plastic surgery is a close second to the importance of your wheels. Why the fuck not?

A car salesman! Could this be my next blockbuster? And off we go to the DMV together.

It didn't take much time before Monty and I ace the audition at Culver City Imports.

Subaru, Hyundai, Mazda, and lots full of used cars to play with here in Culver City no less, the home of MGM where The Wizard of OZ was filmed, and now, "Robert and Monty Sell Cars."

We're buddies on the lot learning the ropes. Every lurking visitor blows us off telling us they're "Just looking." They sure are just looking for the car they desperately need to help define their image.

I snap back to Coney Island Avenue—A boy with his dad exploring endless car dealerships lining this street. It's the time of the year next year's models are about to be revealed. The showroom windows are covered with paper concealing the new arrivals, but up close a few open spaces between the paper drapes let us to get a glimpse of brand new Buicks, Chevys, Cadillacs, Chryslers, Pontiacs, and Fords. I'm thrilled at the sight of new fins, headlights, front grills and convertibles, all spectacular.

A father and son bonding with these discoveries, this rare occasion is when I felt close to him as a child. And it set my fascination with cars early on and now incredibly I'm selling them.

I know every make and model, horsepower, fuel economy, and nameplate. And I also know the personality of each car, buying one must fit who you want to be. You are what you drive especially in LA.

Not put off by the "Just looking" I watch them, inspect them and if need be interrogate them for a clue to point them in the direction of a possible metal and chrome soul mate.

I'm working this gig to the hilt to keep hidden what's just under my surface, the constant pain of losing Don and when unbearable moments hit I just walk off the lot for a smoke.

Monty's good at the game, he's handsome and can be very charming, and I'm doing okay. The salary is next to nothing, it's all about commission and that's not very much. The most important reason I'm here is the company's healthcare policy.

Months are filled with test drives and conversations with strangers confessing their sins and wishes. I document this taking Polaroid's of every customer I sell a car to. I pose them next to their new car displaying their new car keys in ecstasy. This could become something interesting.

Monty is preparing for the production of his silent film taking more of his time and he finally quits, I'm glad for him. He tells me he's got a part for me in his movie. I tell him that sounds familiar.

It's September, I'm still on the lot and I get a call from my mom, my father's not well, the Cancer spread to his bones. I need to go to Miami again and I need to make an overnight stop in New York to see Juan; I hear he's also not good.

I land at JFK and rush to Juan and Paul's loft on Union Square, Sonia, Juan's sister is there, and others I don't recognize, I spot Paul, he comes over to me and whispers terrible news and then I see Juan, he's in a wheelchair alone.

I go to him. "Juan."

"Robert, I'm blind."

"I know... Juan, I love you." I can't find another word, I just try to hold it all in and manage to kiss his forehead and say good bye.

My father is lying on a hospital bed installed in his bedroom; my mother is exhausted being his full time nurse. A nurse's aide comes just an hour a day, the rest is left up to my mom and my father continuously calls her name demanding whatever he needs. I hire a full time homecare nurse. I can't allow my mother to care for my dad without more help.

I go to his bedside and take off my new sneakers and show them to him. Being a shoe salesman at Saks all his life, he takes one and bends it in half and approves, another heartbreaking connection.

Now that she has the extra care needed, my mother insists I go home and take care of myself.

I'm back in LA and back at the car lot for a month now and get a call from Paul.

Juan Ramos died of AIDS November 2nd, 1995.

SEX DRUGS AND VIDEOS

IT'S BEEN A WHILE since Todd introduced me to Brad. And now Brad Chandler has become a close friend with a complicated past. His dad was a wealthy oil tycoon in Texas and relocated to Canada, Brad's mom died when he was six. His father remarried a woman Brad refers to as his "Step Monster" with a daughter from her previous marriage. The story goes she threw Brad out of the house as a kid in freezing mid-winter Canada and bilked his father out of every dime.

The lifelong repercussions become evident. Even

though Brad is a successful realtor, somewhere deep down he doesn't believe he deserves success and this causes self sabotage.

Hard drinking and drugs—especially speed—takes over. I know what that's like. Speed was the drug of choice when I was in my twenties. The rush begins at your toes and rockets to your head and instantly you're Superman with superpowers and your problems are solved brilliantly and you are spectacular.

The crash however is devastating, so speed and more speed and that's addiction.

There are many things about Brad I love, his wit, sense of humor intelligence and imagination. Brad's a rare find.

Being reintroduced to that speed high again is the kind of escape from grief I can't replicate. I'm a veteran at this and know how to keep it at bay; it's lethal if not controlled.

Now there's another powder, you put it into a small glass pipe and smoke it. The first inhale goes directly to your dick, it's a sexplosion. All inhibitions are gone, all is unlocked and it's full tilt boogey spending nights of debauchery in front of the TV watching porno. This isn't love-sex, it's drug-sex, not even full-on sex but it's incredibly freeing.

He's young and can take this way over the limit. I warn him, hold the caution flag up high. This crack is a way AIDS gets in.

There's something that will save him though, it's a resolve to survive. He finds ways and people that help.

He's now living with an older man who's the kind of a father figure he needs. This gives him stability and support to pull himself together, a relationship that's part ambition part necessity.

Drugs are my temporary madness. I've allowed this indulgence knowing it's no cure for my pain it's just a band aid. Brad will realize this for himself eventually, I hope.

I'm grateful to him for loosening chains binding me. We'll be friends for a long time, friends nothing more but that's enough.

And just like that, I'm in an old Hollywood mansion shooting a scene with Jennifer Tilly, as Clara Bow in Monty's silent film. God knows how he put this together. It's a lot of fun in Tyrone Power eye makeup emoting silent picture "acting" trying to bilk Clara out of her fortune so I can open a burger joint. Connie is playing Max von Stroheim. Who knew I'd have a voice in a silent picture? That's Hollywood Monty; one day a used car salesman and next he's directing his silent picture. You never know.

Back at my pool, my landlord Boris announces he sold the house, damn it! I told him if he ever thinks of selling, I'd gladly go into hock for this place. Instead, he sold it to a developer who's going to tear it down and build condos. Eventually this disaster will be known as "The Russian wedding cake! How awful. This is LA, nothing lasts.

I got to move. I have the proceeds from Bellport and Irving Place so it's time to buy something. I call

The Heartbreak of Static Cling

Victor Kaminoff, an old friend from NYC who reinvented himself here as a Realtor. The search begins for a property here in West Hollywood. We find a house on Orlando that could be my dream home, but it's slightly over my budget and needs a lot of work. It's killing me; I know its potential but I have to let it go, oh well.

A few days pass and Victor tells me about a large condo up the street that may fall out of escrow, they're holding an open house and I should go see it.

It's on Kings Road and Willoughby, just a block away. The building looks solid, fairly new and well designed. And when I enter this condo the first thing that comes to mind is, wow, this is West Hollywood? It's more like a very chic large New York City residence, completely redone in great taste, the owner is known for his taste, he's the owner of an exclusive celebrity go to beauty spa. A lot of people are here checking this place out. I take a seat on a sofa, and realize this place is perfect. 851 Kings Road becomes my new home.

Funny, Kings Road no less, flash back to Chelsea and the Kings Road I discovered in London long ago. Now I've landed on Kings Road, in West Hollywood, what a trip getting here. And who knows where this will take me.

Finally all my things are in one place with room to spare. And a very special carton arrives: "AIDS Why Should I Care" is published and I can't believe I'm holding this book in my hands. The next phase begins, I need to get this into as many book stores, high schools, and libraries as possible. Only then will my promise to Don be fulfilled. I got my work cut out for me.

Another move is at hand, Culver City Imports has served its purpose but I'm not done with this business yet. It's mindless but health insurance and some unsteady income is better than none. I want to move on to another dealership in a different location with a different clientele and see if I can make this a fresh experience again.

Now that I'm a "seasoned" salesman, getting hired at another dealership is no problem. Santa Monica Infinity is now my new workplace. This is high end compared to Culver City. So here I am at a new dealership with new and different Santa Monica customers, let's see how long this new lasts.

I just say to myself, "keep moving and you might find yourself."

THE BEST HE COULD

MY DAD, Theodore Abraham Starr was born in 1912 on Cherry Street, lower East Side of Manhattan. He was the youngest of ten siblings. It was a rough life; his father a truck driver, Ted never had a chance at a proper education, no graduating high school, just working with his father driving trucks. Ted has a big heart and he's extremely handsome, actually the best of the bunch.

Ted met Zelda at a party in Bensonhurst Brooklyn and they fell deeply in love. Even though Ted is years older, she found him irresistible and they married. Times were tough, the depression raging but they were in love and started a life.

Zelda always worked, first at the offices of D'orsay Perfume where she was considered a blonde bombshell and constantly hit on. She left D'orsay and became a legal secretary for a local lawyer. And then she began her career in the public school system working her way up from secretary to assistant principle by continually taking additional collage courses.

Ted sold shoes at A.S. Beck in NYC. My sister was born in 1942 and Ted went to war. The child, Carolyn felt abandoned.

Newsreels showed Ted, the military policeman on motorcycle in Japan. Zelda's three brothers are fighting in different parts of the world. Zelda never stopped working. Carolyn is taken care of by Grandma who is on the edge of a nervous breakdown.

Finally the horror of war is over. Ted finds a job at Saks Fifth Avenue. And four years later, I'm born.

Now I'm on a plane to Miami, trying to write something to say at my father's memorial service.

Zelda is somber but relieved Ted's suffering is over. Carolyn sits next to her emotionless in the temple attended by a small assortment of strangers.

I get to the podium and focus on my mom and begin to talk but it seems hollow. My relationship with him was so complicated but I put all that aside and stick to the facts, especially his lifelong devotion and love for Zelda and how he adored Carolyn. Words crafted to make them feel better. I sum it all up by saying, "He always did the best he could."

My emotions run the gamut. Bottom line, he loved me and I loved him. He was my dad.

My biggest concern now is my mom living alone here in North Miami Beach. She assures me she'll be alright. She never would allow herself to be a burden. She could never be a burden to me, she's my heart. I can't leave her to live alone for long and a seed for a plan to get her to California is planted.

SIX FOOT BUNNY CROSSES THE BORDER

MAXWELL, Brad's old buddy and roommate was well connected to Beverly Hills society, before he passed he introduced Brad to Bobby Beverly Hills. Bobby is older than Maxwell and much more connected and much richer. Brad instantly bonds with Bobby who lives in a mansion on Summit Drive in Beverly Hills. Brad introduces me to Bobby and I find his charm, grace and past intriguing. A while ago Bobby sold his Orange and Avocado fields in Anaheim. It's now Disneyland.

Now Brad has another daddy figure and a fresh

supply of intros to endless Real Estate prospects.

Easter is approaching and Brad and Bobby are vacationing at Casa de Mara, Bobby's estate in Acapulco. And surprisingly I'm invited for Easter weekend, a Spring break in Acapulco, with Brad and Bobby Beverly Hills, irresistible.

I pack my bags plus an extra duffle bag containing a gift for my host and take off to another adventure. The plane lands, I get a cab and hand the driver a note paper with the address and we climb the hills over the astonishingly beautiful Acapulco bay.

Las Brisas is a billionaire's enclave. When we approach this exclusive neighborhood and encounter guards armed with machine guns. They inspect the cab and the driver shows the address of our destination, and they see the gringo smiling in the back seat allowing us to proceed up the hill.

Here I am in wonderland, I ring the bell and a uniformed maid opens the door, Brad appears and a butler takes my bags. I hold onto my gift bag as Brad takes me through the mind blowing villa to Bobby who's at the pool on a Cliffside patio with a heart stopping view of the bay and most of Acapulco below.

Bobby seems confused as if not knowing of my invitation. Brad smoothes this over and I embrace Bobby and unzip my duffle bag and present him with a six foot Easter Bunny. Bobby's amused.

The butler announces lunch will be served in a half an hour. Bobby disappears with the bunny and Brad shows me to the poolside cabana stocked with robes and bathing suits. I take the plunge and float in the salt water pool as Brad lounges on a float going over our itinerary, after lunch we'll drive down to the beach and later this evening we're invited to a gala benefit at another cliff hanging estate belonging to at Suzie de Jilli. "Expect the unexpected," Brad warns brightly.

I lose count of how many servants are employed at Bobby's. Lunch is a five course Mexican culinary extravaganza.

After lunch Bobby leaves to take his siesta. Brad warns me to not to take my wallet and watch, just cash, and we get into one of the cars parked in front and drive down to where mere mortals dwell.

Brad finds his favorite sleazy bar and disappears. I'm sipping a margarita noticing some shady guys sizing me up. Suddenly Brad reappears and we jump back in the car and return to Casa de Mara.

We go to my guest room and Brad locks the door and pulls a big bag of coke out of his pocket. Viva Zapata!

Cocktails are at the poolside watching the sun set, Brad and Bobby are dressed in white, I'm in my black NY blazer and jeans and ready for who knows what. Neither of them have a clue of what this gala "benefit" is for. It's probably a benefit for the billionaires' insatiable egos.

We arrive at this architectural masterpiece once owned by Frank Sinatra. It's a tribute to Frank Lloyd Wright's masterpiece, "Falling Water."

The Heartbreak of Static Cling

And the fun begins with the very cross-eyed Contessa making her entrance with her semi cross-eyed twenty something gigolo at her side and that's just for starters, Titans of obscure industries, dowagers with tiny dogs and princes of unknown principalities accompanied by titled and entitled creatures have all emerged from under their gilded rocks wearing many rocks of different colors for this event. What a gift, what an amazing inspiration! So much so I'm transported into a new screenplay written before my eyes, entitled "Eurotrash."

My head is no longer in Acapulco; I'm in Beverly Hills with Holly Lola, the aging Warhol Superstar who had her fifteen minutes of fame years ago. Fortunately she married Kikea Kikatukas, the Greek mega mogul billionaire and owner of the largest movie studio in Hollywood.

A party is given for Holly this evening and it's is a must go according to her publicist, Holly could care less but decides to make an appearance; her husband, Kikea, prefers to stay at home.

After an hour of accolades, Holly has had enough and leaves the party, goes home and finds her husband in bed wearing her hosiery and her favorite Christian Louboutin heels while he's being fucked by their beefy gardener.

Holly in a flying rage and pushes the gardener off of her husband. "How dare you have the nerve to ruin my stockings and stuff your fat feet in my shoes!" Kikea is so terrified he has a heart attack and drops dead.

Six Foot Bunny Crosses the Border 330

In order to quell any scandal, Holly directs the gardener to remove her shoes and tattered hose from dead Kikea and throw him in the pool and declare her poor husband drowned.

At Kikea's funeral, the tenacious pimp, The Barron, introduces Widow Holly to a gorgeous hunk hustler, Paolo. She's immediately taken by him and a torrid affair begins.

Holly decides to be benevolent and plans a gala at her house to benefit bereaved widows of Beverly Hills whose husbands drowned in their pools. The theme of the benefit is aquatic.

And it's a major event covered by the press. All her guests engaged premier designers to create bespoke couture aquatic eveningwear.

Nicolette Von Vilderbeast of Manhattan and Tasmania accompanied by Trey of Salon Coiffure are first to arrive. Nicolette's latest plastic surgery is complemented by her enormous catfish collar. She has whiskers implanted in her face and her Oscar de la Renta gown has dorsal fins. Her companion sports yellow flippers accenting his evening blue Prada rubber thong.

Oxonia Von Kimptenstein and Frederic Von Mole of Bulgaria appear and hesitate in the spotlight at the top of the stairs. Oxonia is wearing an inflated orange Gucci life preserver over her bejeweled black rubber wetsuit gown. Frederic is in a Tom Ford wetsuit tuxedo with swim goggles accentuating his enormous mole.

Next, Countess Rottenteet and Philippe de Vulva

The Heartbreak of Static Cling

of Mexico arrive. The cross-eyed Countess is strapped into Versace sequined aqualungs over her skin tight mermaid gown. Philippe is a vision as a Ralph Lauren shipwrecked passenger of the Titanic carrying a piece of a piano as a flotation device.

Ms. Trinky Nukus and Mrs. Bedsy Bathandbeyond, two of Holly's favorites make their entrance and enjoy the spotlight. Trinky is a giant Chanel clam with a huge black pearl for a bellybutton. Bedsy is all arms in a giant Dior glittering octopus. They descend the stairs to the garden as the Penguin costumed trumpet players sound off.

Paolo is confronted by the Barron who's livid to hear he and Holly are planning to get married. The Barron forbids this marriage and dashes off to find Holly.

And the Barron finds Holly and spills the beans. He declares Holly can't marry Paolo even though he's the best sex she ever had and she's madly in love with him, absolutely no marriage can take place because Paolo is also Holly's son! Yes, Paolo is the baby Holly gave to Andy Warhol to raise because a child would have ruined her career.

Holly thinks about this for a minute and runs through the crowd to find Paolo who doesn't have a clue about this. When Holly finally finds Paolo she insists he takes a vow. "Paolo, promise me you will never ever call me Momma!" Befuddled and in love Paolo agrees and they elope.

This inspirational finale brings me back to the marvelously brilliant successful benefit which has raised a significant number of eyebrows and all are quite pleased with themselves.

And so ends the high point of my Easter holiday with Brad and Bobby Beverly Hills here in Acapulco.

Now I must run back to my glamorous engagement at the used car lot in Santa Monica.

YOU WON'T SEE MONDAY

MY SHEETS are soaked and it's hard to breathe, I haven't been feeling well for weeks but I forced myself to go sell cars and now it's gotten worse. This is a kind of sick I haven't experienced before. Brad drives me to Cedars Sinai and they take one look at me and I'm admitted.

I'm on oxygen and it's like there's something heavy sitting on my chest. Dr. Leland Green checks me out and orders Dilaudid for the pain and schedules a series of tests and procedures to get a diagnosis.

They hook me up to the Dilaudid and give me a handy button to push another dose every fifteen minutes. It's better than morphine, better than heroin, and now it's my favorite drug of all time. The high is amazing.

CT Scans, X-rays, more blood draws, MRI's, full body Tomography scans and a spinal tap for desert. All this takes weeks and still there's no definitive diagnosis and I'm getting sicker. They're sure I'm dying, and so am I, so what?

God bless Cedars and Dilaudid, I'm comfortable in my private room with artwork and a view. Company arrives, Todd, Holly, Connie, Brad, Ilene, BJ, and Jennifer Connelly who snuggles up to me in my hospital bed.

More weeks pass and more tests and still no diagnosis, and doctors tell me I don't have much time left.

And now my mother and my Aunt Dottie and my sister Carolyn, Elda and Holly are here horrified at my bedside. There's nothing I can do but put on a happy face.

Todd appears and he wants me to sign papers leaving him my fortune, that's what friends are for, right? Brad shows up on speed and that makes me mad. I tell him I'm fighting for my life and he's shooting speed. I throw him out and press the Dilaudid button and turn on the Teletubbies. Watching them on Dilaudid is better than any acid trip.

Dr. Green orders lymph node biopsies from my

groin, but they can't get any results and decide to do biopsies from my lungs. I wind up in the ICU with chest tubes in both lungs and an audience of friends watching Frankenstein hooked up to machines breathing heavily through my oxygen mask.

Funny how perfectly fine I am with all this, except who called my mother? She doesn't need to see this.

Finally they yank the chest tubes out of my chest and I'm back in my room with more Dilaudid.

This is a teaching hospital and interns arrive and discuss possible reasons why I'm dying. Still with all the tests and procedures, no one has a clue.

Elda, Carolyn, Mom, and aunt Dottie are in my room as the interns appear again. I hit the Dilaudid button and tell these young doctors exactly what is wrong with me. "Last month I was on safari deep in Africa's Congo. In the thick of the jungle I discover the hidden grave of Patrice Lumumba. I exhumed the corpse and contract Lumumbalella! Lumumbalella! Lumumbalella! And do you know how Lumumbalella is transmitted? It's transmitted at will!"

The horrified pale white interns run out of the room. My mom and Dottie are in hysterics, Mom pees her pants and I continue, "And I want my body donated to Jiffy Lube!" Now my sister and Elda are doubled over hysterically laughing and run out of my room. You just need a sense of humor when you're dying.

Next day a somber Dr. Green arrives with news finally. "We have a diagnosis."

Great, it's just taken three weeks.

He continues, "Robert, you have a virulent case of Non-Hodgkin's Lymphoma. You need to begin chemotherapy."

"I don't want chemotherapy, I've seen what chemotherapy did to my friends and I don't want it."

He replies, "Robert, today is Friday, if I don't get you on Chemo this evening, you won't see Monday."

Now that's a dramatic sales pitch, similar to, "Buy this product or we'll shoot this puppy." But Dr. Leland Green is not known for hyperbole, it's just the facts and that's one of the reasons he's held in such high regard at Cedars.

Dr. Green continues, "The first dose must be administered very slowly, you could have serious reactions to this. A nurse will be at your side continuously overnight monitoring you. You'll be sedated. Take a rest now, we'll begin at 6PM."

He's about to leave the room when I ask what exactly am I going to get?

He replies, "CHOP," that's the name for the combination of chemotherapeutic drugs necessary, an anachronism for Cycloposhamide, Doxorubucin, Vincristine, Prednisone, plus he's adding Bleomycin. "If you were diagnosed five years ago, you wouldn't have had the benefit of these drugs."

Realizing my Uncle Moe and Jackie O died of exactly this, I reply, "Okay, Doc, chop me up."

Satisfied, he leaves the room.

The Heartbreak of Static Cling

Did I make the right decision? Why should I fight this and for what reason? I had a life, a very interesting life but it's not so fabulous lately, wouldn't I be better off dead? Isn't this the perfect way for me to go, and what's so important about seeing Monday? I hate Mondays.

The resolve comes as I recall vivid images of Don fighting for his last breath. I have to fight for my life to honor him and also I realize my death would kill my mother. So, fuck this cancer. I decide to live.

I fall into waves of Dilaudid euphoria floating between life and death. The day passes and a team of doctors finally appear. They unplug me, inject sedatives and move me to another room.

A fat sweaty male nurse hovers above me, he tells me he will be at my side every minute over night. I manage to tell him to mop his brow, lose weight and do something about his horrible breath. He's surprised, but my comments are well taken. I've never been so grateful for Listerine.

He hooks me up to bags of radioactive orange colored liquids slowly making their journey into my body hunting and killing cancer cells and who knows what else? I've decided to welcome this invasion with determined sincerity.

More sedation and fade to black.

Flip the switch and turn on the sun and I'm back in my room. I discover a nurse has placed the Delaudid button in my hand. Before I push it I realize something odd, the elephant isn't sitting on me any longer. I take a deep breath of pure oxygen from my mask and decide this nightmare is over, could this be actually true? Who the fuck knows but I feel great. I reach for the phone and call Rosemary. But just for fun I press the Dilaudid button first and get stoned out of my head to celebrate. I have no idea what I'm saying to her, but her voice is like icing on a cake.

Dr. Green shows up and he's actually smiling. "You tolerated it very well, how do you feel?"

"Fabulous, you did it!"

"Not so fast, this needs to continue for at least six months twice a week."

"With Dilaudid?"

"No Robert, we need to wean you off that before we can release you from the hospital."

"Release me without Dilaudid? Does it come in pill form for me to take at home?"

"No Robert, you have a long road ahead, your treatments will be administered at our infusion center, pain management won't be necessary."

"None?"

"If things go as I expect you'll beat this."

"Can't I stay here and do it and have my Dilaudid?" He just smiles and leaves the room.

I really don't want to leave the hospital, I'm comfortable and I have company every day and amazingly the food is good. Boy I'm glad I stuck it out at the dealership, this hospital bill has got to be hundreds of thousands and it's all covered, thank God.

And here is my relieved smiling mother with her sister, my aunt Dottie. I love them both; Dottie is like my second mom. Zelda tells me she's going to stay with me at my place all throughout my infusions, I'm forever so grateful but we'll see about that, she's not my nurse, she's my mother and I can't allow her to burden herself.

A week of observation passes and the time has come, I'm being released. Why am I so sad about this? There's got to be a good reason I've survived, I hope I'll find out what it is. Right now the glow of relief on my mother's face is enough.

Good Bye Cedars Sinai, Dr. Green and my dear friend, Dilaudid.

Back home in my own bead, weak and getting used to breathing regular air which seems heavy compared to pure oxygen from a mask. But I'm okay, just tired and my pillow is covered with hair. Mom brings me a clipper; I'd rather just shave it all off myself than wait for the inevitable. Luckily shaved heads are in style, but no eyebrows no eyelashes and no hair anywhere is daunting. I'm a chemo poster child emaciated and hairless. But I like being thin, I've always thought it's more elegant.

Zelda is a wonder and my great companion. She's energized by this caretaking. And surprise company, Jennifer and her fiancé Paul Bettany come for a visit just before they go off to a castle in Ireland to be wed. Sorry I can't attend, chemo you know. Mom loves Jen and instantly falls in love with Paul. Zelda is so proud to show them my art collection, taking them room to room pointing out the Antonio's, Malcolm Morley's and Keith Harring's, all such wonderful art given me by these incredible artists. I'm so grateful for those friendships including Jen and now Paul. Both are truly beautiful in so many ways, I'm thrilled for them.

The chemo routine continues and I'm strong enough to take a cab by myself to the infusion center at Cedars. Zelda doesn't need to see this.

The infusion room is a festive affair. Cancer victims in all stages of decay are happily hooked up intravenously relaxing in reclining club chairs, I'm shown to mine and here comes the day-glow liquid hanging from a rack and the nurse gets a vein quickly, that's all she does and she does it brilliantly.

Again I welcome the chemo cocktail with open vein and get lost in endless catalogues my neighbor provided me for distraction.

The procedure takes about an hour and a half, there's no immediate reaction so I'm able to cab it back home and go to bed. I'm drained and weakened and drift off. Hours pass and I'm okay and happy there's no nausea or pain. Dr. Green cautioned the affects are cumulative, but he also assured me he added another ingredient to avoid the worst of it.

A few weeks pass and actually I'm feeling okay. I can't allow my mother to continue being my caretaker; I have friends who are willing to help if necessary. It takes some convincing, she's stubborn but she relents and goes home to Florida.

I'm determined to move her here when all this is finally over. She can't live alone much longer.

I think I can see myself almost normal again, whatever that is. This saga is coming to an end and so is my last chemo cocktail, I should have a party. Instead I have to see Dr. Green to get his green light to live again. I do and he does. So now what?

Eyelashes, eyebrows and tufts of hair are growing back slowly. How can I use this long recovery? I'm mining for inspiration. I need another creative ship to build.

When it was believed the world is flat, those with vision built ships to sail the seas for the slightest chance of discovery and the possibility of finding riches, however improbable the prospect was that belief was undeniably motivating. The more ships the better. Some ships will surely fall off the flat earth into oblivion, but there just might be one ship that finds a new world and return. Even those with limited means would build at least one ship and launch it with hope in their hearts.

Everyone in LA is a screenwriter building their ships to sail to the abyss of rejection. Eurotrash has sailed, why not build another?

I dig deep and find LA itself to be the inspiration. And here she is, Essence Shapiro. Essence is the embodiment of many LA women I've encountered. She's holistic and spiritual, she's an environmental activist she's blonde and set for life with her ex-husbands alimony.

Essence is my heroine who doesn't need heroin because she has CUDA—her three thousand year old Etruscan guru who guides her through traffic on the 405.

Essence is in touch with the Universe but not her own heart. She lives alone comforted by CUDA and her Buddha's. And she has followers amassed at The Bodi Tree, a spiritual bookstore on Melrose Avenue.

One fateful night at Gelson's parking lot, CUDA appears from the universe and challenges Essence with the most important mission of her life.

CUDA hovers above captured frozen Essence and begins, "Essence, Essence Shapiro, this message is for you, a test of your will. Essence Shapiro in exactly ten days, *The Big One* will hit. This quake will be so violent it will crack LA off the continent. What will you do with this knowledge, Essence Shapiro? I CUDA will be watching you."

CUDA evaporates and Essence falls to the ground, grabs her groceries and crawls to her BMW.

"The Lady Who Saved LA" becomes a perfect way for me to recover. Now I can escape into a world of incredulity absurdity hilarity panic pathos downright craziness and heartfelt discovery. Who needs Dilaudid?

Even so, a nagging reality lurks, every day I get insurance statements in the mail itemizing the cost of thousands of procedures, drugs and hospital expenses, the numbers are mind blowing and co-pays are mounting. I've got to get back to work.

I'm indebted to the dealership for the healthcare coverage. I have to go back there for enough time to be able to pay off my part of the medical bills. I wonder if I can tolerate being a car salesman again, it's no longer a novelty.

Every day I take a walk and I'm getting my full strength back and also my hair. Time is coming soon for me to face the music and get back to selling cars. Is this what I decided to live for? I guess I have to step backward in order to move ahead to whatever is in store for me. It's always been a surprise.

Nobody believes Essence, not even her most ardent followers. No matter what she comes up with to warn them of the impending doom, nobody listens. Even her devoted followers think she's nuts.

But there is one person who gets it and believes her, he's known as T-Shirt Man, a burnt out advertising executive who abandoned his position in a successful agency in New York and his coke empowered copywriter ex-wife. He now lives in a trailer in Venice and sells his custom made t-shirts on the beach, each one emblazoned with conjoined advertising slogans, such as, "Where's the beef, don't leave home without it," "Things go better with Coke, it's the quicker picker upper," "Betcha you can't eat one because you're worth it," "Reach out and touch someone, it's finger lickin' good, just do it," "It melts in your mouth, not in your hands, have it your way, only your hairdresser knows for sure," and "This is your brain on drugs, it's you, only better."

T-Shirt Man speaks his strange language and it takes awhile for Essence to realize he's making perfect sense but even so, he's too nuts for her.

So at least when I go back to the car lot, I'll have Essence and T-Shirt Man's adventures for an escape.

Three weeks back at work and I've had it. The dealership guys are happy to see me again and recovered. And I've actually met a few Santa Monica crackpots shopping for cars that would be perfect to include in Essence Shapiro's world, but it's not good enough for me to remain in character as Robert the car salesman.

LET'S HAVE LUNCH

BRAD INVITES me to lunch with him and Steven Solomon, a very successful Real Estate agent Brad has attached himself to for the benefit of his career. Steve's originally from London and works his effete English accent to impress Beverly Hills billionaires who change homes like we change underwear, Steve knows his stuff.

Steve opens the conversation, "Robert, you would be very good at Real Estate. You have a good eye, know architecture and know how to sell."

"Oh, really?"

Brad chimes in, "He's right, you should get your license and we'll help."

I'm silently mulling this over, who knows where this could take me? The commission selling one good house would be about the same as selling a hundred cars, but... "Steve, there's a problem, I really hate cell phones and driving."

Both laugh this off and Steve adds, "We'll help you get started, you should really consider this."

Why not? It's a challenge, Brad and Steve are friends, maybe they would help? Robert the Realtor, why the hell not?

I could think of a lot of reasons why not, but fuck it, what else is there for me to do?

Not so fast, not so easy, this takes commitment. I have to enroll in Real Estate school and that will take weeks and weeks of courses before I can go downtown and take the dreaded test to get a license, I've heard this test is no piece of cake. I can't remember the last time I had to take courses and pass a test. Okay sign me up, I got nothing to lose, this is just another unexpected turn in the road and it could turn out to be fun or a complete disaster, it doesn't matter.

I'm signed up and buy the books, a lot of books and I'm a diligent student. I'm amazed at the scope of topics, from legal issues to contracts to categories of ownership, architecture, appraisals and also the language of land surveying. Do you really need all this to sell a house? Well to get a license in California you must. So I read the books do my homework and immerse myself completely for the slight chance this world isn't flat.

I'm up bright and early, I feel prepared but nervous as hell as I drive downtown for the big test. The place is packed with even more nervous Real Estate wannabes lined up for the slaughter of convoluted questions.

The Real Estate market now is ramped up, it's a feeding frenzy and we're all here to get a chance for a piece of the pie. The room is big enough to accommodate a hundred hopefuls of every age and description.

I take my seat, the door closes and the thick test is handed out. The room is silent and it begins. I read the first question and wonder if it's written in English. I re-read it and it still makes no sense, I read it again and decide it's a trick question and skip it not wanting to waste time trying to decipher nonsense. And then I'm off to the races, all the hours of intense preparation is coming back and I'm flying confidently, questions page after page are answered quickly and then I decide to revisit the first question and see if I can decode it. I actually read the riddle backwards and the puzzle is solved, so there, got you motherfuckers!

I never imagined I would feel this good after taking this test. I sing "Hallelujah" with Leonard Cohen's CD driving home, but I'm still not sure I want the part.

Kids are asked, "What do you want to be when you grow up, a doctor, a lawyer, fireman, what?" You are what you do, so what am I doing? I'm trying to do whatever it takes to live with a shredded heart and survive the horrors I've lived through.

I've had a great creative career lasting more than twenty-seven years and now it's over... So I try things I would never have considered and now this. I was challenged and accepted it, and I have a Real Estate license. I'll find out soon enough what I can do with it and what it will do to me.

I call Mary Kay to tell her the news about my license and she tells me she has a present for me, the listing of her house in Echo Park. She's been renting this house out for awhile and now she wants to sell, and she wants me to be her agent! Wow, I have my first listing and I'm not yet associated with a Real Estate company.

I walk into Caldwell Banker Real Estate, a new agent with a listing and a buyer pending. And here I am, Robert the Realtor.

And I'm no longer a virgin realtor, Mary Kay's house sells in a week, on December 7th. That just happens to be Don's birthday.

STEALING ZELDA

ZELDA'S ninetieth birthday is coming up. My plans are in place, I've organized a wonderful celebration and an even more wonderful kidnapping.

I'm determined to give her some of the best years of her life. She knows I'm coming for her big birthday, but has little idea what will come next.

A life of hard work and constant caring... Zelda will be celebrated. Here's the plot: a cousin works at a luxury hotel in Ft. Lauderdale where I'm setting the stage for the big party. Uncles, aunts, cousins and all whose lives have been touched by her will attend. It will not only be a party but also a premier screening of 'The Zelda B. Starr Story,' a short movie I produced and plan to distribute on CDs to all of our guests.

The B is for Brodis. The Brodis family is all I've known. The Starr family has been mostly nonexistent in my life. Those who are still alive are loathsome. David Starr, Dad's older brother had a chain of appliance stores in Minneapolis. He lured my father to work for him just after he and Zelda married. David treated my dad like a slave and he hated Zelda. He actually tried to bribe her to leave Ted. My sister Carolyn was born in Minneapolis and finally Ted and Zelda had enough of Dave's abuse. They returned to Brooklyn, and soon after Ted goes off to war.

Zelda never stops working, it's an absolute necessity. Not only Ted but my mom's three brothers go to war, deployed to Burma, Italy and Japan.

Dave sells his Minneapolis stores and moves to Houston where he makes his fortune in oil. Other members of the Starr family are a dim vague memory. So this party is for Zelda and her Brodis family.

Disappointingly hurtful, Carolyn is a no show at the party. There wasn't a blowup between her and Zelda, it's just that Carolyn can't get out of her own way and this is sad.

Mary Kay helped me shop for a special birthday outfit for Zelda and I bring it with me. Humble and frugal, Zelda would never succumb to extravagance, I'm forcing her hand. And I have a bigger surprise. Never wanting to impose, Zelda will not agree to share my home. Instead I've secured an apartment for her that surpasses her lonely condo in Miami Beach and It's just a two minute walk from my place on Kings Road and big enough for all her furnishings and a spare room for me when necessary. There's also a big terrace with a great view of sunsets and most of West Hollywood, Zelda will have a new life in California.

As soon as I arrive in Miami my investigation into her financial affairs begin. Home values in Florida have plummeted leaving Zelda's condo under water, meaning she owes more than it can be sold for. I also discover she's been bamboozled by a predatory lender who manipulated her to take a forty thousand dollar home equity loan and now she's trapped.

After weighing every option and consulting local Realtors, lawyers and accountants, I make a tough decision. We're walking away, the bank can foreclose her condo and the other sleazy lender can shove it. They deserve this, taking advantage of a ninety year old diagnosed with Alzheimer's. I'll deal with the consequences whatever they may be.

This kidnapping has taken on an enhanced element of escape; we have to be a little deceptive. I inform the condo board we are taking an extended cruise and putting her valuables in storage. I begin editing her furnishings, selling things off and arrange movers to do their thing in stages so it doesn't look like a total move. We need to slip out carefully, not ringing alarm bells with the Condo management that could interfere. Nothing is going to stop me from saving her life.

It's time for the celebration. We arrive at the hotel early and settle into our suite. Zelda looks fabulous in her new outfit, feeling years younger. But she's nervous about the whole thing. I hold her tight, she knows how much I love her and she trusts me.

Zelda's big birthday party is wonderful. A family get together so rare I can't remember ever seeing all of them in one place, each sharing memories that touch her heart.

Happy birthday, Zelda! And now Zelda get ready for the rest of your life, it's going to be real good.

As the weight lifts from my mother's shoulders, it is transformative for me as well. I'm finally doing something again that matters deeply. I've found a purpose that relieves a lot of my pain, her happiness is mine. I'm dedicated to bring her joy, whatever it takes, just like she has done for me all my life.

We get on that plane to California and a different, renewed life for me and my mother.

I've learned so much from Don, seeing how bravely he lived his life and how he was so completely thorough he was investigating every possibility of survival. I've learned those hard lessons well applying that knowledge to my arsenal against Cancer. Now I'll use it to care for others. Maybe this is the reason I survived.

SLEEP OVER

I'M IN BED with my mother. She turns to me and asks, "Where's my stuff?" I convulse in hysterical laughter, this strikes me as a really twisted, John Waters movie. She repeats, "Where's my stuff?"

Finally through guffaws I reply, "Somewhere in the Midwest, it takes time for the moving van to cross America with your stuff."

Satisfied, she turns and drifts off to sleep.

Yep, I'm in bed with my mother, I have to be, the bed in my guest room is too high for her to get up and go the bathroom, so is my bed but I made her promise to nudge me so I can assist. My place is foreign to her and I can't take any chances, I'm in bed with her until I can replicate her condo down the block and move her in and stay with her until she adapts. Sleepovers can be really fun with your mother.

Zelda quickly has a new family; Connie, Brad, Holly, Todd and Mary Kay all adore her, and of course she's in love with them all. And there's Carolina, my faithful housekeeper who now is Zelda's companion caring for her when I have to work. Carolina and Zelda are great together.

I'm looking forward to taking Mom on road trips exploring California. But Ziggy, my little Volkswagen isn't comfortable and so underpowered I never use freeways. I mention this to Brad, he's a car nut and surprisingly he is interested in buying Ziggy. He comes over and takes it for a test drive.

And the next time I see Ziggy it's impounded and a total wreck. Brad is continuously distracted by his cell phone and he rear ends a truck on his test drive and that was that.

Fortunately I have great insurance and get more than Brad would have paid for Ziggy. So now I've decided to tap into a no interest home equity loan, add the insurance money and get the car I've dreamed about, a Mercedes convertible, a present to me for surviving, it's a great set of wheels to chauffer Zelda and a necessary front as a Realtor. I wish my dad could see this.

One of our first excursions is to Santa Monica.

The Heartbreak of Static Cling

Along the Ocean Avenue promenade is a place called "Inspiration Point," offering breathtaking views of the beach below and the endless Pacific.

Zelda is awestruck. I watch her expression brighten. "Robert, this is different."

"What's different?"

"It's so different from the Atlantic, that has always made me sad. Do you know what Pacific means, Robert? It means peace."

I understand this well. As a young girl she and her family escaped Poland and traveled across the Atlantic by freighter to America. When they landed, my grandmother found out her entire family was wiped out by the Nazis and had a nervous breakdown. Zelda, the oldest of five siblings, had to become their mother figure. No wonder the Atlantic always made her sad.

Finally the moving van with all her "stuff" is here. Carolina will take care of her and keep her away so I can unpack and prepare her new home down to the last detail. This is not easy, but it's a great joy setting her up in comfortable familiarity with added luxury all her own. I know I'll be spending more time here with her than at my place and that's fine with me.

I steal Carolina to help put the finishing touches on Zelda's new home. Three days hard work is complete and now the reveal. I document every blessed minute with my camera as Zelda discovers what has been created for her. It's one of the most fulfilling moments of my life. The joy the incredulity and genuine happiness is hers, it's the new beginning I promised.

I'm with her continuously for the next few weeks insuring she's settled in and fully acquainted with her new surroundings. This gives me a chance to make all the calls needed to enroll her with new health insurance and connect her with a team of doctors associated with Cedars Sinai. A major change from the horrible healthcare she had in Florida.

Scheduled maintenance: I plan appointments with doctors, dentist, specialists and whatever is needed. These appointments become our outings and are actually fun. Her doctors are wonderful and she enjoys their care, a level of care she never had.

Fortunately now she's in great shape and ready for good times.

Dr. Dale is her primary doctor and a good friend of Connie and Holly. Zelda tells him how much she loves to gamble and he invites us to his house in Palm Springs not far from a casino. Zelda is astounded and thrilled beyond words.

Stephanie is a good friend of Dr. Dale and she drives us to Palm Springs. This is a long road trip for my mom, I'm apprehensive but Dr. Dale assures me she will be fine.

I'm relieved Zelda enjoyed the trip without a problem. Stephanie is wonderful with her. And here we are at Dr. Dale's. The house is a mid-century sensation and Dale has given Zelda the master suite overlooking a spectacular pool, towering palm trees and mountains in the distance. How incredible, Zelda's in paradise with her doctor friend here for her.

A short rest, an early dinner and it's Zelda at the slots!

Zelda plays penny slots and wins almost every time! Dale gives her a hundred bucks worth of chips and won't let her give it back. Now Zelda ups her game. I'm glad Dr. Dale is close by, she's hyperventilating. He calms her by asking her to rub his forehead for luck. She's laughing her head off rubbing his head and drops a ten dollar chip in the slot, pulls the lever and *BANG ZOOM* bells are ringing five hundred bucks! Zelda pees her pants. Thoughtful Stephanie brought Depends and escorts her to the bathroom.

Zelda returns ready for more but luck has taken a turn, and before she loses all the winnings, Zelda knows how to quit while she's ahead. No casino will get the better of this dame.

What a night! Singing and laughing in the car back to the house. I jump into the pool fully dressed for added amusement. I promised we'd have fun!

Zelda's California adventures have just begun big time.

JUST ONE DRUNKEN NIGHT

CONNIE CALLS, sounds upset, he tells me needs me to meet him for a drink... "Now."

I get myself together and walk fast to the Silver Spoon, a former hangout of Shelly Winters and her gang.

Something's wrong, really wrong. Connie doesn't get rattled easily. I spot him downing a glass of wine with a dismal expression. I catch the waitress and order two more glasses and take a seat. "What's up?"

He doesn't answer.

"What's going on, Connie? What's wrong?"

Tears well and he puts his drink down. "I got it, I'm positive, just got the test results."

I hold back stuffing a gamut of outrage. How the fuck could he let this happen? He fucking knows better goddamn it! But I know all it just takes one drunken night.

I finally respond, "You're lucky, very lucky Connie. Now you can take some pills and be okay, it's a whole different world. You are so very lucky, I would have killed for these pills for Don."

That slap in the face sobers him. "No use beating yourself up. Just take care of yourself, take the pills and get on with your life." I motion to the waitress for another round.

And Connie fills me in on more news. "Brad's got it too."

"How do you know?"

"I told him my results and he confessed."

"You didn't?"

"No, not with Brad, it was some trick; I was blitzed out of my head."

"What else is new Connie, you got to cool it."

"Yeah, I know."

We finish our drinks, hug and part company. Walking home I try to squelch the pain brought up by this. Brad, Connie and so many more will escape the horror of it all with just a few pills.

A few pills, damn it!

I decide not to contact Brad. I know he'll tell me when he's ready. The few people close to me are all killing themselves. Holly is drinking herself to death, that's nothing new; Connie is now beginning to realize the consequences of his craziness; Brad isn't dealing well with his demons, and he's also on self destruct. I get it, it's taking all my might to keep from offing myself as well. It's not easy.

I just listen to my own advice and get on with my life. I got a mother to take care of. And tomorrow's Halloween.

Drag queens, cops and an obnoxious dyke: Zelda's first West Hollywood Halloween. We find a seat on the steps of a closed shop on Santa Monica Blvd. Zelda is thrilled by the parade of proud queens and all the fanfare, she loves every minute of it.

Suddenly an aggressive dyke approaches Zelda with a video camera. "I'm doing a documentary, can I interview you?"

Zelda takes this as a compliment and agrees.

The dyke gets near for a close up and asks, "What's your name?"

"Zelda Starr."

"So, Zelda Starr, tell me what it's like to have an orgasm."

"Hey, this is my mother!" The dyke ignores me and repeats her ridiculous question.

Zelda hesitates and then replies, "Orgasms are wonderful, but you must be careful. Girls get AIDS, too, and they can spread it." The dyke looks like her head just got slammed into a brick wall.

I'm doubled over laughing at her reaction. "That's my mom, Zelda Starr!"

We decide to take a walk and for some reason Zelda is a magnet for drag queens. They adore her and pose for pictures with her and she loves them of course. "They're so glamorous."

"Right, Ma."

We cross La Cienega and encounter leather queens in jock straps and chaps, and Zelda is in heaven thinking she's in Vegas at Chippendale's. They hug and kiss her, causing a commotion that catches the attention of West Hollywood cops who think she needs some help, but when she asks them if those leather guys are the Village People they crack up and a gorgeous cop actually lifts her onto his motorcycle and that becomes Zelda's first West Hollywood photo shoot.

Enough excitement for the day and I take mom home, Carolina is waiting for us with dinner waiting and I've arranged for her to stay overnight with Zelda. I have plans.

BJ, Frank's wife, called a week ago to ask if I know any drag queens who would like to make some money. Her friend is having a Halloween party and all guests are to be dressed as the opposite sex. The host will pay two hundred each for drag queens to attend. Do I know drag queens that would go to a party for two hundred bucks? What a question, immediately I call Holly, Connie and Todd. None of them are drag queens, but they are very inventive women when they want to be, especially when money is involved. Of course they all agree to get in drag and go to the party, a limo is included! It strikes me, why not, why not me too?

Holly Woodlawn, Warhol Superstar is on the high wire with no net and no panties. Connie is the bald bad beauty, the celebrated severe host at the infamous, Bar Marmont. And Todd is in the mood as hilarious Zsa Zsa Gabor glamour in a gay gown with a thick Long Island accent.

And who am I? In less than a minute lightning strikes and I'm Rosalie, Rosalie Cuntadina the tomato paste heiress from Bayonne, New Jersey! Rosalie Cuntadina, that low down cheap slut with big tits and big hair teased to an inch of its life and Rosalie Cuntadina is equipped with a can of tomato paste in her purse to prove her lineage if there are any doubts.

I'm at Holly's for my transformation. I get a black leatherette mini skirt from Connie, Holly loans me her cheapest plunge neck blouse and extra large falsies stuffed in a bra and a load of tawdry cheap jewels. Todd supplies ripped fishnets, but shoes are a problem... Fuck it, I'll wear my cowboy boots, they have heels! Connie creates my makeup somewhere between Joan Crawford

The Heartbreak of Static Cling

as Mommy Dearest and Baby Jane Hudson, perfect. Now that big ratty fried blonde wig gets a workout and voila! A vision to behold. What a joy, what a relief what an escape from me! Let's party, we're ready and the limo is here!

It's a tony Brentwood bash and when we arrive we turn up the "tone." BJ is a handsome man in a mustache and motorcycle jacket. Frank is what, Laurence of Arabia? I guess some men don't have the balls to be a woman.

Rosalie Cuntadina makes her entrance to their shock and terror. As I pluck my tomato paste can from my pocketbook, I'm concerned my hair isn't big enough, but BJ says it's fine.

Us girls do the Frug, the Mashed Potatoes, The Jerk, and The Watusi! Frank is mesmerized by Zsa Zsa Todd; I think he's in love!

I refuse my greenbacks feeling I should pay them for the liberation. I've never dressed in drag, and now I know what I've missed. It's one thing being an advertising exec, a pencil pusher, a car salesman and a realtor; it's entirely something else being Rosalie Cuntadina, the tomato paste heiress from Bayonne, and that's exactly what I needed.

The party winds down and we're just winding up, we've powdered our noses with the magic powder in the powder room and now for the after party! We decide to go to my old haunt, The Polo Lounge at The Beverly

Hills Hotel, why not we got a limo?!

Four dazzling demented drag queens arrive in style and we're treated like royalty! We're given the best booth in the place, the piano man is in heaven at the sight of us and Martinis keep coming from admirers.

I wish I could have foreseen this vision years ago when I actually lived at this hotel while shooting commercials in another life.

FAST LANE DETOUR

I'M SITTING in my dentist's waiting room about to get a tooth pulled thumbing through magazines. Turning the pages of MotorWorld magazine I find an invitation to compete in a writing contest. It's a call for entries for articles about your car experiences. Winning entries will be published and will attend the Indy 500 races and write a review of the new Jaguar X-Type. I rip the page out of the magazine and pocket it.

Now at home without a left molar and I revisit the call for entries and decide to enter, another why not?

What comes to mind is the one thing that brought me and my father close, his 1954 Kaiser Manhattan. The ache in my jaw is actually helpful recalling 1 the pain of my relationship with my dad as a kid.

And just when I finish the final draft, Brad calls. He's in dire straits asking if he could move into my guest room for awhile, he offers to pay rent. I tell him I'll call him back.

This isn't an easy decision, Brad's been strung out on drugs and his career is on the skids. It's another roller coaster ride of great success and an inevitable plummet blowing it all. I care for him greatly, I understand the depths of his problems and reoccurring self sabotage. Could I help? Could I give him safe harbor without this bringing me down the rabbit hole as well?

After weighing it all I decide to give it a chance, there's too much good about Brad to ignore his plea for help. I'm strong enough now to give it a shot.

I make room on the shelves and closets in the guest room. My place is big enough and he'll have his own bathroom and privacy. We'll see.

Brad moving in is a bit of a shock, cartons and cartons of collector books and wardrobes of binge bought designer clothing and Max the wonder dog, a Brussels Griffon.

This doesn't seem like a temporary move and it's alarming but I've made the commitment, let him settle in and I'll settle in as well. Somewhere inside I wish this was more than what it is but I know that will never happen.

Just as I suspected I'm spending more time at

Mom's than my own place. I take Max when Brad is working and Zelda will have an adorable puppy visit her often.

This seems to be working; Brad is getting back to a healthier routine back to work. Good to see this change. And for now we're not getting in each other's way.

A letter arrives announcing a big surprise I'm going to the races the Indy 500! The article about my dad's Kaiser will be published and I'll get to test drive Jaguars on that famous racetrack. Life takes an unexpected detour to the fast lane.

I make arrangements for Carolina to care for Mom while I'm gone. Gentlemen, start your engines!

Turns out I'm one of five winners. Each assigned a category, mine is design. That's what I'm to cover in my review of the X-Type. Others will write about things like engineering, performance, power and marketing. Good. Jaguar is all about design. This X-Type is a baby Jag sedan, kind of retro and that's what I like about it, I can't wait to get acquainted.

I'm on the plane to Indianapolis fantasizing about racecar drivers.

A chauffeured big new Jaguar picks me up at the airport and whisks me off to a pretty good hotel. I find my itinerary in a welcome package including a frosty bottle of Champaign. I immediately pop the cork and here we go again.

Nothing's on the agenda for the first night so I decide to explore the hotel and find the bar where I

Fast Lane Detour 368

discover my competition. There's a Yale business major, a computer nerd, a race car driver wannabe and a gal whose dad is a master mechanic and so is she. It's an interesting group, very congenial except for the hyper competitive numbers guy from Yale. We toast to our upcoming adventure and I turn in early. Tomorrow morning we get to meet the Chief Editor of the magazine and his entourage and the Jaguar people at the track.

It's 9 AM and I'm in front of the hotel, there's a lineup of Jaguars, red, white, blue, silver and of course, British racing green, with drivers ready to chauffer each of us individually, how thoughtful. I make a dash for the green one.

And here we are at the famous Indy 500 racetrack to meet our hosts, Ed, the chief editor of his magazine introduces us to his staff and the Jaguar people. And we're also introduced to the subject of this event, the new Jaguar X-Type.

There are five models each with different levels of trim, engine power, and both automatic and manual transmission models. We will each get to test drive all of them on the track. There will be a race car driver in the passenger seat just in case. Ed encourages us to take the cars to the limit.

I'm terrified, a stick shift?! The last time I drove one I almost went off a cliff in the French Rivera driving a car the size of a suitcase. I never got good with a manual transmission, how embarrassing will this be?

This test drive is choreographed like clockwork, each of us get a car and take it around the track and get out and get into another car rotating every different model for us to test drive. My heart is pounding, would I dare opt out of driving the manual? That would be unthinkable but even more embarrassing would be trying to get that thing in gear! I decide to just shut up and take my chances.

First round and thank God it's an automatic. I floor the thing noticing this doesn't feel like a Jaguar, this baby Jag is a bit underpowered and I'm appalled by the interior, it's definitely not Jaguar quality.

Now I'm empowered showing them I can handle the track at top speed but my heart is sinking as the next Jag for me pulls up and it's a damn stick shift! Okay... I get in, step down on the clutch and the brake, put it in first and rest my foot on the gas and release the clutch... *clunk clunk clunck* and it stalls! I try again and the same damn thing! My copilot racecar driver is laughing his head off. He finally calms down and coaches me and finally I get the fucking car in gear. And when I get up to top gear I floor the damned thing, so there!

So glad that's over, Ed's gang is amused but nice, the Jaguar people just grin at me. Okay, what's next? They lead me to a steel blue X-Type for my close up examination.

This X-Type is a retro design referring back to a great car, the Jaguar MK2 of the mid sixties. It was a small four door sedan with great panache. A real beauty, compact and sophisticated and the interior that was magnificent, fine leather, thick wool carpeting and burled wood all over the place including the inside of the window sills, real Jaguar luxury.

From afar this X-Type kind of resembles its predecessor, but up close it's a totally different story, shocking fit and finish, but this could be overlooked as this Jag is priced at the low end of the spectrum. But open the door and that interior is a complete let down, nothing about it is in the vocabulary of Jaguar it's more like a Ford, Jaguar's new owner. There goes a legend. I make notes.

I inspect the hood ornament, it's a throwback classic called "The Leaper" a sinuous chrome Jaguar cat in motion. I ask one of the Jaguar crew onlookers if he has a measuring tape. He hands me one and I measure the cat from tail to snout and turn to my hosts, "I'm impressed; this Jag has a ten inch pussy!" They needed a laugh.

So ends our first day, we get back to the hotel for a drink and a rest, later tonight we'll be taken to dinner like a congenial team. The gal mechanic and I bonded, the rest keep their distance especially the numbers guy who has his competitive fangs out pulling Ed the editor into his web whispering to connive a victory. You see there's another prize to capture. Beyond our articles published, the author of the piece considered the best review will win the use of a new X-Type for a year. I could care less, I'm not a fan of this car, and it's not like winning the damn thing so you can turn around and sell it, so let Mr. Yale do his thing, I'm here to have fun. But I need to decide how real to be with my review of this Ford in Jaguar's clothing.

The Heartbreak of Static Cling

At seven sharp the Jag limos are in front again ready to take us to dinner with Ed and the MotorWorld team.

The restaurant is an upscale steakhouse perfectly manly for car nuts. Since my stick shift debacle and my ten inch pussy comment I've detected some ill concealed snickering from Ed and his team. I just chalk it up to macho stupidity, let them be amused, especially Ed who's sitting next to me.

The menu is steak and more steak so I decide to order the steak. And when it's served, I'm startled at my plate.

How Ed the Editor managed to pull this off this juvenile prank is anyone's guess. There in front of me on my plate is a sizzling steak in the shape of a dick and balls! I decide not to indicate any reaction instead I consider every possibility, from absolutely ignoring it to something better than that. Finally expressionless I take my steak knife in hand and cut off the head of the dick, fork it and chew it with a broad smile and hold up my wine glass as if I'm making a toast. I then get up excuse myself and visit the restroom to plot my next move. No one makes a sound.

I return to my seat and I cut off the left ball and politely place it on Ed's plate. "It's really a good piece of meat, have a taste." Oh, look, he's blushing!

Today's the day we visit the pits where the Jaguar racing team is prepping their cars for the big race. This pit crew is capable of getting the Jag's back on the track in seconds no matter what. They're just as fast as the cars they service, this is vital to win a race. Engines explode to life screaming and fine tuned. From this vantage point I can see the Ferrari, Maserati and Lamborghini teams preparing their ferocious machines.

Start time approaches and we're taken to our prime seats and given earplugs. The stadium is jam-packed and the excitement is ramping up.

Thirty three snarling growling beasts emerge from their lairs and take their positions ready to explode to over two hundred miles per hour in seconds. Cool headed pilots sit in their low to the ground open cockpit seats just large enough for their bodies. They rev their engines to ear splitting decibels declaring their territory like snarling beasts ready to attack.

My chest is vibrating; I decide to remove the earplugs to get the full impact and blast off! Crackling howling screaming high pitched ear splitting screeching engines clenches my teeth. Adrenalin pumping, endorphin surging cool as ice drivers calculate life or death maneuvers every second fearlessly on this crowded track just inches from each other. Speed freaks now at 170 MPH and still accelerating so fast they become a slow motion time warp blur at hairpin turns and straightaway's louder and louder, crazy loud. Heart stopping disasters are narrowly avoided with precision, unlike rush hour on the 405.

I'm hyperventilating leaping from my seat blindly speed dialing my cell phone trying to share this sound, it's impossible to know if anyone picks up. The whole stadium is on their feet yelling seemingly on mute overpowered by the mega decibels of power careening to record speeds in front of us. It's surreal my ears are ringing chest vibrating and my brain is scrambling, this is better than any ride in Coney Island, even reaching Mach 2 on the Concord doesn't compare. The speed keeps building, The Jags and Lambos are inches from each other and Masarati is fractions behind as they blast past one another. Flags fly, a winner is declared by an inch and it's hard to breathe.

Now that's a day at the races!

I have no idea who won and it doesn't seem to matter.

And to think, it was just yesterday I was driving—well, stalling—a Jaguar on this very track. I'm so glad I got that molar removed.

Exhausted elated and deafened it's back to the hotel bar and dinner in bed.

Our last day together and we're taken back to the track. This time we're greeted by Ed and his magazine team. They're standing behind a long table covered by a sheet concealing something.

Ed makes a speech thanking us for our efforts and lifts the sheet revealing custom trophies for each of us with our names engraved and topped with a scale model of the Jaguar X-Type. Big applauds as Ed presents the trophies and reminds us to get our articles into his office by next Friday.

Champaign pops for our final toast at the track of the Indy 500.

This was a great escape even though any hopes of

becoming an editor at MotorWorld and traveling the planet from one Grand Prix to another will never happen.

Let them eat steak.

SEEING RED

CAROLINA is upset, very upset. She pulls me over and away from Zelda and tells me she was at my place earlier today to do a light cleaning, Brad wasn't home. As she reached the top of a tall cabinet to dust and she was stabbed by a hidden used syringe in Brad's room. My stomach flips, that son of a bitch! Immediately I make a few calls and set up an HIV test for her. Goddamn it.

I do my best to calm Carolina and myself. I thought this shit was over, well think again. Brad is a master of deception but I won't stand for it one more minute. Not only is he late with his rent, he's using again and now he's put Carolina in jeopardy. Get ready Brad, I'm nobody's fool.

I get home and I find him sitting on his bed speeding his head off working his laptop. "Do you have any idea what you did to Carolina?"

"What?"

"Motherfucker, she got stuck by your fucking works! Proud of yourself? And where's your rent?"

He slyly answers, "I'll pay you when I feel like it."

I plant myself on his bed and let him have it, "Get the fuck out of here, this is my room, this is my place, you get the fuck out now!"

He springs out of bed and grabs my arm trying to pull me up and out of the room. His goddamned nails claw my arm, I'm bleeding, and I see *red*. I jump to my feet and plow my fist in his face knocking him back almost off his feet. "I'm calling the cops, get your shit together and get the fuck out!" He just stands there dumbfounded and I dial 911.

Cops arrive, I give them the lowdown, and they cuff me and walk me out to the hallway! What the fuck? I tell them I own this place, he's a junky refusing to pay rent, and he attacked me. I'm furious and bleeding. One cop remains with me, the others go back to Brad. I hear him scream, "He's a drunk!" The cops make Brad pack a bag, take his dog, and escort him out of the building.

A cop takes my cuffs off and I'm back in my place vibrating with rage. It takes a lot to get me to explode and when I do, watch out. I went right for his jaw with all my might. Just don't fuck with me, I can be dangerous.

I go to my room and collapse on my bed. How sad, how infuriatingly sad.

The last time uncontrollable rage took hold of me I was twelve in a playground. Carl, a dirty little creep classmate attacked me from behind wrapping his filthy hands around my face and digging his nasty fingernails in my face. Blood dripped down my cheeks. I saw red for the first time in my life and I turned and grabbed him by his ears and slammed his head full force into a brick wall.

My capability of unleashing uncontrollable violence is shocking. I promise myself never to allow this again. I can't live with it and I'm so sorry. I drift off trying to forget the whole thing.

The phone rings me awake, it's Connie. "Is it true?"

"Is what true? I can hardly hear you, where are you?"

"I'm at drag queen bingo in the East Village, wait I'll go outside to talk... Brad called me he said, 'Starr punched me in the face!'"

"I sure did, and called the cops and threw him out."

"What happened?"

"Long story, did he tell you where he is?"

"Le Parc Hotel."

"Thanks, I'll call you later. "

I guess he needed a shoulder to cry on. Of course, he wouldn't tell Connie the whole story.

I think about it and finally decide to call his new

hotel. "Brad, you really know how to push my buttons, and this time you went too far. I lost control, couldn't help it, I'm sorry. Get some sleep, come back tomorrow, we'll talk it over."

"Okay."

I thought it was daybreak, but actually it's 2 PM when Carolina calls. The test results just came back and she's negative, thank God that horror is over.

Shortly after Carolina's call, guess who's knocking on my door? There he is, holding adorable Max in his arms, a suitcase by his side.

Brad's sorry and so am I and we decide he'll stay here until he finds his own place, best for our friendship, best for the both of us.

It doesn't take Brad long, just two weeks pass and he finds a place of his own, and it's pretty terrific, a top floor two bedroom in a vintage Spanish duplex with an enormous garden, not far from my place. The rent is steep but Brad's again on a roll with real estate deals. He's really good at it even through all his craziness.

I knew being a realtor wasn't for me but there have been moments of fulfillment connecting clients with their dream homes. I have run into some interesting crackpots, some of them believing their home is worth twice the market price because they themselves selected the wallpaper.

And there's the business set up, selling cars you get a small salary plus commission and healthcare. A realtor gets nothing but mandatory Real Estate Association dues and more fees for Errors and Omission insurance, and weekly pep rally sales meetings prompting you to knock on doors of strangers, send endless postcards and sit other agents open houses.

The commission split varies with the agency you're with. So I jump from Coldwell Banker to Rodeo Realty to a small boutique agency and then to Teles Properties. Each move increases my commission if and when I finally make a deal. Turns out I'm paying more than I'm earning just for the privilege of calling myself a realtor.

There are big earners whose passion for this business started early, like Brad. They hold tight to their connections, and their competitiveness and I'm just not one of them, never will be.

I know enough is enough and eventually I cut my losses and chalk it up to experience, a good try. What's next? Maybe I'll try twirling signs on street corners. Who the fuck knows?

There's a reason for everything—happenstance. The secret is to allow things to happen. The reason exposes itself eventually. Good to remember when you're lost.

HOLLY'S FIREWORKS

MY TIME with Holly is priceless, we have the comfort of knowing each other's past. Holly's unique perspective on life is insanely awe inspiring. I guess that comes from her absolute resolve to be herself against all odds and at any cost, a very difficult accomplishment she perfected long ago. I don't know another soul who could survive Holly's lifestyle and thrive with a vengeance as she does effortlessly.

During the depths of grief and difficulties finding myself again Holly has been here for me. We spend hours just the two of us on her tiny terrace drinking "fish piss" and she never fails to inspire me. Especially as she chain smokes, lights firecrackers, and throws them off the terrace in the path of dykes walking by her abode. Oh Holly, only you!

"You're not a fucking salesman, you're an artist. Flush the goddamned toilet, artist!" Holly's words of wisdom, what would I do without her?

Holly got rid of Lurch in similar fashion to what happened between me and Brad. "He deserved it, that should teach him a lesson."

Now that she has the apartment to herself and has come into a windfall from the sale of the movie rights to her book 'A Low life in High Heels,' Holly is on a decorating binge. She shows me pictures of her purchases; leave it to Holly to find a catalogue filled with Cleopatra's fantasy furnishings to choose from. Any day now she's expecting delivery of the ink blue velvet Chez Lounge framed in gold Egyptian icons. She plans to have Nubians carry her onstage lounging on it for her next nightclub appearance, whenever and wherever that may be. Great idea, Holly can't walk now, something about her back and other undiagnosed problems she ignores.

To complete the look she's ordered two King Tut gilded to the max arm chairs. No IKEA for this Puerto Rican diva of many disasters! I'm thrilled for her. Long ago I lectured her about the importance of keeping a roof over her head, it's finally sunk in.

Her birthday is coming up and she's having a soirée and wants Zelda to attend. The two of them have become an item.

This is the third time he's called in five minutes, this time I can't ignore it. "Okay, Brad what's up?"

"I'm dying."

"What?"

"I'm dying, come over."

"Shit, Brad, okay." I hang up. "Holly I got to go, he sounds awful."

"Crack a bottle over his head."

"That might work, I'll call you later." What the fuck is with him?

I'm banging on his door and there's no response. I hear moaning, the door is unlocked and I find him sprawled on the sofa dripping in sweat and not breathing right.

"Fuck! Did you do drugs?"

He shakes his head no.

I know what this is, I've seen it before. "I got to get you to the hospital. You have insurance?"

Again, "No."

Shit!

I call Carolina. "Tell Zelda I need you to help me with some work and drive over to Brad's now." I have a plan, but I can't call an ambulance. There's no guarantee they'll take him to Cedars, he's got to be admitted to Cedars and with no insurance ambulance charges are ridiculous. Ten minutes pass and Carolina arrives.

"Brad I need your wallet and your keys, where are they?" He points to the console table I grab his things and get one of his jackets. He's shivering and I stuff him into it. "Carolina, open your back door." I lift him off the sofa and drag him to the car and lay him down on the back seat and we speed off to Cedar's.

"Brad, don't say a word to anybody, I'll do the talking. Do not try to get out of the car, let them take you out of the car and carry you inside. Carolina, stay right here, don't move the car."

I run into the emergency room like a maniac in full panic. "He's not breathing! Help, he's not breathing!" This is the only way to get him admitted quick. No way is he going to sit in a crowded emergency room for hours.

My performance works and three doctors rush to the car with oxygen and a stretcher and they carry him into the hospital. They try to ask Brad endless questions, he doesn't respond, good boy. "He's HIV Positive, he can't breathe, he's in and out of consciousness, admit him and I'll give you all his info." And they transport him to a room upstairs.

I run back to Carolina. "Go to Zelda, tell her I'm in the middle of a business deal and I'll see her later tonight."

"I'll cook dinner and stay with her until you come back."

"I love you."

She takes off.

I go up to his room, he's not there. A nurse tells me they've taken him for a series of tests. I just wait and catch my breath. Hours pass and finally he's wheeled into the room now connected to several IV drips. He's out of it but breathing easier with an oxygen mask. Two doctors arrive. I was right, it's Pneumocystis Pneumonia. That sonofabitch wasn't taking his damn meds. Recovering won't be easy, back when, recovery wouldn't be possible—a lot has been learned since.

There's nothing more I can do, he's barely conscious. I decide to leave and return in the morning.

I arrive early and I make arrangements to see a social worker. When I get to his room he's sleeping, there's little change he's still not breathing normally but better than yesterday. Brad senses I'm here sitting beside him, he awakens and actually manages a smile.

"A social worker will be here soon, don't say a word. This is critical, let me deal with this, it's a matter of you either getting thrown out of Cedars, charged a fortune, or getting off the hook. So just make like you're unconscious, you hear me?" He nods yes.

Finally an hour later she appears, I explain the situation, and ask for a financial hardship application. She tells me a letter should accompany the forms which will be presented to the Board of Directors for their decision. She disappears to get the correct forms to fill out and I begin writing in first person as if Brad could dictate a letter.

I carefully lay out how AIDS has destroyed his successful career to such an extent he became unable to pay his rent and was evicted from his apartment and had to sleep on a friend's couch. As a realtor you're considered an independent contractor, therefore you have to pay for your own healthcare insurance and that also became impossible.

"And now suddenly diagnosed with AIDS related pneumonia I'm completely debilitated, and at the mercy of Cedars Sinai for financial consideration."

I continue the letter attempting to be even more compelling, we'll see. I read it to Brad and have him sign it.

The social worker returns and hands me the official financial hardship application. I hand her the letter, she reads it and seems impressed. That gives me some hope.

"When can we expect a decision?"

"I can't say for sure they have a lot to attend to."

Doctors appear and tell me he'll get through this, it'll take a few weeks on heavy meds in the hospital. "Good thing you got him here when you did." They check his IV connections and vitals and leave.

"Brad, when this is all over never ever again skip any of your meds!"

He rolls his eyes and nods.

"I got to go back to Zelda, I'll see you later. You don't need company now, just rest. And by the way, the food here is good. I'll see you tomorrow."

I feel a tremendous sense of relief. That was a close call, too close. Now go take Mom for a walk, lunch at an outdoor café and later make dinner, watch TV and put her to bed. Then go home and put yourself to bed.

Day three he's visibly better, his color's returned and he's sitting up, good. And surprise, in comes the social worker.

"News?"

"Yes, they've approved it."

"What does that mean?"

"The decision is to forgive all costs."

"All costs?"

"All costs."

It's hard to believe and even harder to contain myself, I manage restraint and thank her several times before she leaves. I close the door and sit on his bed. "Brad, we did it!"

He's confused.

"They're not charging you anything!"

This sinks in and he's overwhelmed, he grabs my hand, a rare showing of gratitude.

Back with Holly I fill her in on all the drama as she lounges on her blue velvet Egyptian chaise with a bottle of fish piss at her side, though she's out of firecrackers.

"You didn't listen to me."

"I'm saving that if he doesn't take his meds," she gestures to one of the empty gallon wine bottles at her side, "take this, keep it for the occasion, and mention my name when you crack it over his head."

"I'll send him your love."

"You missed my party."

"Sorry, I was busy saving a life."

"Zelda is a star!"

"Zelda is Zelda Starr."

"She was filmed by Craig Highburger, he's making a documentary and she was brilliant! We'll have

The Heartbreak of Static Cling

a screening as soon as Craig gets it edited. And Carolina is an angel, at Zelda's side every minute."

"She sure is, I couldn't do this alone."

"What about your sister?"

"What about her?"

"Forget it, you're doing fine, Zelda's having a ball."

I check the time. "I got to get back home, Connie's coming over to give Zelda a makeover and get her ready, Debbi Mazar invited us to the set of 'Dancing with the Stars' tonight."

"Give that dollpuss a big kiss for me and tell her 'break a leg.'"

"Perfect, Holly!"

Connie is working his magic, Zelda's getting the full treatment, makeup and hair taking years away transforming her and reminding her of her heyday.

And here she is in a great outfit wrapped in a faux leopard coat ready for her night out with Debbi Mazar at Dancing with the Stars.

On our way we pick up red roses for Debbi and when we arrive at the CBS studios on Fairfax we're escorted to the set. Debbi arranged great seats for us and the show begins, all glitter mirror balls and fabulous dance numbers, Debbi is great!

It's hilarious watching Zelda trying to shoo the cameras away from blocking her view, I tell her their doing their job so the poor people at home can see this, Zelda can't stop laughing, she's so lifted by it all, I almost expect her to get up and do the Mambo!

A big finale and Debbi comes in second. As soon as the show ends, Debbi runs over to us, Zelda stands and holds the roses up high. Debbi yells "Zelda, Zelda!" and they hug. Debbi Mazar is truly beautiful making this night a miracle for my Zelda.

SLOW MOTION

IT'S HARD to believe Zelda's apartment three year lease is coming up for renewal. Time has come for her to move in with me, although subtle her Alzheimer's has progressed. I gently convince her it will be better for both of us for her to move to my place and finally she gives in and agrees.

The process begins, paring down unnecessary things and most importantly keeping whatever is truly precious to her. I know how to make this happen smoothly without her needing to see all the work involved.

    This will be her last move and it's difficult for me emotionally but she won't see that, I just cover my thoughts of inevitable heartache with a façade of excitement and happiness; this is what I have to do.

    I've furnished her room with everything loved and familiar to her. She's here with me now and settling in.

    Her routine doctor appointments continue and what's best are often visits from her West Hollywood fans and Carolina continues to fill in giving me a break and a chance to try to work. Mary Kay also brightens Zelda's days taking her on shopping sprees.

    I've done my homework and we begin low impact workouts prescribed by physical therapists. We dance the Mambo keeping her young and continue our daily walks to Kings Road Park. We have great lunches at nearby cafes and for dinner, incredibly I've become a good cook adhering to all the constraints of her diabetes. I read books to her and play word games, everything contrived to combat the oncoming dullness.

    It's now nearly a year since she's moved in with me and we host a dinner party to celebrate Zelda's 94th birthday. Holly, Todd, Brad, Connie and Mary Kay are here and it's a wonderful loving affair.

    This time living with my mom is so valuable, I'm so fortunate to be able to make her life here enjoyable filled with California wonders she never had and so many new loving friends.

    And before we know it more months pass. One

evening I decide we should try to play cards after dinner. I deal the cards and play both hands trying to teach her the game. It doesn't matter she can't quite get it she's enjoying the challenge and we play a few more hands until it's finally time to go to bed.

I think by now she can find her way to her room. She gets up and I watch her slowly walk to the open terrace doors. I call out, "Where are you going?" She stops, turns around to face me and in slow motion she crumbles and falls to the floor screaming painfully. My heart stops, I can't believe this is happening. I don't dare to move her it could make things worse and I call 911.

Paramedics arrive give her pain meds and carefully place her on a stretcher, they tell me possibly she's broken her hip. I sit next to her in the ambulance trying to calm her and myself but I know, this is the beginning of the end.

She's seen immediately by a surgeon, x-rays confirms she needs hip replacement surgery immediately. They explain she will need to be hospitalized for a couple of weeks and then transported to a rehabilitation facility for even longer and they suggest a place in Santa Monica.

All this is heart-crushing. Everything is changed, now my mission is to investigate all options to make this as easy and comfortable as possible get her the best care there is and be with her through it all.

I sit with her in recovery. Eventually she awakens and I take her hand and manage a big smile, I hold back tears and kiss her cheek. "Robert, I'm okay, go home."

And she returns to a peaceful sleep.

The doctor arrives at her bedside and he tells me she'll be out for the night and I should come back tomorrow afternoon.

In the cab on my way home and plan to get up tomorrow early to drive to Santa Monica and check out that rehab facility they recommended. I'll make a quick decision and get back to the hospital by noon.

I'm expecting the worst, a rehab nursing home from hell, something I promised my mother long ago she would never have to suffer.

I drive by a ranch house at the corner of Second Street and Washington, in Santa Monica, this can't be it. I continue down the block and there's nothing but private homes, no ghastly institutions. I double back to that corner ranch house. I pull into the driveway still not believing this can be the right address but it is. I'm greeted by a well dressed man, the director of the rehab and he takes me on a tour.

This place is clean bright and homey with plenty of outdoor space. He shows me the well equipped rehab workout area like a boutique gym and also a screening room for daily movies and to top it off he shows me a comfortable sunny private room which would be my mom's if I decide this is the place.

The doctor's at Cedars told me the staff here is exceptionally qualified for the kind of physical rehabilitation and care she needs and her doctor visits here often. Adding all this up in my head I'm also realizing eventually I can take her for outings in a wheelchair two blocks away to Inspiration Point on the promenade overlooking the wide white sand beach and her big blue peaceful Pacific, and that seals the deal. A very welcome miracle—I can't wait to get back and tell her all about our new "beach house."

Back at Cedars I turn the corridor and I can't believe my eyes, Zelda is walking with a walker held up by two male nurses assisting her. She sees me and is even more encouraged to show off her progress. Wow how great is this, no pain, smiling and walking!

The nurses guide her back to her room and help her get back in bed. I give her a big kiss and she's beaming and so am I as I tell her the good news. She's excited to get out of the hospital. And my enthusiasm about the "beach house" makes this move something she's actually looking forward to.

They tell me she'll be ready to leave the hospital in a few days and I call Santa Monica to secure her private room. I stay with her while she has an early dinner and dozes off watching her favorite TV show. I'll be back in the morning.

SMASH HIT AT THE GETTY

I'M BONE TIRED, emotionally exhausted and finally home after another day at the hospital, I get in bed and the phone rings, it's Connie. The Getty is having a major Robert Mapplethorpe exhibit in concert with LACMA and Connie is invited to be a guest speaker at both museum events. The Getty affair is first and it's taking place tonight in their main auditorium where big slides of all the Mapplethorpe photographs of Connie will be projected as background while he describes what it was like being a Mapplethorpe muse. Connie insists I attend.

The Heartbreak of Static Cling

I want to be there but I'm torn, it would really be good to get away from my routine and escape to see Connie perform at the Getty, it will definitely be memorable, but something is telling me not to go. I stubbornly ignore whatever it is that's holding me back.

Connie needs to be there early for sound checks and staging, so I'll have to drive there alone. And here it is again, the "don't go" voice in my head. It's almost like being a kid hearing my mother yelling "Don't go there you can get hurt." And this convinces me to go.

It's nearing seven I get into my car and I'm on my way to the Getty in Malibu, actually enjoying the drive.

I make a right off Wilshire and onto Sepulveda, there's no traffic and I get to a red stoplight. "Getty Drive" is a left turn, the light turns green and I make the turn and out of nowhere, speeding like a bat out of hell without headlights, a Honda slams into my car at full speed.

I saw it coming and I didn't care. The voice in my head warned me not to do this and I went ahead anyway wanting to crash and wanting to be killed. This way it would be considered an accident, not suicide. The voice in my head warned me and I knew it was saying, "Don't do it!"

No, I'll have someone else do it. It'll be better that way.

In slow motion my foot is barely touching the gas, I could have gotten out of the way, but I didn't want to. "Come on, hit me!" And it happened killing my car and not me. Damn it.

This is where my head's at and it's really no good and I know it. I'll take this crash as a hit and run to find whatever it takes to go on from here.

The gal who doesn't believe in headlights or breaks walks over to me to see if I'm alive. I ignore her and just demand her license and call my insurance. The cops won't show up because no one is dead.

The tow truck arrives, I say farewell to my car and I walk to the auditorium where Connie has already begun. I march to the front row shaken and steaming and take a seat.

I'm trying to forget what just happened and enjoy Connie shocking the audience with the lurid details of his relationship with Mapplethorpe. Connie's a big hit, very entertaining. The audience erupts in big applause. But all I hear is that Honda slamming into me.

Now that I've had a big car crash, survived a major earthquake, cast in a film and dumped and failed to reinvent myself again and again, I can be considered a true Angelino.

THE BEACH HOUSE

TWO AND A HALF WEEKS at the beach house rehab and progress is slow but steady. I finally get permission to take her on an outing. It's a spectacular blue sky day and I'm carefully maneuvering Zelda in her wheelchair across a few streets. And we're here taking deep breaths of cool ocean air Zelda is mesmerized by the expanse of the Pacific.

There are so many things I want to tell her, but she knows. I just sit beside her on a bench silently. She squeezes my hand and smiles. That's all that's necessary.

All is good.

She knows I'll be there every day watching her get stronger and this keeps her going. Sometimes when I arrive I see her sitting alone almost in a trance until she recognizes me and comes to life.

Her doctor tells me it won't be long before she can leave this place. This is great and terrible news. She will need more care, the kind of care I can't give her at home. My search for the next move has been very disappointing. I've looked into hiring a full time home care nurse but the cost is impossible. I wish she could stay here at the beach house, but this place is for rehabilitation not long term care.

I'm about to go see another place for her when I get a call from her doctor at the beach house, he tells me her hip has become displaced and she needs another surgery. They're preparing to take her to the hospital. I'm devastated speechless. What the hell?!

I come to my senses and ask every question I can think of. Her doctor answers everything. This happens, damn it. She doesn't know and she's not in pain. I beg them to make it seem routine and tell her she needs an "adjustment"—just don't call it surgery and they agree. She's scheduled to arrive at Cedars in an hour. I get my broken self together and go to the hospital to meet her.

I'm there just as she's about to be wheeled into surgery. She's under sedation but knows I'm here.

Chain-smoking on a bench, I'm praying this setback won't trigger more complications. There will be weeks in the hospital, and more rehabilitation necessary at the beach house. This would be a difficult ordeal for someone much younger, is she strong enough? I just have to believe she is.

She's in recovery semiconscious. Her doctor reports she did well and should be okay. That's what they told me the last time. I stay with her through the night, she seems comfortable and I leave, it's early morning and I need to grab a couple of hours sleep.

When I return she's awake, I tell her how proud of her I am and she brightens. I realize I'm falling apart under this weight but I can't show it.

So the routine starts all over again and slowly she regains her determination to show me her progress, it's impressive.

Rosemary's voice is in my head. "Do something for yourself, Robert." I miss our conversations but our time is over, her help has been enormous. But for the life of me I can't think of a thing to do for myself. Maybe I'll take a hot bath for starters.

Drifting in the tub, I realize there is something I need to do for myself, get a car. I got my insurance settlement, enough to replace my totaled Mercedes with a pre-owned one, and it's nuts to continually Uber it. I search online and find one a few years newer with low mileage. This convertible is silver with the same black leather I love. Connie comes with me to find the dealership in Fullerton, wherever that is.

Finally, the saga of my car wreck is over and I'm in my new car ready to chauffer Zelda to new adventures when she's ready. And now I can try to be a Realtor again, yeah sure.

This will be a longer stay at the beach house. Alzheimer's has taken more of a hold on her, but she's still determined to do her best to get back on her feet. I'm with her every day cheering her on.

It's close to a full month of rehab at the beach house and her time here is coming to an end and I've still haven't found another place for her to move.

On the corner of Willoughby and Crescent Heights is a twenties Spanish style home behind tall hedges and it's within walking distance from my place on Kings Road, a major plus. Could this be it? All the places I've investigated were disgusting nightmares. It's absolutely criminal how the elderly are treated and charged a bloody fortune for the privilege.

But astoundingly I believe I've found the place. It's a comfortable home with just nine in residence, the staff is personal and professional and there's a pleasant backyard garden. Sure it could be a great deal better but I hope this could work and I make arrangements to move her there when she's ready.

I'm holding on by a thread, I thought I was strong enough to handle this, but now I'm not so certain.

MONSTER UNLEASHED

NAGGING dangerous frustration and bitter sorrow grows and I can't shake it. It's impossible to be comforted by past accomplishments when everything feels completely dismal. Nothing I've tried worked and now I'm losing my mother.

There's a painful churning in my soul ready to erupt and all it would take is a trigger, it comes by invitation.

Raleigh Studios Hollywood, where I shot many TV spots in my heyday is where Frank Steifel has his production offices. The legendary studio is turning one hundred and the studio will celebrate its centennial with a major bash. Frank can't make the party and hands me and Todd invites. Could this be my escape, could I become someone else for a night, would this free me?

The glass bubble, that's where they live and thrive on their talent, celebrity glamour, fame, riches, and beauty. They did it, they broke into that that impervious glass bubble. And we watch them like a movie fantasizing about their lives.

My demons rage to a full boil and a terrible imposter is born. Suddenly I'm one of them right here with them inside the glass bubble. Endless martinis fuel the fire at this magnificently glamorous evening's event amidst Hollywood's elite.

He's tall, handsome, sexually confident, and enjoys beautiful men—and occasionally beautiful women who can't keep their hands off him. He's a young, hot new director at Frank Steifel's production company and everyone is aware of this newcomer's enormous talent. Every inch of him oozes success and he's thrilled to occupy the glass bubble.

He loses Todd in the crowd and works the room. They all seem to notice his stature and he enjoys the recognition.

Finally he's free of the weight of the troubled world he's abandoned for the night. He comes across a spectacular fountain in the middle of all the magnificent décor and decides to sit at its edge and enjoy the view sipping another martini.

And like a magnet, she's attracted. Gorgeous young sexy and just as successful as he, she plucks a martini from a waiter and sits beside him. They click glasses and embrace like lovers. That's what happens in the bubble. We're all so desirable.

Like a thirties film they throw their empty martini glasses into the fountain and enjoy a long deep sensual Hollywood kiss. She's a producer, he's a hot new director, how perfect.

This made for the silver screen romance continues with brilliant conversation passionate heated embraces and more martinis.

Alarm bells sound when he realizes they're about to elope and the charade will be over. He springs to his feet and dashes away through the crowd. She's stunned.

He finds Todd, grabs his arm and they run out to the parking lot and jump into Todd's 1965 Lincoln convertible he named, "Holly Lola."

"Who was she?"

"I'll tell you later, let's get out of here."

"Give me the ring you borrowed." I look at my hand, no ring.

"I don't have it."

"You gave it to her."

"No, I didn't."

"Yes, you did, get it from her." Todd spots her at

the valet waiting for her car. "There she is, get my ring, she has it."

"I didn't give it to her, did I?"

"Get my ring."

I get out of the car and run to her. "You got my ring?"

She's puzzled. "You didn't give me a ring, what's with you?"

"I did give it to you, I need it back."

"No, you didn't!" She comes closer to me and I push her away she stumbles and falls backwards to the ground staring at me in disbelief, I freeze. A crowd in horror witnesses this imposter molester.

I bolt back to the car and we speed off. A terrible completely unforgivable disaster and it's about to get much worse.

My phone pierces the fog of my hangover in bed this afternoon. It's Frank in a solemn tone, disguising his rage, informing me he received a call from my victim. Humiliation and disgust envelope me, there's no explanation, no excuse possible. I want to kill myself but realize I already have.

The damage is done, most hurtful is the wreckage of our friendship, I love Frank and there's nothing I can do but manage to say I'm sorry and hang up. I'm reeling with the pain of it all, what the fuck have I done?

My unleashed monster is killed by exposing it to the world. This tragic imposter is destroyed, purged

The Heartbreak of Static Cling

forever lanced like a festering boil. Lesson learned, face it all in the mirror and deal with it, that's the only thing that works.

I roll over in bed pull the covers over my head determined to write Frank a letter, eventually. I have to hold on and hope our friendship might be healed with the passing of time.

A "TEMPORARY" MOVE

ALL THAT CAN be done has been done at the beach house. She can walk with a walker, but more likely it's a wheelchair from now on. It's killing me that I have to move my mother to the house on Crescent Heights but I have no choice.

I tell her this move is part of her rehabilitation and her stay here will be temporary. It would be too dreadful for her to understand this is not true. Again I assure her I'll be there every day. Her faith in me is unwavering.

She's settled into her room, familiar things and flowers are placed at her bedside. I hug and kiss her as she drifts off to sleep. I leave and walk up Crescent Heights, turn the corner and collapse to the sidewalk in a flood of tears.

I've put my trust in these caretakers but every day I make sure they know I'm keeping track of their every move. She seems to be settled in putting on a happy face for me when I visit. I ask her about the people caring for her but it's getting harder for her to remember. She just tells me they're very nice.

We take outings around the neighborhood, I point out different styles of houses, names of trees and flowers and the history of the neighborhood. This is the best time of her day and mine. For now she seems good.

Several weeks pass and I'm spending more time every day with her. She's not eating very much, sometimes refusing to eat at all. They serve meals family style at a large table, maybe that's the problem, I have her meals delivered to her room and I try feeding her, this seems to work somewhat.

Her doctor's checkups reveal nothing more than advancing Alzheimer's. And I begin another search for a facility specializing in Alzheimer's care. I don't know what else to do.

One morning surprise, Mary Kay stops by and wants to come with me to visit Zelda. This is great, Mom loves her. We walk over to Crescent Heights and what we find is devastating.

Zelda's unconscious. How long has she been in

this state?! Why haven't they called me immediately? I'm furious but control my panic. Mary Kay whispers, "She's dying."

"No she's not, I've got to try!" I call an ambulance, they arrive in minutes. I climb aboard say goodbye to Mary Kay and we speed off to Cedars.

She's in intensive care and I'm pacing the halls not allowed to see her. Hours pass and finally a doctor approaches. "She's stable, sedated and on antibiotics, it's an infection, she will pull through."

I enter the ICU she's hooked up to bags of IV fluids sleeping peacefully, I kiss her forehead. The doctor tells me to go home and they'll call if anything changes. She should be much better by morning. On the way home I decide she's not going back to that house on Crescent Heights. I will beg, bribe and do whatever it takes to get her back to the beach house.

Her progress is slow but it is progress. It'll take a week or two before she can be released from the hospital.

After continuous calls I get a meeting with the director at the beach house and he finally allows her return. I'm more than grateful.

With bills piling up I'm forced to do whatever possible to save my home, I realize I need a roommate.

She has a pleasant voice over the phone and I invite her to come over. Marilyn is in her early fifties, she's from Texas, has a son she's very proud of in the Army and a job in Santa Monica at a financial consulting firm. All good things, especially the job assuring me she's responsible with paying rent. Marilyn is attractive, smart, black and well put together.

Marilyn asks, "What are you looking for in a roommate?" I answer, "Respect, respect for my home and privacy, the kind of respect I will have for my roommate." And that sealed the deal.

It's helpful to have a new person in my life with a new perspective; she's sympathetic and kind regarding the situation with my mom. I don't see much of her, she gets up early makes her smoothie and goes to work. I wish someone would invent a quiet blender, but I'm fortunate that's the only complaint.

Finally Zelda is released from Cedars cured of the infection that almost killed her but she's fragile and weak. She's being closely monitored at the beach house. I'm there every day telling her she's beautiful and how much I love her knowing this isn't going to get any better.

Eventually her doctor demands she needs a feeding tube and suggests we begin hospice care. I thought I would be prepared but I'm not.

I'm at her side, she smiles up at me and I begin to sing the song she sang to me as a child. "I love you a bushel and a peck, a bushel and a peck and a hug around the neck." I repeat these lyrics, the only words I remember and amazingly she sings with me, bringing her back to long ago. We sing together until she drifts off.

On the way home I recall another song called Nature Boy, it's the song my mother felt was about me. There's a line in it that has stayed with me, "The greatest thing you'll ever learn is just to love and be loved in return."

Next morning Carolina calls from her car driving to Santa Monica to see Zelda. I tell her I have some errands to do and I'll be there this afternoon. I get myself together and walk to the supermarket and my cell phone rings. The director of the beach house tells me my mother passed away. I can't respond, I'm just holding the phone looking up to the sky. He asks if he should have the funeral people wait for me to come before they take her. I manage to tell him no and hang up. I can't have the image of my mother dead ingrained in my soul. I just need to remember singing with her and all the rest of her throughout my life.

I call Carolina she's not there yet. I tell her and she says she wants be there to say goodbye.

I've been killed by so many tragic deaths. This is different, this was an inevitable natural death not a tragedy. But this is my mother and I never felt this kind of sorrow and this kind of alone. I turn around, walk home and get into bed.

Zelda B. Starr
September 3rd 1919—March 16th 2013

I'm at the far end of the Santa Monica pier searching through binoculars hypnotized by shimmering sunlight on the ocean. it's a spectacular day. And there it is, the ship making its way toward the horizon, I recognize the insignia "Neptune" and its passenger is about to become one with her beloved blue Pacific.

The Heartbreak of Static Cling

"This is different—this is the Pacific. Robert, Pacific means peace."

I find a bench and try to catch my breath. Finally, I walk back through the pier's thrill rides, concessions and souvenir stands, so many familiar sights sounds and smells recalling my earliest memories with my mother as a kid in Coney Island. A childhood never imagining the life I would have.

Wherever I travelled I searched for a unique butterfly pin for Zelda, she loved butterflies. Eventually there are many all shapes and colors and they're here waiting for guests arriving for her memorial at my apartment.

All her California loved ones share their favorite moments with Zelda. My neighbor, Jill sings the Jewish mourner's Kaddish. And each is given one of Zelda's butterflies.

MARIE'S CRISIS

CONNIE has a rich doctor friend, Louis, who invites him to New York for his birthday every year at Christmastime. I've got to get out of LA, I really need a change of scenery and there's unfinished business I have to take care of in New York.

      Connie's reluctant to lean on Louis more than he does. But I'm determined to convince him to ask Louis to let me stay at his loft just for a weekend. I like Louis, he's smart kind and generous, I'm hoping he'll realize how much I need this now.

The Heartbreak of Static Cling

Connie finally asks Louis and I get the invite.

On the plane I'm filled with a sense of relief and caution. This escape from the pain of losing my mom is also a chance to confront the ghosts in New York. I need a private final conversation with them to be free after all these years haunted.

The cab from Kennedy pulls up to Louis's address on 22nd Street. I find the intercom and press the buzzer and Connie answers and to his surprise I say, "I'm here." His hello is tentative like he really didn't think I would come and he buzzes me in.

The loft is luxurious but it has only two bedrooms, I'll have to share a room with Connie, no big deal for me a bigger deal for him, oh well. Louis is welcoming and gracious, I tell them I have meetings with old friends lined up from my past to visit tomorrow, I don't go into details. Connie seems relieved, he too has plans and Louis is always busy at work.

We have a few drinks and go out to a neighborhood Italian restaurant, the kind that doesn't exist in LA for a great dinner. Afterwards Connie goes night crawling in the East Village. I return to the loft with Louis and excuse myself needing to go to bed and get up early. I'm eager to begin my ghost hunt.

It's seven AM and I slip out of bed trying not to disturb Connie passed out under his comforter. I leave the loft quietly and head for a diner on 23rd Street for of a pot of coffee, I need the fuel to cover a lot of territory today.

Finishing the last drop I decide to begin my

mission on 13th Street.

The "family" that captured me with and all their drama is long gone. The townhouse is now a condo with several units, only the façade remains the same. I look up to my bedroom window remembering the feeling of that room and that house.

I summon the ghosts, I can feel them, they won't show themselves, but they hear me declaring a strong and final farewell and "Go haunt someone else!"

I continue east cross town on 13th Street to the corner of University Place where Carol, Don and I lived. I envision Saint in his car with Truman Capote sitting next to him waiting for me. And I turn around and there they are, pale gray transparent amorphous shapes moving toward me, or is it just steam from a manhole? I tell them I've moved on and I'm okay, just in case.

Walking through Union Square Park I pass by Antonio's loft and Warhol's factory just a few buildings apart. Another lifetime, I was so lucky to have that. Their spirits are free and so are mine.

Crossing Park Avenue South I spot a nondescript deli and stop dead in my tracks. That was Max's Kansas City! Funny to think it was so much a part of my life and now it's just a dumb deli. All the ghosts are there and seem settled in, this deli must have better chopped liver than Max's.

On to Irving Place and this is the hardest. Pete's Tavern will never change and I need a drink. I pay my bill and walk up the street to 82 Irving Place. This was our home and life together. It's now just a building that has grown a new appendage, a deep blue awning elevating the façade. I take a last look through the glass of the front door and see the small lobby has barely changed. That life I'm forever grateful for. Now I declare detachment from this place, and a final release.

A few steps away and there it is, our Gramercy Park. It was a cold winter late night and things were getting bad, when I said, "Come on, Don, let's take a walk." We bundled up and walked to the gate. I unlocked it and we're in the empty private park now for us alone. Gravel pathways led us to a bench and we sat huddled together in the cold, silently praying for a miracle.

This is the hardest good bye.

I continue to 23rd Street and stand across the street from the School of Visual Arts watching a new generation of aspiring young artists enter that building that shaped me, imagining the life they might have before them.

And now the subway takes me to 50th and Madison, just like it did going to work every day for so many years. I arrive at the station where I met Keith Haring drawing crawling babies with chalk on a black blank subway poster space.

Here I am again at 437 Madison Avenue where my office was on the 44th floor at Doyle Dane Bernbach Advertising Worldwide. I walk into the lobby past banks of elevators to the rear of the building and find the small newsstand is still here. I notice a rack of magazines and remember seeing my face on the cover of Advertising

Techniques Magazine when I was in my twenties. I get a pack of Marlboro Lights, walk through the lobby and watch the parade of ad execs, young art directors and copywriters crowding elevators to their careers. DDB is not the same, nothing's the same but in a way everything is still the same. I decide not to anonymously join the elevator crowd and leave the building for the last time. These ghosts now embolden me.

One block away is a trinity, Saks Fifth Avenue, where my father spent his working life, St. Patrick's Cathedral where every good New York Jew would go to at Christmas to light a candle, and finally the one and only Rockefeller Center with its iconic Christmas tree. All three landmarks are here and alive in my heart and always will be. I walk into Saks and take a deep breath of the perfumed air of old world New York luxury remembering my dad. Then on to St. Pat's to light a candle for all my New York City ghosts. And next stop a bar at Rockefeller Center with a much needed martini in hand toasting the memory of past Christmas trees and feeling changed, free of a lot of weight.

It's time to celebrate these long overdue visitations and I head back to the loft to have some fun in the city with Connie.

Connie and I plan to see what's left of the West Village starting with Julius, the landmark bar that began in 1864 now the oldest gay bar in Manhattan, speaking of old haunts. And it's just as remembered, cheap drinks and greasy burgers. It's packed with old gay devotees, New York's tenacious survivors.

Connie turns to me. "Too bad you can't get coke in New York."

"Really, is there a problem?"

"It's impossible."

"Shit, I'd love to have one last hurrah, don't you know anyone?"

"Nope not anymore, c'mon finish your drink, lets go to Marie's Crisis."

On the way to Grove Street a small jewelry shop window catches my eye. Unique handmade objects are calling me and I look at one in particular up close. I buy the silver pendant, a gift for my sister Carolyn. I will always be disappointed about her disregard for Zelda, but it's time to let go of a lot of things. I plan to visit her tomorrow in Brooklyn and take her to a great seafood restaurant in Sheepshead Bay for dinner. Connie approves the gift and we continue on our way to Marie's.

Marie's Crisis is a below ground bar that opened in the 1850's as a den for prostitutes and became a boy bar in the 1890's "Crisis" came from The American Crisis pamphlets written by Thomas Pain published in 1776, Thomas Paine died in the this house. Ghosts have been seen down in the cellar's original rusting kitchen. This place has soaked up its share of memories and then some. Don loved piano bars especially Marie's Crisis and we became a part of its history.

The place is packed and the crowd is singing "I'm Still Here," along with the piano player, how appropriate.

And then I spot her and turn to Connie. "See that

redhead at the bar looking like Bette Midler?" I point her out yakking her head off to everyone at the bar. "Okay, Connie, you said you can't get any coke in this city, just watch me."

I make my way through the crowd to the bar. "Hey Bette!" She turns hyperventilating and stares at me. "You look like a young Bette Midler, you're divine!" She cracks up. And I just go for it, "Got any coke?"

"I know how to get some, interested?"

"You bet, Bette."

"Come with me."

She pulls me toward the door and I yell to Connie, "I'm on a mission!" We run out the door, Bette finds a phone booth, she quickly dials and makes arrangements and asks me for cash. Somehow I trust her and hand over a wad of bills.

"Stay here, I'll be back in ten minutes, I can't bring you with me."

"Okay, just don't try anything, you be back in ten, you hear?"

"Don't worry, doll..." She splits and I'm wondering if I just got taken, but it's worth the risk.

Twenty minutes pass, I'm still at the phone booth convinced I was just ripped off. I'm about to go back to the bar but out of nowhere Bette appears, she grabs my arm and shoves a ton of coke in a baggie into my hand. She is divine!

Back at Marie's I pull Connie away from a hot guy and shove him into the bathroom. And holy shit! The best coke we ever had and that's saying something.

The Heartbreak of Static Cling

There's so much of the stuff I decide to turn on the whole bar starting with a couple of bartenders who show us an ancient staircase to the cellar, the perfect place for debauchery. And *POW!* The night lights up at Marie's Crisis and the bartenders return the favor with endless free drinks.

Nobody does coke anymore, this isn't the eighties but this night is a throwback to celebrations past and to all the farewells.

We get home around 3 AM buzzed out of our minds. Fortunately Connie has "sleeping pills."

Today we have plans to explore the city. We start early because I'm going to see Carolyn this evening. We agree to ignore the stash I have with me at the coffee shop but Connie slyly asks to see the vial I invented, it's a straw inserted into the vials cap so it becomes an effortless quick coke dispenser. I hand it over and he splits for the bathroom, of course.

Before Connie returns to the table, I call to Carolyn to confirm our dinner reservations. She tells me she doesn't want to go out to dinner, she would rather have me to take the one hour subway ride to her apartment in Brooklyn and she'll order Chinese and I'm furious. I tell her I'd rather not and I'll send the gift I have for her when I get back to California and hang up. What is wrong with her? The restaurant is literally two blocks from her place. I guess I'll never see her again.

Connie returns from the bathroom bright eyed and bushy tailed, he pulls up his chair and I grab the vial out of his hand. He sees I'm crazed. "What's wrong?"

"I'll tell you when I get back." I dash to the bathroom.

"Forget it Robert, that's her problem, let's go ice skating in Central Park." Somehow this seems to be a perfectly good idea even though it's about eight degrees with a wind chill below zero. But with the help of our magic powder that isn't a problem, in fact we decide to walk to Central Park from our cozy café on 23rd Street.

We power walk dozens of frozen long New York blocks and finally get to Central Park South. What seemed like ten minutes was more like two hours fighting the wind and I can't feel my face, so what. We soldier on to the Bethesda Fountain, I take a picture of Connie posing like a Popsicle and decide ice skating isn't a great idea after all, so we continue east through paths of glistening icicles and finally get to 5th Avenue. Connie pipes up, "I want a martini."

"We'll get one on 5th Avenue, darling."

I forgot what 5th Avenue is like getting closer to Christmas. The sidewalks are so jammed with tourists and we're forced to walk in baby steps sandwiched in by the crowd like frozen sardines determined to get martinis.

Eight torturous blocks later we finally get to Rockefeller Center but it's impossibly jam-packed and no way to get a martini so we give up and take the bus downtown to find a nice warm bar thaw out and check for frostbite.

Tonight's my last night in the city, I'm taking Louis and Connie to one of my favorite haunts The

Odeon, for a thank you dinner to show my appreciation for their invite that got me here and afterwards it's a late night flight back to LA.

I'll always be a New Yorker, it's part of my DNA. But this city is no longer my home and may never be again. It's the greatest most powerful city on earth providing every possible opportunity to fulfill dreams of those who have the ambition, drive, strength, talent and guts to overcome every obstacle. I did it all here.

Gershwin's "Rhapsody in Blue" magnificently portrays this city's dynamic soul moving me deeply through my headphones as I view Manhattan's skyline below from my window seat, good bye New York.

I'm flying back to my future in LA unencumbered by ghosts.

STILETTO GLADIATORS

ILENE CONNELLY calls as she's driving from San Francisco to LA. She has a check for me from the sale of my old tank watch she took to her jeweler in New York who pays top dollar for vintage watches. I expected her to mail the check weeks ago, I'm a little pissed, I needed that money as soon as possible. She asks if she can stay at my place for a few days, but I explain Marilyn and I have strict house rules, no sleep over's. I'm sorry about that; we've had a lot of great times together when she stayed at my place in the past. She understands and tells me she'll stay at Todd and Richie's and she'll stop by to see me on the way to their place.

I'm sitting on my front steps and spot her getting out of her car. I haven't seen Ilene in awhile. Wow she looks good, model thin and hiked up tall on the Valentino gladiator strapped spiked heels she hunted down at an upscale consignment store. She's great at that, but how the hell do you drive from San Francisco to LA strapped into Stiletto gladiators?

Big hugs and she hands me the check for the watch. I ask her why she didn't send it by mail. Uncharacteristically deadpan she just tells me she decided to bring it to me. She seems a little strange, like something else is occupying her thoughts, so I let that slide. I have to get to the bank and ask her to give me a lift. I get into her little rent a car and we pass by Crossroads on Santa Monica Boulevard, her favorite consignment store and she can't resist, she pulls into the parking lot. I can't spend hours with her on safari hunting through racks of gently worn designer wear. I need to get to the bank and deposit this check. We kiss good bye and I continue on foot.

Later that evening she calls me from Todd's and asks if I would like to come over. It's late at night, I'm tired in bed and not really wanting to drive to Todd's, I tell her I'll come by tomorrow and say good night wondering what's up with her, she sounded a bit somber.

Early next morning my phone rings, it's Todd and he can barely talk. "I found her slumped over on the bathroom floor, Ilene's dead."

"What!?" I try to question him but he just hangs up. The shock hits me like a hammer. I should have driven to Todd's when she asked me to, maybe I would have detected something terrible was wrong. I'm flattened on my bed reeling trying to make believe this didn't happen.

A month earlier I called Ilene in New York. She was on her way to the hospital to get a pacemaker implanted, and Jen was with her. This was astounding to hear, she never mentioned any problems with her heart. The only thing concerning her was the placement of the device. She said her doctors agreed to implant it where it wouldn't be noticeable. And now she's gone.

Jennifer calls and asks if I would agree to be a pallbearer. Stunned, I say yes. She's arranged services at Hollywood Forever and asks if I would like to say something at the service, I tell her I don't think I could keep it together, she asks for some thoughts about Ilene, So many thoughts and memories come to mind, but I finally I say, "Ilene could find treasure in a sea of shmatas." A metaphor Jen understands.

Hollywood Forever, the final resting place of luminaries is quite a place. This gathering is situated on a small island accessed by a footbridge over a pond. The surreal beauty of this is amplified by a woven basket covered with hundreds of fragrant gardenias. It's an exquisite unique casket lying on the grass in front of seats filled with guests. Jen's husband, Paul Bettany approaches me and whispers he will also be a pallbearer and he'll show me what to do.

Jen appears on the footbridge with her angelic baby, Agnes by her side. I go to her and we embrace. Her two sons, Kai and Stellan are seated with Paul. I walk her to the podium and get back to my seat. I notice Frank and BJ seated behind me and nod to them. Time has somewhat mended our friendship. And I spot Todd trying to compose himself with the help of his partner Richie, and I spot Brad and Connie sitting still   and speechless.

Jen begins and she's beautifully eloquent plainly speaking her heart. And when she quotes me, it adds some needed levity.

Todd walks to the podium and tries to say something but he just breaks down, that's all he can do. My heart goes out to him imagining how horrible it was to discover Ilene that morning.

After all is said, Paul, Kai and Stellan pick up guitars and sing, their talent has no bounds.

And now Paul and I join two other pallbearers and I take hold of one of the handles attached to the woven basket coffin covered in gardenias and we walk away carrying Ilene's body over the footbridge through a field of green to a waiting hearse.

I wonder when I'll wake up from this nightmare.

YOU GOT TO MOVE

HOLLY got a new apartment. She's been on the list for a rent subsidized place for four years and she's finally hit the lottery. It's $250 a month on Westmount, a great street just a few blocks from my place. It's small but livable with a view of West Hollywood's gym rats parading to 24 Hour Fitness for their "workouts" as Holly yells "Free Pussy" from her balcony.

The building was converted from a cheap hotel built in the seventies, now it's a bit institutional occupied by old Russians and the like, Holly calls them Kreplachs.

427 The Heartbreak of Static Cling

She tells me she couldn't care less. She's thrilled her Welfare checks now cover much more than her rent.

And now that she's confined to a wheelchair she's also entitled to a part time caretaker, she's gone through three of four already. Holly can be very demanding, mostly demanding cigarettes and booze. So she's snared a new caretaker/fan of hers who is more willing to please, Holly is "she who must be obeyed." We'll see how long this one lasts.

I get there and find her apartment down an endless hallway. I ring the bell, bang on the door and no answer. Finally I hear something and Holly in her wheelchair appears in a stupor. There's no caretaker to be found and her place is a pigsty, empty gallon wine bottles strewn everywhere, piles of cigarette butts smolder in plates glasses and ashtrays. She's semi coherent.

All I can say is, "Holly what the fuck?"

She ignores me and rolls herself toward the balcony.

"Damn it Holly, what are you doing?"

"None of your business." Where's your caregiver?"

"Getting fish piss, gimme a cigarette." Shaking she pours herself the last of the Vandage rotgut into a paper cup and lights up a Marlboro. "Did you bring wine?"

"No, I didn't, and you're smoking my last cigarette."

And with that, Holly turns, and when Holly turns

watch out!

I love the bitch madly, but right now I got other shit to deal with, my doctor tells me I need an operation and I don't have the energy to deal with her. As I'm leaving, the door opens and her "caregiver" is back from CVS with more cheap booze and cigarettes, perfect. I read him the riot act and leave.

I'm fuming. I've seen Holly in this state many times over many years but now those years of depravity are catching up. There are no cabaret acts to prepare for, no scripts to learn and she's trapped in that fucking wheelchair and blitzed on booze.

Once I deal with my newly diagnosed problem and regain my strength I'll set her straight, we'll work together again to adapt her book 'A Low Life in High Heels,' into a screenplay that will snap this lowlife back to life.

I get home to find my roommate Marilyn is moving back to Texas. This is not good, my money is getting thin and her rent is really necessary, shit!

But right now I have to deal with my Urologist who tells me the reoccurring urinary tract infections I've been suffering are caused by an enlarged prostate. He's given me pills for it that I really hate because they've made it impossible to ejaculate. He gives me an option of a surgery called TURP. This procedure reduces the size of the prostate. This should fix it so I decide to have it done. At least it's not prostate cancer.

It's déjà vu, I wake up after an operation in a penthouse suite, who knew Cedar's even had one? But

I'm terrified, there's got to be a reason for this and it's probably bad news.

Dr. Bender arrives at my bedside and delivers a mind bender. "You're very fortunate you decided to have this operation, we found lesions on your bladder. It's cancer."

I snap to a seated position. "There's no way in hell I will allow anybody to remove my bladder, I would rather drop dead!"

"Calm yourself this is curable, we caught it early it hasn't spread and there's no need to remove the bladder."

I don't believe him. "I'm a dead person, I'm a dead person, I refuse to have a tube attached to my body emptying piss into a bag strapped to my leg! I'm a dead person!"

He leaves the room and returns with a shrink. I'm now out of bed and sitting on a sofa reeling from this news. "So what now, chemotherapy?"

"No, there's BCG, it's a bio engineered drug that kills cancer cells and it also sets up immunity. It's proven very effective but you'll just have to see me very often for the next six months."

I quiet down and the shrink leaves. Bender tells me we can start this BCG next week.

Okay, this is only my third cancer, very amusing.

Bender's office calls to tell me he just retired. I guess after my freak out he decided enough is enough. I'm referred to a Dr. Daskovitch. I do my homework, he's extremely well respected and handsome and I make an appointment.

Dr. D fills me in on the details of the BCG treatments. I almost pass out when he shows me a twenty inch tube that gets inserted into my penis reaching the bladder to infuse the BCG. And this is done with no anesthesia. Oh really?! After the infusion which must be repeated once a week for six weeks at a time for six months and possibly more, I'm to go home and lie on my back for fifteen minutes then turn on my side for another fifteen and then the other side and then repeat before peeing it out. Modern medicine meets medieval torture.

"Okay doctor, there's no way I'll go through this without anesthesia."

He finally relents and offers a script for Valium, not good enough, and Oxycodone, breakfast of champions! Then he tells me he doesn't do the procedure, he sets up my infusions with his associate, Dr. B.

And so the fun begins. Fortunately I'm well versed in pills. I take two Valiums and two Oxy's one hour before I see Dr. B and when I arrive at his office I'm flying and they can shove a freight train up my dick and I wouldn't feel it.

But it is humiliating, why do these urologists have female assistants do their job? Oh well, I'm so blitzed I make instant friends with her. How and why she has this job god knows, maybe she gets off on it. At least she's good at what she' does. Somehow I'm going to get used to this routine, I have no choice.

Back at the ranch my latest mortgage statement

reveals good times are almost up because my payments are about to balloon to the moon. It once was easy and simple to refinance, no longer, and I'm being forced to sell my place and move to where? Great, what else do I have to do?

    This is more torture than the BCG. I don't want to sell my place, I desperately want to stay but whatever option I investigate it all leads to list it and move on, damn it again I have no choice.

    Coming to grips I begin the necessary steps to insure netting top dollar for this place, it needs some updating. I tap funds from my home equity line of credit for this and I'll pay off at the sale.

    And soon after all the new shiny appliances are installed and the place is painted, I get a top dollar offer and accept it. The quicker the transaction the better, it's like ripping off a bandage.

    I have a month to find a new place to live. I start a search for the cheapest rental I can tolerate until I find another property to buy, and I find it where else but back on Alfred Street.

    This faux Cape Cod was built in the eighties. It's a ten unit apartment building. The one available is a top floor one bedroom with a small terrace. Okay, it's cheap and temporary. I put most of my furnishings in storage and just take a bed a dining table and chairs, a couple of dishes, my coffee maker and my art collection. The cost of insuring the art is prohibitive so I'll have my "friends" with me in crates keeping me company in this dump.

It's been almost six weeks of BCG torture and I'm used to it, actually I look forward to my Wednesdays with Oxy and Valium dulling the pain of the procedure and the loss of my home.

MOMENTS OF TRUTH

MONTHS OF INFUSIONS and now it's time to find out just how effective the BCG has been. I'm admitted for a surgical look see. Dr. D is at my bedside telling me he'll be with me when I recover, I cross my fingers and they put me out.

       Propofol is a pleasant death or as close to death you can get without being dead. You're completely unplugged, no thoughts, no visions, no dreams, nothing. Time doesn't exist, you don't exist. There's something actually fabulous about this.

When you snap out of it there's no sense of how long it's been since consciousness, a minute, an hour, a day a lifetime? And here's Dr. D looming over me. "Robert we found a couple of lesions."

"Wonderful, thanks, now what?"

"We can try another immunotherapy or continue with BCG." More BCG means more Oxy and Valium.

"Let's give it another try and see."

He agrees.

Four weeks into this new round of BCG I get a cough and take some powerful cough medicine and go to bed. I get up to pee and pure blood is streaming full force out of me and it won't stop. Freaked out I call an Uber to get me to the hospital, I wrap myself in towels but that doesn't work the blood keeps coming in torrents, I call 911 I need an ambulance not an Uber.

I'm in the emergency room doctors surround me trying who knows what and it's not doing any good. Dr. D arrives and he arranges surgery immediately. Before I'm wheeled out for the procedure Brad pokes his head into the emergency room where I'm covered in a pool of blood, I wave "hello" and he almost passes out. I'm shot up and blacked out and taken away.

It wasn't an easy operation, Dr. D tells me he was about to wake me for approval because he couldn't stop the bleeding which would mean bladder removal but he finally managed to repair the damage and saved me that horror.

This event put a tear in my confidence as well. All that blood felt like my life draining from me. What else is to be expected in the battle of the bladder? Okay I'll answer that question right now, I expect to be cured. I've done it before I'll do it again. It's just cancer.

The second round of BCG treatment is put on hold for a few weeks allowing time to heal and recuperate. So I decide to use this break to investigate every real estate listing daily. There's no use, garbage is being snapped up for millions. I need to reset my expectations and realize this Alfred Street dump will not be so temporary.

Lipstick on a pig, why not try it? I recall tiny rat holes in New York I've seen turned into jewel boxes. I realize I can do that here. I'm at my wits end living like a prisoner of my dreams without a pan to fry an egg.

I have all my stuff delivered from storage and keep crates of things that just won't fit in the garage to deal with later.

I can usually picture things clearly but the transformation of this motel 6 box is better than I thought. Alfred Street is now comfortable and astoundingly a bit chic, it's amazing what artwork and furnishings can do. It's still a dump, but it's my very convenient dump and I can finally make an omelet.

THE PROXY

TWO MONTHS into this second round of BCG I'm home enjoying the vestiges of my Oxy Valium high and the phone rings, it's David Chic, Holly's new and best caregiver so far. "Holly's in the hospital unresponsive." He discovered her on the floor an hour ago and tried to revive her but it was just no use, he just called 911. Damn shit!

    I pull myself together fast and find her room in Cedars. She's attached to several IV's. Holly's two "husbands" Joey and Michael—devoted fans—hover by her bedside, clueless.

I run to the nurse's station demanding to see her doctor and all I get is a look of disdain like, who are you? Well, they're about to find out.

"Look dear, get Holly Woodlawn's doctor here now, you hear me!"

"Are you related to him?"

"Her! You bet I am, page her doctor." Finally the nurse relents and I go back to her room.

She's unconscious and her dumbfounded "husbands" pace the room, finally a doctor and a nurse arrive and they adjust her infusions. "I need to have a consultation with you now." Again they ask if I'm a relative, I just stare them down until they ask me to follow them to a small conference room.

"Okay doctor, what's going on?"

The doctor begins, "He—"

"Excuse me, your patient is Holly Woodlawn, Holly Woodlawn is *she*, don't be fooled by her big Puerto Rican dick! And Holly Woodlawn will survive because she has cockroach blood running through her veins."

That pushes the pause button for a moment and the doctor continues, "She has ammonia on her brain caused by Cirrhosis of the liver. We're treating this and it should bring her back to consciousness. She also has lung cancer that has a metastasized to her brain."

"Is that all?"

"Spinal stenosis."

"Is any of this treatable?"

"We're waiting for lab reports. Do you know of a

relative who can make medical decisions for her?"

"No, but I can."

"When she's able to communicate there's a form she needs to sign naming you her proxy."

"When will she be able to talk?"

"Tomorrow evening possibly."

Holly has an uncle in Puerto Rico who I'm sure can't handle this, and none of her friends or fans really know their way around doctors, hospitals, insurance and all the rest. So it's me and I'm determined to use everything I've learned and dealt with to save Holly.

I leave the hospital and begin researching her diagnoses to equip me for another round with her doctors and start searching for top specialists at Cedars, I'll also contact Dr. Green, for now that's the plan.

I do as much as I can and take a break, the aftermath of my recent BCG treatment and Holly's dilemma has taken its toll.

A few hours of sleep was enough to gather my strength and I get up and go to back to the hospital.

Color has returned to her face and she seems more alive and just sleeping hooked up to even more infusions. A nurse appears and tells me she's been awake and coherent. I hold vigil at her bedside.

An hour passes and I see her stirring. "Holly, Holly, it's me Holly, open your eyes you gorgeous thing." She turns her head looks at me and smiles. "Okay, Holly, you did it this time, you really freaked me out, welcome back to the living, how do you feel?"

"Oh, I'm okay, how the fuck are you?"

The Heartbreak of Static Cling

"Fabulous now that you're awake."

"Was I babbling?"

"No darling, you where in a coma somewhere on planet Woodlawn."

"Got a cigarette?"

"Cedars doesn't have a smoking lounge, relax."

"How long am I gonna be here?"

"That's up to you, just listen to the doctors and be patient, give yourself time to recuperate."

"From what?"

"From being Holly Woodlawn. Listen honey, there's a lot of decisions that need to be made about your care, dealing with doctors, insurance all that crap. You should name someone to take charge—a proxy."

"They told me I got cancer."

"Big deal, I have cancer, fuck cancer. You and me will fuck cancer together you hear me?"

"How?"

"You'll see, I got a lot of experience with this shit."

"Okay proxy, fuck my cancer."

"My pleasure dollpuss, now relax."

And Holly drifts off.

I leave the hospital making mental notes. Once that proxy thing is signed I need to get into gear, questions need answers. An aggressive treatment strategy needs to be set in place. I'm not losing her.

News travels fast and I get a call from Penny Arcade. She tells me Connie called her about Holly. I haven't heard from Penny in years. In 1971 Penny was featured with Candy Darling, Jackie Curtis and Holly Woodlawn in Andy Warhol's, "Women in Revolt" directed by Paul Morrissey, Holly hilariously portrays a nymphomaniac who loathes men despite being attracted to them. Morrissey also directed Holly in Andy Warhol's "Trash" in 1970 with Joe Dallesandro. Penny is a devoted friend of Holly's and shaken by the rumors of her condition.

I fill Penny in on the details; she's devastated and tells me she's starting a GoFundMe page. I have no idea what that is, but she explains it and it sounds perfect, Holly doesn't have a dime, and her minimal insurance won't cover the kind of care she needs. Penny asks if I would be willing to be the beneficiary and manage the funds since I'm being named Holly's healthcare proxy. Penny is aware of my acquaintances with cancer and how much I care for Holly. I agree, money is desperately needed to get Holly through this.

Connie and I check out Holly's apartment before we go to the hospital. The place is a horrific fifthly mess, nothing can be salvaged. We throw out tons of garbage but I realize I have to hire an industrial cleaning company to get this place habitable for Holly's return. She needs a new bed, new sheets towels new clothes, all her things are torn filthy rags and her Holly Woodlawn wig looks like she set it with Raid.

We get to Cedars and find Holly more clearheaded and happy to see her "Sister Connie" and me. First thing she asks for is the proxy papers for her to sign. I go to the nurses' station and find a social worker and she tells me we'll get the documents this afternoon.

Holly is having a good time with Connie and it's great to see her brighten up. Doctors arrive and ignore me and Connie. They just check the IV's and leave. I'll begin their full interrogation as soon as that proxy is signed.

Sunny California is visited by what's called an atmospheric river and LA is getting drenched, it just keeps pouring and cars keep crashing, no one here knows how to deal with serious rain. There's a lot to do whatever the weather, the disaster team is at work sterilizing Holly's apartment and I'm out shopping for everything she needs. It's astounding how fast funds are gratefully amazingly coming in from her devoted fans through the GoFundMe page Penny set up. When Holly is able to go home it will be ready including nursing care.

I'm back in the hospital for a meeting with her doctors. We gather in a small room and I present the signed proxy. I begin with "What's the plan?" And they just run down a repeat of her diagnosis, they add now that the ammonia on her brain is gone they want to release her. What?

"Okay doctors, which one of her conditions is the most immediately life threatening?" They look at each other in silence. I know the lung cancer, the brain tumor, and the Cirrhosis is all lethal, but there has to be a way to slow things down. Finally, they reveal the brain tumor is most likely to take her life quickly. "What about radiation? What about operating? What about doing something about this? I want a consultation with a neurologist!" And they have the nerve to mention her insurance. "Fuck her insurance, we have the funds to cover her care, damn it! Now, what about a liver transplant?" They tell me she's not eligible due to the lung cancer. "Okay, I'll consult Dr. Leland Green." They get a little red in the face. "And have you taken into consideration that she also needs to detox from alcohol and you want to send her home?" Another dead silence. I get up and leave the room steaming.

Dr. Green confirms she isn't a candidate for a liver transplant and he gives me a referral to the top neurologist at Cedars. I immediately call and schedule a consultation.

I've done everything to make her return home possible, but I know it's wrong. She'll become a nightmare with home nurses demanding fish piss and cigarettes defeating any medical intervention. But I'm powerless if they decide to release her.

Thankfully this neurologist gets on the case quickly and schedules brain scans and whatever other tests he needs delaying her release for a week. He tells me operating is out of the question but radiation will slow the growth of the brain tumor giving her more time. She'll be fitted with a custom mask to protect her head and face from the radiation and then a series of weekly treatments will begin. Great! We're beginning to fight back.

But he tells me she doesn't need to stay in the hospital after all the tests are done, radiation will be out patient and in a few more days she'll be released, damn it.

Divine intervention. I've always been skeptical, but this turn of events changed my mind.

Holly is to be released from the hospital day after tomorrow. And then it happens, the constant torrential rain collapses part of the roof of Holly's apartment building. The City of Los Angeles owns this place and is relocating all residence to a nursing home in the Valley for at least three weeks while repairs are made. Holly can't go home, and Holly isn't going to some dump in the valley either. I contact the city authorities and explain the situation and they finally agree to cover costs of a facility closer to Cedars for access to her radiation treatments.

I have just a day and a half to find a place, a social worker recommends a few, I check them out and the best I can find is on Melrose, their nursing staff includes physical therapists, it's not the Ritz but it's perfect for now.

Holly's okay with this, she's looking forward to the radiation determined to put up a fight for her life. She admits she's enjoyed the attention she's had at the hospital and I assure her the Melrose place will be even better. "Physical therapy just might put you on your feet again!" This brings an unexpected tear, she never complained about being confined to a wheelchair. Awhile ago somehow she got an electric wheelchair and terrorized the boys on Santa Monica Boulevard before crashing it into a mailbox. The girl just knows how to have fun.

For her trip to the Melrose place I buy her several new outfits, Ralph Lauren preppy, the style she loves. And more gifts, her favorite Shalimar perfume and a new wig, she's thrilled.

Melrose greets her with open arms and she is energized and determined to make her mark with all the "guests" and the staff, especially her new physical therapist who is a hunk and a half. She quickly notices there is an outdoor patio where smoking is allowed. "Off limits, Holly!"

She loves her radiation mask and models it for me, very attractive. Weekly sessions begin tomorrow. One of the nurses will bring her to Cedars and back and Holly can't wait.

And I'm looking forward to my last BCG treatment. After that I get admitted to Cedars again for Dr. D to put me under Propofol and surgically take a look see if all these treatments actually worked. What fun! I tell Holly it's my turn to be treated at Cedars and I'll be back in a week. "Go take care of yourself and don't worry about me, I got this covered."

Connie is on his way to visit Holly with makeup and the latest Chateau Marmont gossip to enjoy. I decide to leave, there's nothing more I can do here.

With mixed feelings I down what may be my last Oxy and Valium cocktail in preparation for my next and last BCG fest. Oh well, day after tomorrow we'll find out what Dr. D's surgery reveals and I'll just take it from there.

I'm being prepped for Dr. D's surgery and he

arrives at my bedside reassuring me he'll be with me as soon as I recover.

The anesthesiologist begins with a delightful shot of feel good and they wheel me into surgery and roll me onto the operating table and lights out.

I'm startled awake still on the operating table. The procedure is over and I'm surrounded by smiling male nurses. "What happened?"

"You're good, all clear, nothing was found." And they wheel me back to the recovery room.

Ten minutes pass Dr. D appears and confirms he found no tumors and my bladder is clear, the BCG worked. I manage to sit up and hug him. What a relief! Sure I'll have to undergo another look see in three months and then if all is good and no cancer, follow ups every six months, fine by me.

Recuperating at home Penny calls. "Have you seen what's going on?"

"What?"

"Take a look at Facebook, it's ridiculous, we're being attacked!"

I open Facebook still on the phone with Penny and there it is: "It's a Hoax, Holly Woodlawn is just running a scam for money," "What is Robert Starr doing with all the funds?" "Penny Arcade is colluding with Starr in this scam!" And on and on. What?!

Penny is furious. I'm initially astounded but not surprised, these jokers have no clue, some don't even know Holly, certainly they don't know Penny and they don't know me. What drives their craziness? I guess when they see the amount of money being donated every day it brings out the worst in them.

I'm fine with just ignoring it, but Penny is launching an online counter attack. And so are Connie and Jane County and others who know exactly what's going on. Good let them, I can't be bothered, I have a lot on my mind and a great deal more to do for Holly.

When I finally get back to see Holly, low and behold she's walking, barely leaning on her walker. She smiles showing off to her new adoring fans at this venue as she continues down the corridor followed closely by her physical therapist, wow!

I decide just to share good news about defeating my fucking cancer. She needn't get caught up in social media wars. She's thrilled I did it again and I'm amazed at her being able to walk! "I told you so, Holly."

"Yeah ya did, that radiation is doing its stuff, let's go outside." She sits back down in her wheelchair and takes me to the garden to meet her new best friend sitting on a stool by a small round table. He's a double amputee, no legs. How he was able to seat himself on that stool is beyond me. And then I realize how they became friends when he pulls out a pack of Marlboros and gives one to Holly. I don't make a fuss, Holly will be Holly and nothing can stop her, shit have a smoke. At least I didn't see a bottle of booze nearby.

The director of the Melrose place spots me outside and gestures for me to come in. She tells me once Holly completes her radiation treatments week after next, she'll have to go home. LA county authorities informed her Holly's building will be repaired by then. She adds, Melrose is a rehab facility, not a long term care facility, as if I didn't know, still my stomach turns. If she can find a way to bum a cigarette here, imagine what she can manage when she gets back in her apartment. I ask the director if Holly's smoking can be discouraged by a nurse, "She has lung cancer you know."

I got two weeks to figure this out, there may be nothing I can do, but at least her apartment is spotless and ready for her return. I begin interviewing home nurses. I have to find the strongest.

Here Comes the Rain Again—That's a great song title but this deluge repeat performance is way beyond divine intervention. And don't you know, that newly repaired roof at Holly's apartment building collapses again and the damage is worse than before and it will take months to fix. Holly can't go home, again!

But Holly can't stay at Melrose, so I have to find something more permanent, more like a home for Holly. It's another miracle we have the funds now to pay for a good one, a really good one.

I've trudged to rat traps, and outrageously expensive joints that were just not worth it, and finally I discover a place on La Brea. It looks and feels like a luxury condo. It's immaculate and done with great taste. Her room is large on the fourth floor and it has great natural light from big windows with a view of the Hollywood sign in the distance, the en suite bathroom is large and almost luxurious. There's a comfortable attractive dining room a floor below, meals also can be delivered to the room. And to top it all off, take the elevator to an enormous roof terrace to lounge and entertain. And there's a nursing staff, perfect. I wish I could of have had my mom here.

Holly and I have a good laugh when I tell her of the second roof collapse. And she's excited to move to La Brea, it's so much better than her apartment.

But the Cirrhosis is getting worse, at first it's deceiving, just a weight gain which could be perceived as healthy but I know this is due to a failing liver and I pray this doesn't advance quickly. Holly is in such good spirits, there's no need now to talk about any of this.

Instead as a distraction I let her in on the ongoing slings and arrows posted online. We both have a big fat laugh about that. I must say, Penny's counter attacks are quite fabulous and so are all the other posts from those who know better. What's life without scandal and outlandish entertaining drama generated by those who have nothing better to do?

Radiation treatments are completed and Holly moves to La Brea, she's in a very good place, comfortable and happy. Her friends and devoted fans are impressed when they come to visit. I wish there is more that can be done.

Holly's birthday is coming up, her sixty-ninth. I plan to give her a fabulous party on the rooftop terrace. Sadly we both know this will be Holly's last birthday party.

We begin to compile a list of guests. I'm surprised when I ask her if she would like to include her costar in Warhol's movie Trash and she refuses because she's not a fan of his wife who actually called me demanding a spread sheet accounting of expenditures from the GoFundMe account. However the guest list is quickly growing for her grand party.

 Several weeks quickly pass and all is set for the celebration but Holly's condition has noticeably worsened, the bloat has increased and her energy is diminished, but not her spirit, nothing can get her down nothing ever has, that's how she's been able to live her life.

 One evening we have a more serious conversation when I ask if there is anything she would like me to do. She tells me she wants her ashes placed in the tomb beside her mother Minta, in Puerto Rico. And if there is money left in the fund after she's gone she wants it to benefit homeless transgender teens. I compose myself and assure her this will happen. The conversation turns to having a cigarette and a glass of wine on the roof. And that's exactly what we do.

 It's October 26th and Holly is getting ready for her party. Connie is doing her makeup, styling her wig and helping her choose her wardrobe and no one is allowed in her room but Connie.

 I'm upstairs on the roof wondering where the fuck is the caterer. I'm organizing the bar, tables and chairs and inspecting the incredible cake that has just been delivered. It's an Egyptian temple with tall golden candles and a portrait of the Goddess Holly Woodlawn, she who must be obeyed.

Guests are arriving and Holly is still in hair and makeup with Connie. The sun is setting and the view is spectacular, the Hollywood Sign is lit and the moon is full and finally the food arrives, the caterer is setting that up with the help of a few adoring staff members Holly invited. Everything's ready for that Lowlife in high heels. Lou Reed's signature song, 'Walk on The Wild Side,' featuring Holly's journey from Harold to Holly is cued for her entrance.

And here she is all dolled up blowing kisses and guests applaud. It's showtime!

Holly chooses to position herself a bit remotely so guests can come and adore her without crowding her highness. She's having fun, there's so much love for her here.

The temple of Woodlawn is placed on a platter, the golden pillars are lit and it's wheeled through the crowd to Holly. I've rarely seen Holly stunned, her awe at this creation will remain with me forever. Happy Birthday Holly!

More hugs kisses and pictures snapped, and soon after Holly asks me to take her to her room. Connie comes with us to help her get comfortable. Holly's nights of party till dawn are no longer.

I leave the party determined to find something, some intervention, somehow there has to be something that can be done. I book consults with oncologist's neurologists internists and investigate drug trials that might make a difference. It all leads to the same place. All that's left is to monitor her and make sure she's in no pain. That means eventual hospice care. It's very hard to come to terms with this. But now even though her energy is waning, Holly is still Holly with all her wit and humor, loving her life.

I see her every day, when I visit in the evening I realize nurses are only looking in on her a few times a night and I hire a full time night caretaker to be at her bedside continually.

Constant visitors are exhausting her. I make a list of a few friends allowed to visit and give it to the front desk. Others will have to call me to make an appointment to see her.

We spend a lot of time on the roof terrace reminding each other of our past lives loves and escapades.

She tells me how much Don meant to her. I treasure every minute with Holly. "He's still with us."

"I know."

Three months pass, her condition has been stable and then suddenly she's having difficulty breathing. Her doctor tells me she needs oxygen and it's time for hospice care to begin. She'll have round the clock nursing care and pain meds—Morphine—if she needs it and there will be no discomfort.

I get a call the next day from Joe Dallesandro's wife, Kim. She tells me Joe wants to visit Holly and could I give the desk his name. I ask if she will come with him, she says no. I tell her I'll put his name on the list as soon as we hang up.

Joseph, and Michael, Holly's two "husbands" are

with her. I decide to give them time alone with her. I plan to come later this afternoon.

It's around 3:30 and I'm just about to leave my place and go see Holly and the phone rings. It's her nurse in tears, "Holly died." She tells me guests are still there, I tell her to get them to leave and I'll be right there. She tells me she's made the call and will delay them from taking her until I arrive.

Holly is surrounded by nurses and staff of the La Brea home. They leave me alone with her. All our years, all of our past together flash back at me as I kiss her forehead.

Holly is gone and this hurts deep.

A SEND OFF AND THEN SOME

THE ONE AND ONLY spectacular bum, Holly Woodlawn will never be forgotten. Everyone who loved Holly needs to kick up their heels and celebrate her life. That's what Holly would want, no maudlin memorial. And with the help of close friends, plans take shape.

Connie's tenure as the bad bald beauty hostess of Bar Marmont pays off when he contacts Phil Pavel, the general manager of the Chateau Marmont and he gives us bungalow 1 and also provides waiters and wine for the celebration of Holly's life.

A Send Off and Then Some 454

This couldn't be more perfect. The Chateau Marmont, that tawdry elegant glamorous legendary haunt of star studded debauchery and mayhem hosting the celebration of that tawdry elegant glamorous degenerate lowlife Andy Warhol Superstar Holly Woodlawn.

There's much to do and Bryan Rabin, producer of spectacular events and films comes to the rescue. He organizes an extensive guest list and creates the invitations. He researches and secures the big black gospel girls, a must for a special performance.

Bungalow 1 hardly describes this two story 1920's Spanish villa situated at the Chateau's poolside. The main floor with tall vaulted beamed ceilings is large enough for any event. It has the same funky chic atmosphere as the hotel. Brian has candles lit in every window. Two banks of chairs are divided by a wide aisle leading to a platform with a pedestal displaying a large urn containing Holly's ashes.

As the moderator I need to organize a way to keep this very Holly Woodlawn. Holly told me long ago what it was that inspired her as a young boy to become who she is. Her uncle Julio would take her to the movies in Puerto Rico and before the movie a short film featured her idol, Lola Flores on the silver screen singing her heart out and that did it. Her song, 'Ay, Pena, Penita, Pena' is a torrid performance of emotional sorrow and fierce determination.

The Heartbreak of Static Cling

With the help of a great friend Denise George, a computer genius and DJ, we were able to find that film of Lola Flores singing this song. And it hits, these same emotions are on screen in a film Holly did long time ago called 'Broken Goddess.' Holly is in a slip, barefoot emoting silently in black and white at the Bethesda Fountain. There's no dialogue, no voice over, just a Debussy symphony as soundtrack. With Denise's help we take the Lola Flores film and create a split screen with Holly as Broken Goddess and we ditch the Classical music for Lola's performance and it's magic.

All is set, the day has come and Bungalow 1 is filling with guests including John Waters, Greg Gorman, Pat Loud, Alexis del Lago, Connie, Todd and Ritchie, Brad, the "two husbands" Michael and Joseph, Bryan Rabin and Holly's uncle Julio is here to bring her urn back to Puerto Rico as she requested.

Dozens of friends and fans arrive including the director and staff of the Los Angeles LGBT Center attending for a special announcement. And to give blessings we have a lesbian rabbi who at my insistence will say the prayer for wine.

I begin with, "Thank you for coming to celebrate the life of Holly Woodlawn," and the crowd erupts in hoots and hollers and applauds! Let the fun begin.

I keep my talk short and show the Lola Flores/ Broken Goddess film, then ask who would like to say a few words. The two husbands, one at a time, come to the podium and a few others follow, and then Pat Loud, mother of Lance Loud and dear friend of Holly, adds her thoughts. And then Alexis Del Lago now stands but is unable to walk to the podium. I bring the microphone to the legendary transgender dowager and she begins, "Holly Woodlawn was not a man. Holly Woodlawn was not a woman. Holly Woodlawn was a way of life." And after that brilliance, no other guests dare to add anything more.

    I decide it's time for an announcement, "Holly's last wish was to allocate all funds remaining in her go fund me account to support transgender youth." And so, The Holly Woodlawn fund for Transgender Youth is established at the Los Angeles LGBT Center. The director and staff of the Center stand to applause.

    I quiet the crowd. "Listen, listen. I hear angels, I hear angels." The front doors swing open and a group of big Black gospel gals enter belting 'Amazing Grace' as only big Black gospel singers can. They continue up the isle singing and arrive at the pedestal holding Holly's ashes and then Amazing Grace morphs and becomes 'do da do da do do da do da do... Holly came from Miami, FLA, hitchhiked her way across the U.S.A. Shaved her legs and then he was a she. She says, 'Hey babe, take a walk on the wild side! Hey honey, take a walk on the wild side! And us colored girls sing, do da do da do, take a walk on the wild side, *Holly is free!* Take a walk on the wild side, *Holly is free*" They sing and shout this to heaven walking down the aisle belting Lou Read's song memorializing Holly until they're out the door, and the crowd goes wild.

"Let's party!" Fish piss flows and everybody's dancing to "96 Tears" by Question Mark and the Mysterians.

Now that's a proper Holly Woodlawn send off.

AMONG THE STARS

SOME OF HOLLY'S ashes have been added to smaller urns to tribute her here in LA and New York.

I get a surprise call from Hollywood Forever, the legendary resting place of legendary stars. They want to honor Holly by placing her smaller urn there, and they will do whatever it takes to help make this happen.

Connie and I meet with the director for a tour to find just the right place for Holly and we decide on a niche in a wall overlooking the lake. Holly's portrait, her favorite photo is transformed into a permanent plaque affixed to her resting place. Flowers flank her photo and Holly will be among the stars at Hollywood Forever.

I thought it would be no big deal, but when I arrive at the interment service there is a tent erected over folding chairs filled with fans. Connie and I bring flowers and a giant bottle of Holly's favorite fish piss to place beside her niche.

I manage a few impromptu words and the small urn is placed and we add roses and a few handwritten notes. A strange older woman hands me a card and asks if it could be included. I read the loving tribute written by an adoring fan and include it. And the vault is sealed.

Holly Woodlawn Forever.

SAIL ON

THE SHIP is sleek and fast. The captain knows why I'm aboard with no destination chartered allowing the wind to fill our sails and take us to the edge of this flat world and then some.

A few friends are onboard to catch me if I crumble. But I won't. This decision as hard as it is has been made, I'm committed to it. After all these years it's come to this.

We sail on carrying two passengers, Holly who showed me the strength of being your true self. And

The Heartbreak of Static Cling

Don, the love of my life.

Two bouquets of roses are at my side waiting. Miles off the coast of Santa Monica our sails release the wind and we come to a silent drift. Holly's small urn is in my hand, and 'Walk on the Wild Side' slyly fills the air. And the particles of Holly take flight and settle softly among blood red roses floating on Technicolor Pacific blue waters. She is beside her mother, she will be eternally adored at Hollywood Forever, she will find rest in New York City and now also she's a part of the world's largest ocean. Kick up your heals in heaven, Holly.

Our sails catch a strong determined wind pushing us on and Holly's roses disappear in the distance.

I'm travelling at a million miles an hour with images imbedded in my heart crystal clear of Don, our lives our love, our years, so many years, so many years ago.

We slice through waters beyond the Pacific Palisades and miles beyond Malibu and I see the distant landscape return to its natural state, nothing but pristine cliffs and lush greenery. Here, we're here.

Jesse Norman's operatic lullaby fills the air and I feel Don's soul embrace me. I hold tightly to my chest the box containing his ashes I've kept at my bedside for twenty-five years. Can I do this?

Pale yellow roses of Texas float on softly rolling waves and Don's ashes take to the wind becoming a low white cloud travelling descending and vanishing into the Pacific blue.

Untethered and silenced I'm now adrift in a sea

of uncertainty with no purpose and no destination in sight wondering what lies ahead.

"But wait, there's more. Act now. Don't miss this once-in-a-lifetime opportunity... Robert, put it all in writing."

Okay, Don.

EPILOGUE

AND HERE IT IS, my life in living black & white, for all to see. I believed once written my life would be over, that's why it took so long to commit it to paper. Instead, I'm naked as a new born beginning again.

There have been so many unforeseen events and chance encounters with the most extraordinary who shaped my life and I'm so grateful.

Every life is full—document yours, it's freeing. I recommend it. Build your ships, set them off to sail unchartered waters, you never know what you might discover. Thank you for coming aboard my ride.

Expect something wonderful to happen, because if you do, something wonderful will happen. When you least expect it, and when you need it most.

INDEX

Aguirra, Carolina 354-355, 361, 367, 375-376, 378, 382-383, 387, 390, 410
Arcade, Penny 439-441, 445-446
Arias, Joey 147-148, *247*, 282, 436
Bernstein, Richard 18
Bettany, Paul 339-340, 424-425
Bodrov, Sergei 289, 291-293, 302-304
Boman, Eric 121-122, 124-125, *247*
Canawati, Monty 313-314, 316, 320
Capote, Truman 30, 59, 62-64, 414
Caranicas, Paul 98, 101, 103, 160, 164-165, 206-208, 210, 218, 220, 229, *246*, 307, 316-317
Chow, Tina 164-165, 207-208, 210, 233, *246*
Connelly, Ilene 130, 140, 146, 182, 232, *247*, 262, 266, 306, 334, 422-425
Connelly, Jennifer 130, 140, 146, 182, 232, 233, *247-248*, 263, 266, 268, 270, 272, 274-276, 320, 334, 339-340, 424-425
Croland, David 18-19
Curtis, Jackie 59, 440
Cutrone, Ronnie 3-4
Darling, Candy 59, 440
Dockweiler, BJ 20-23, 27, 267, 271, 276, 277, 280, 334, 361, 363, 425
Drella 74-78, 82
Drew, Deanna 105-106
Ehrlich, Carol 40, 46, 49, 53, 61-62, 66-68, 70-74, 78, 81, 109-110, *236*, 414
Emerson, Eric 59
Fauci, Dr. Anthony 142, 160

Forcade, Xavier 101, 113, 116-117, 142, 146, 164-165, 213-214
Frechette, Mark 41-43, 51, 86, 100,105
Frere, Tony *247,* 282-283
Friend, Leon 67, 68, 71, *236*
Geyer, Todd *248, 271,* 281, 283-284, 287, 292, 313, 318, 334, 354, 362-363, 390, 402-403, 423, 425, 455
Gifford, Horace 123, 128, 147, 163, 181, 233
Glasser, Helen 126, 127, 128, 129, 130, 131, 137, 138, 139, 146, 203, *248*
Gorman, Greg 455
Green, Dr. Leland 333-336, 338-341, 438, 442
Grubbs, Samantha 25, 29, 145
Hackett, Pat 76-77, 107-108, 455-456
Hall, Jerry 90, 94, 102, 130, 204-205, 207-209, 218-220, *241, 246*
Hayes, Ed 126, 141, 191-192, *246*
Hockney, David 17
Huston, Angelica 209, 220
Jagger, Mick 19, 75, 207, 208, 209, 219, 220, *246*
Johns, Jasper 6, 13, 20, 39
King, Bill 89-94, 100, 102-103, 166, 182, 204, 224, *239, 242*
Krim, Dr. Mathilde 142, 160, 188
Lange, Jessica *246*
Lennon, Bernard 101, 113-114, 116-117, 164-165, 173, 213, *246,* 251-252
Lenz, Bob 145-146, 181, 192, 217
Lopez, Antonio 98-99, 101-102, 141, 164-166, 168, 182, 206-210, 218, *246,* 288-289, 306-307
Mapplethorpe, Robert 164, 188, 284, 394, 396
Mayhew, Mark 145
Mead, Taylor 129
Morley, Malcolm 3-4, 17, 101, 123, 125, 141, 164, *238*

Morrissey, Paul 76, 440
Pinnell, Max 182, 184
Rabin, Bryan 454-455
Ramos, Juan 98, 101, 103, 141, 160, 164-165, 206-208, 210, 218, 220, 229, *246*, 316-317
Ruskin, Mickey 60
Schlesinger, Peter 17-19, 22, 24-25, 121-125, *238*, 247
Sherman, Robert "Constance Cooper" 284, 320, 334, 354, 356, 358-360, 362, 377, 387, 390, 394-396, 399, 412-413, 416-420, 425, 439-441, 444, 446, 449-450, 453, 455, 458-459
Sonnabend, Dr. Joseph 164, 169
Starr, Carolyn 146-147, 151, *235*, 262, 293, 303, 324, 334-335, 350, 417, 419
Starr, Ted 7, 9, 13, 147, *235*, 287, 316, 323, 324, 350, 366, 416
Starr, Zelda B. 7, 9, 13, 95, 147, 194-195, *235*, *248*, 287, 323-324, 339-340, 349-352, 354-357, 360-361, 367, 375, 381-383, 385-388, 393, 397, 399, 407, 409-411, 417
Steifel, Frank *248*, 271, 276-277, 280, 282, 363, 401, 402, 404-405, 425
Stiletto, Elda 59, *243*, 334-335
Tippin, Cory Grant *246*
Toland, Katrina 8, 9, 59
Warhol, Andrea "Whips" 59, 60, 74-78, 81-82, *237*
Warhol, Andy 3, 4, 5, 37, 56, 59, 63, 74, 75, 100, 283, 293, 331, 454
Waters, John 131, 353, 455
Weisal, Robert "Bobby Beverly Hills" 326-327, 332
Wilson, Prime Minister Harold 5, 6
Wilson, Patty 182-184
de Winter, Orion 37-39
Woodlawn, Holly 59, *243*, *248*, 283-285, 287, 292-294, 299-300, 302, 310-312, 329-331, 334, 354, 356, 360, 362, 380-382, 386-387, 390, 403, 426-428, 437-441, 443-461

www.ingramcontent.com/pod-product-compliance
Lightning Source LLC
Chambersburg PA
CBHW070042080526
44586CB00013B/884